IMPERIUM ROMANUM

Imperium Romanum is the first full-length book in English on the organisation of the Roman empire for over fifty years and will provide the student at all levels with a conspectus of the latest research on all its aspects. Much important new material is now available; Andrew Lintott brings to light and discusses recent discoveries of documents preserved in inscriptions and on papyrus.

The classic books on the Roman empire emerged in a period when imperial enterprise was generally exalted. These works transferred the values and preconceptions of the British empire on to that of the Romans. They stressed territorial control, defined frontiers, clear divisions of responsibility and channels of communication. More recent research, by contrast, highlights how flexible, casuistic, personal and (sometimes deliberately) ill-defined the principles and methods of Roman imperialism were.

Andrew Lintott provides an up-to-date assembly of the evidence and suggests new interpretations of this material. How far did a system arise from this apparent lack of system? How far did Rome's subjects grow into a unity, which transcended the results of direct Roman coercion?

Andrew Lintott is Fellow and Tutor in Ancient History at Worcester College, Oxford. He is the author of *Judicial Reform and Land Reform in the Roman Republic* (1992), *Violence, Civil Strife and Revolution in the Classical City* (1982) and *Violence in Republican Rome* (1968).

IMPERIUM ROMANUM

Politics and administration

Andrew Lintott

London and New York

First published 1993
by Routledge
11 New Fetter Lane, London EC4P 4EE

Simultaneously published in the USA and Canada
by Routledge
29 West 35th Street, New York NY 10001

© 1993 Andrew Lintott

Typeset in 10/12pt Garamond by Witwell Ltd, Southport
Printed in Great Britain by T.J. Press (Padstow) Ltd, Padstow, Cornwall

British Library Cataloguing in Publication Data
Lintott, Andrew
Imperium Romanum: Politics and
Administration
I. Title
937

Library of Congress Cataloging in Publication Data
Lintott, A. W. (Andrew William)
Imperium Romanum: politics and administration/Andrew Lintott.
p. cm.
Includes bibliographical references and index.
1. Rome—Politics and government—265–30 B.C.
2. Rome—Politics and government—30 B.C.–A.D. 284.
3. Rome—Provinces—Administration.
I. Title.
DG241.L56 1993
930'.0971237—dc20
92–26011
CIP

ISBN 0-415-01594-4
0-415-09375-9 (pbk)

For my colleagues and pupils

CONTENTS

ILLUSTRATIONS

PREFACE

Over a number of years while I have been teaching Roman history I have regretted the lack of an up-to-date book which would explain to my pupils the structure of the Roman empire and how it worked. In an attempt to fill this gap for them I became interested not only in the mechanics of the administration but in the conceptualisation of the empire both by the Romans themselves and by modern scholars. This led me to deliver a paper, which in turn persuaded Eyre Methuen to commission a book. The delay in its appearance (during which Eyre Methuen was incorporated into Routledge) may be in part explained by my desire to finish some work on Republican legal texts first as a foundation for part of the argument, partly by the need to assimilate new documents, largely preserved in inscriptions, which have appeared in profusion during the last decade, partly also by my diffidence, when I realised what I had perhaps too confidently undertaken. One aim of the book which has gained in importance over these years is to bring to the reader's notice the accumulation of new evidence. Another is to provide an introductory overview of an historical subject which, like the Roman empire itself in its time, has expanded phenomenally and is hard to conceive as a coherent intellectual entity. I would like to think that, while attempting this, I have also been able to make some contribution of my own to the new thinking about the empire, whose fertility may be found in many modern works on particular aspects of it, and which is very far from exhausted.

I have learnt much from a number of contemporaries and it would be invidious to limit this in a brief list of names. I am, however, particularly grateful to Greg Woolf for reading the typescript and making a number of useful suggestions. Much of the work on the latter half of the book was done when I was a visiting scholar at the

Institute for Advanced Study at Princeton in 1990 and it is pleasant to record here my thanks for the hospitality I received and for the assistance and stimulating discussion provided in the Department of Historical Studies.

ABBREVIATIONS

Abbreviations of periodicals in general follow the system of *L'Année Philologique*, with one important exception: *ZSS* for *Zeitschrift der Savigny-Stiftung für Rechtsgeschichte, romanistische Abteilung*.

Abbreviations of papyri in general follow those in E. G. Turner, *Greek Papyri: an Introduction* (Oxford, 1980), 159ff.

AJ	F.F. Abbott and A.C. Johnson, *Municipal Administration in the Roman Empire*, Princeton, 1926
ANRW	*Aufstieg und Niedergang der römischen Welt*, Festschrift J. Vogt, ed. H. Temporini and W. Haase, Berlin and New York, 1972–
Braund, *AN*	D.C. Braund, *Augustus to Nero. A Sourcebook on Roman History 31 BC-AD 68*, London/Sydney, 1985
Bruns	G. Bruns and O. Gradenwitz, *Fontes Iuris Romani Antiqui*, 7th edn, Tübingen, 1919
CAH	*Cambridge Ancient History*
CIL	*Corpus Inscriptionum Latinarum*
Claros I	J. and L. Robert, *Claros I: les décrets hellénistiques*, Paris, 1989
Corinth	*Corinth. Results of the Excavations by the American School at Athens*, Cambridge, Mass., 1932–
CPJ	V.A. Tcherikover, A. Fuks and M. Stern, *Corpus Papyrorum Iudaicarum*, 3 vols, Cambridge, Mass., 1957–64
EJ	V. Ehrenberg and A.H.M. Jones, *Documents*

	Illustrating the Reigns of Augustus and Tiberius, 2nd edn, with addenda, Oxford, 1975
ESAR	T. Frank, *Economic Survey of Ancient Rome*, 5 vols, Baltimore, Maryland, 1933–9
FGH	F. Jacoby, *Die Fragmente der Griechischen Historiker*, 3 parts, 11 vols, Berlin and Leiden, 1923–58
FIRA	S. Riccobono, *Fontes Iuris Romani Anteiustiniani*, 2nd edn, Florence, 1968
IDélos	F. Durrbach *et al.*, *Inscriptions de Délos*, Paris, 1926–
IEphesos	H. Wankel *et al.*, *Die Inschriften von Ephesos*, Bonn 1979–
IErythrai	H. Engelmann, *Die Inschriften von Erythrai und Klazomenai*, Bonn, 1972–3
IG	*Inscriptiones Graecae*
IGB	G. Mihailov, *Inscriptiones Graecae in Bulgaria repertae*, vol. 1, 2nd edn, vols 2–5, 1st edn, Sofia, 1958–70
IGRR	R. Cagnat *et al.*, *Inscriptiones Graecae ad Res Romanas Pertinentes*, 3 vols, Paris, 1906–27
ILAfr	R. Cagnat *et al.*, *Inscriptions latines d'Afrique*, Paris, 1922
ILLRP	A. Degrassi, *Inscriptiones Latinae Liberae Rei Publicae*, 2 vols, 2nd edn, Florence, 1966
ILS	H. Dessau, *Inscriptiones Latinae Selectae*, 4 vols, Berlin 1892–1916, reprinted 1954
ILT	A. Merlin, *Inscriptions Latines de la Tunisie*, Paris, 1944
IOSPE	B. Latyschev, *Inscriptiones Antiquae Orae Septentrionalis Ponti Euxini Graecae et Latinae*, 3 vols, 2nd edn, St Petersburg, 1916
ITrip	J.M. Reynolds and J.B. Ward-Perkins, *The Inscriptions of Roman Tripolitania*, London, 1952
JRLR	A. Lintott, *Judicial Reform and Land Reform in the Roman Republic*, Cambridge, 1992
Levick, *GRE*	B.M. Levick, *The Government of the Roman Empire: A Sourcebook*, London, 1985
Milet	Th. Wiegand, *Milet. Ergebnisse der Ausgrabungen und Untersuchungen seit dem*

	Jahre 1899, Berlin, 1908–90
Mitteis, Wilcken *GCP*	L. Mitteis and U. Wilcken, *Grundzüge und Chrestomathie der Papyruskunde*, 4 vols, Stuttgart, 1912, reprinted Hildesheim, 1963
Mommsen, *Ges.Schr.*	Th. Mommsen, *Gesammelte Schriften*, Berlin, 1904–13
Mommsen, *Staatsr.*	Th. Mommsen, *Römisches Staatsrecht*, vols 1 and 2, 3rd edn, vol. 3, 1st edn, Leipzig, 1887–8
MRR	T.R.S. Broughton, *The Magistrates of the Roman Republic*, 2 vols, 2nd edn, New York, 1960; vol. 3, Atlanta, Georgia, 1987
MW	M. McCrum and A. G. Woodhead, *Select Documents of the Principates of the Flavian Emperors*, Cambridge, 1961
OGIS	W. Dittenberger, *Orientis Graeci Inscriptiones Selectae*, 4 vols, Leipzig, 1903, reprinted Hildesheim, 1960
ORF	H. Malcovati, *Oratorum Romanorum Fragmenta*, 2 vols, 4th edn, Turin, 1976–9
PIR	E. Groag *et al.*, *Prosopographia Imperii Romani saec. I, II, III*, 2nd rev. edn, Leipzig/Berlin, 1933–
RDGE	R.K. Sherk, *Roman Documents from the Greek East*, Baltimore, Maryland, 1964
RE	Pauly–Wissowa, *Real-Encyclopaedie der klassischen Altertumswissenschaft*
RGE	R.K. Sherk, *Rome and the Greek East to the Death of Augustus* (Translated Documents of Greece and Rome 4). Cambridge, 1984
RIB	R.G. Collingwood and R.P. Wright, *The Roman Inscriptions of Britain*, vol. 1, Oxford, 1965; vol. 2, Gloucester, 1990
RRC	M.H. Crawford, *Roman Republican Coinage*, 2 vols, Cambridge, 1974
SEG	*Supplementum Epigraphicum Graecum*
Sel. Pap.	A.C. Hunt and C.C. Edgar, *Select Papyri*, London, 1932
Smallwood, *GCN*	E. M. Smallwood, *Documents Illustrating the Principates of Gaius, Claudius and Nero*, Cambridge, 1967
Smallwood, *NTH*	E.M. Smallwood, *Documents Illustrating the*

Principates of Nerva, Trajan and Hadrian, London, 1966

*Syll.*³   W. Dittenberger, *Sylloge Inscriptionum Graecarum*, 4 vols, 3rd edn, Leipzig, 1915; reprinted Hildesheim, 1960

Welles, *RC*   C.B. Welles, *Royal Correspondence in the Hellenistic Period. A Study in Greek Epigraphy.* New Haven, Conn., 1934; reprinted Chicago, Ill., 1974

The following legal texts may be referred to without further reference.

Frag.Atest   *Fragmentum Atestinum*, CIL, I², 600; FIRA, I, 20.

Lex agr.   *Lex agraria*, CIL, I², 585; FIRA, I, 8; JRLR, pp. 171–286.

Lex Ant.Term.   *Lex Antonia de Termessibus*, CIL, I², 589; FIRA, I, 11.

Lex de Delo   *Lex Gabinia Calpurnia de insula Delo*, CIL, I², 2500; C. Nicolet (ed.), *Insula Sacra*, Rome, 1980.

Lex Flav.mun.   The combined text of *Lex mun.Mal.* and *Lex Irnit.* (see below)

Lex Irnit.   *Lex Irnitana,* J. Gonzalez, *JRS*, 76 (1986), 147–243.

Lex Iul.agr.   *Lex Iulia agraria* (or *Mamilia Roscia Peducaea Alliena Fabia*), FIRA, I, 12.

Lex mun.Mal.   *Lex municipii Malacitani*, CIL, II, 1964; FIRA, I, 24.

Lex mun.Tar.   *Lex municipii Tarentini*, CIL, I², 590; FIRA, I, 18.

Lex osca Bant.   *Lex osca tabulae Bantinae*, FIRA I, 16; Bruns, 8; new fragment, D. Adamesteanu and M. Torelli, *Arch.Class.*, 21 (1969), 1–17.

Lex portorii Asiae   H. Engelmann and D. Knibbe, 'Das Zollgesetz der provincia Asia. Ein neues Inschrift aus Ephesos', *Epig.Anat.*, 14 (1989), 1–206.

Lex prov.praet.   *Lex de provinciis praetoriis (de piratis)*, FIRA, I, 9; new fragments, M. Hassall, M. Crawford and J. Reynolds, *JRS*, 64 (1974), 195–220.

Lex rep.	*Lex repetundarum, CIL,* I^2, 583; *FIRA,* I, 7; *JRLR,* pp. 73–169.
Lex Rubr.Gall.	*Lex Rubria de Gallia Cisalpina, CIL,* I^2, 592; *FIRA,* I, 19.
Lex Urs.	*Lex Coloniae Genetivae Ursonensis, CIL,* I^2, 594; *FIRA,* I, 21.
SC de Asclep.	*Senatus Consultum de Asclepiade, CIL,* I^2, 588; *FIRA,* I, 35.
SC Calvisianum	*FIRA,* I, 68, V (pp. 409–14); *SEG,* IX, 8.
Tab.Heracl.	*Tabula Heracleensis, CIL,* I^2, 593; *FIRA,* I, 13.

INTRODUCTION

When the Greek historian Polybius looked back about the middle of the second century BC on Rome's recent acquisition of the dominant position in his world, the Mediterranean lands and their neighbours, he found two general explanations for it. In part it was the work of fortune (*tychē*) which had so associated and combined events that they had come to point in a single direction, in part it was the logical outcome of the efforts of the Romans themselves and a fair reward for their military and political strength.[1] At the same time the notion of a Roman destiny to universal rule was already developing both among the Greeks and the Romans themselves. According to Cicero, in the funeral oration written for Scipio Aemilianus by his friend Laelius in 129 BC it was asserted that the land in which Scipio lived was bound to rule the earth. Earlier, though whether in the third or second centuries BC is disputed, there was incorporated in the Alexandrian poet Lycophron's play about the fall of Troy, *Alexandra*, a pseudo-prophesy about the race sprung from Trojan seed who were to take revenge on the Greeks for the humiliation of their mother-city by imposing their power on the eastern Mediterranean.[2] This theme was only fully elaborated in the time of Augustus. He himself recorded his own achievements, *Res Gestae*, under the rubric 'the achievements by which he subjected the whole world to the *imperium* of the Roman people', while Vergil in the *Aeneid* immortalised Rome's rise to power, showing it to have been ineluctable, because decreed by heaven, and claiming in further justification that it was in governing others that Rome's true talent lay. The argument that some people were naturally fitted to rule and others to obey was especially powerful in an intellectual and moral climate where similar arguments were used to justify slavery, pre-eminently in Aristotle in *Politics* Book I.[3]

1

Augustus' boast that he and Rome now had the world under their sway would not have seemed exaggerated to his contemporaries, even if the rhetoric in such a claim was betrayed by the fact that it had already been made over 100 years earlier. It is neatly illustrated by the silver *denarii* showing Rome with her foot on the globe, like a football referee before a game[4] – a type which first appears under the Republic in the 70s BC but is frequently reused on the coinage of the emperors. Yet Roman ideas may seem transparently false and overinflated now. The territorial extension of Roman rule even in the hinterland of the Mediterranean basin fell short of complete dominance, while the lack of strict central supervision and elaborate administrative machinery both under the Republic and the emperors casts doubt on the quality of the control. This can lead to contrasting value judgements. The strength of the empire, it may be said, lay in the liberty it afforded its subjects, its weakness in the licence it allowed its officials and local potentates to rob and oppress. There is, moreover, the irony that at the point when central control of administration and life itself is apparently at its most elaborate in the later Roman empire, the empire is traditionally regarded as in decline.

The present work does not aspire to tackle this final period because of the mass of material and special problems this entails. It seeks rather to clarify the nature of the empire during the epoch when in the Roman view it was self-evidently a success. The starting-point is how Romans understood the concept of *imperium* and could reconcile it with considerable flexibility both in the formal relationships between themselves and their allies and in administrative practice. Following this, we consider how the empire worked – the well-worn topic of 'provincial administration', which, although its scholarship stretches back for 400 years (Carlo Sigonio's *De antiquo iure provinciarum* of 1568 was the pioneer text), is continually being illuminated by new documentary evidence. Finally, an attempt is made to assess the nature of the relationship between Rome and her allies and subjects. Of course, neither forms of organisation nor administration remained static over the period between *c*. 250 BC and *c*. 150 AD. There was a general tendency towards the restriction of independent action by Rome's allies or subjects combined with a diminishing differentiation between them and their Roman rulers. Yet at all stages the internal coherence of the empire and the influence of Roman hegemony is in my view greater than one may be led to suppose by the absence of elaborate governmental machinery.

2

Part I

1

THE GROWTH OF EMPIRE[1]

At the time of the expulsion of Tarquinius Superbus and the beginning of the Republic (*c.* 500 BC) Rome was merely one city, ·albeit a powerful one, among those who formed the Latin League in the plain east of the Tiber and on its surrounding hills. Her military achievements in the next 160 years were of three main kinds: first, co-operative enterprises with other Latins to protect their frontiers against the neighbouring hill-peoples such as the Volsci and Aequi (these involved the joint founding of colonies as strong posts on or outside the Latin borders); second, wars with her own Latin neighbours which no doubt had various pretexts but were essentially to determine primacy in the League; third, wars with her Etruscan neighbours immediately to the north and west of Rome through rivalry and the need for self-protection. In spite of a major set-back at the time for the Gallic capture of Rome in 386 (or 390) BC the Romans had some forty years later become the dominant power in the Latin League. In the meantime they had eliminated their dangerous Etruscan rivals Fidenae and Veii, annexing their territory, while Caere, another Etruscan city nearby, had become their ally. Furthermore, fourteen colonies had been created, the majority of which ringed Latium to the south-east, while two provided strong points west of the Tiber in south Etruria. About this time Rome began to reach beyond her immediate hinterland through alliances with the Samnites and Campanians. These proved incompatible, and when the Campanians turned against the Romans, some of the Latins joined them. Victory in this war (338) allowed Rome to consolidate her hold not only over Latin territory but over much Campanian and Volscian territory as well, and their organisation of these conquests was to provide the foundation for their future success through the territorial buffer and the financial and militry resources it afforded.

In the half-century that followed the Romans extended their power by a combination of campaigning and alliances throughout peninsular Italy. A quarrel with the Greek city of Tarentum led to the arrival in 280 of their first opponent from overseas – Pyrrhus, king of Epirus and former claimant to the Macedonian throne. He and his superb army, modelled on that of Alexander the Great, were initially victorious and he sought Roman recognition of his hegemony in Italy. Rome rejected his diplomatic overtures and he had not the resources to press home his advantage. He diverted into Sicily, but his operations there were unsuccessful militarily and politically clumsy. On his return to Italy he was defeated and forced to retire to Greece. This allowed the Romans to take control of southern Italy (Tarentum eventually fell in 272) and to confirm their position in Etruria, Umbria and on the Adriatic coast as far north as Ariminum. The victory over an overseas opponent marked the end of one epoch in Roman expansion and pointed the way to a new one.

Eleven years after Pyrrhus' withdrawal the Romans deliberately involved themselves in Sicilian affairs, provoking a conflict with Carthage, the Phoenician-founded city in north Africa which had dominated the seas in the western Mediterranean for at least three centuries. This set in motion a struggle, which over two wars and an uneasy peace between brought first Sicily, then Sardinia and Corsica and finally the more accessible parts of the Iberian peninsula into the Roman orbit. Victory in the first war in 241 allowed Rome not only to secure Sicily but to exploit Punic weakness in the following years so as to acquire the other islands. Moreover, victories over the Gauls (especially in 225 at Telamon) led to the occupation of their land on the Adriatic coast and later in the Lombardy plain: the first Latin and Roman colonies in Gallia Cisalpina, the Po basin, were founded in 218. Hannibal did not require much Roman provocation in Spain to launch a revanchist war the same year, invading Italy with the aid of the Gauls in order to break the foundation of Roman power, her network of Italian allies. His ultimate failure and the subsequent defeat of Carthage on African soil left Rome master of the western Mediterranean. It was this victory, according to Polybius, that gave the Romans the strength and confidence to embark on what was for him world-conquest.[2]

Between the Punic Wars they had campaigned across the Adriatic in Illyricum, securing allies there. Hannibal's alliance with Philip V of Macedon in 215 led them to acquire allies in Greece, such as Sparta, Messene and the Aetolian League, and in the eastern Mediterranean,

Rhodes and Attalus I of Pergamum. Individual Romans and Italians had already for some time been in contact with the east. It was a Roman ship bound for Syria that rescued the Achaean statesman Aratus (*c.* 250) and carried him to Asia; the Rammii family from Brundisium are attested in Thessaly from the mid-third century BC. Diplomatically, the Romans began relations with Egypt in 273.[3]

Rome's war with Philip was renewed after Hannibal's defeat in response to appeals from Rome's allies. After defeating Macedon in Thessaly, Rome proclaimed herself the following year (196) the liberator of the Greek cities from the Hellenistic kings. This liberty was originally on the whole freer than the autonomy that the cities had been allowed to exercise under the kings of Macedon, Syria and Egypt, but this was more *de facto* than *de iure* (it was expressed in terms borrowed from the diplomacy of the kings). Even if formal alliances (*foedera*) were rarely concluded, the Greeks were regarded as friends and allies of Rome[4] and this involved the Roman expectation that, when it mattered, they would conform to Rome's will.[5]

The Aetolians' resentment of the implications of the settlement of 196 led them to appeal to Rome's most dangerous rival, the Seleucid Antiochus III of Syria, whose kingdom covered much of Alexander the Great's oriental empire. However, not only were the forces that the king landed in Greece defeated in 191, but also his fleet and a more formidable army the following year, this time on Asiatic soil. Rome was now in a position to dictate terms to Antiochus, which eliminated his influence from Europe and most of Asia Minor. In consequence, Greece itself fell more securely under Roman influence. When Macedon under king Perseus began to reassert her power. Rome picked a quarrel in 171 and after some reverses defeated the king at Pydna (168). In the same year she asserted her influence further east when an ambassador expelled a Syrian army from Egypt by the threat of reprisals.

The extent of the belief in Roman power beyond the Mediterranean itself was shown by the terms of the treaty between Pharnaces II of Pontus and the city of Chersonesos in the Crimea, made in 179 or 155 – 'on condition that they maintained their friendship with the Romans and did nothing contrary to it'.[6] It was this image of Rome too which led the Jewish rebels against Seleucid Syria to ally with Rome in 161.

Now Judas had heard of the fame of the Romans, that they were mighty and valiant men, and such as would lovingly accept all that joined themselves unto them, and make a league of amity with all that came unto them ... how they destroyed and brought under their dominion all other kingdoms and isles that at any time resisted them, but with their friends and such as relied upon them they kept amity ... also that, whom they would help to a kingdom, those reign, and, whom again they would, they displace.

Some of the statements about the Romans by the author of I Maccabees, writing perhaps some forty years later, are inaccurate in detail, some are pointed and shrewd ('what they had done in the country of Spain for the winning of the mines of the silver and gold which is there'), but the overall impression left by the chapter must mirror the sentiments of the Jews and other peoples of the Near East at the time.[7]

Nevertheless, the exercise of Roman physical power was intermittent in most regions and in the most remote areas Roman activity was merely diplomatic. Before 150 BC they only undertook to rule directly as *provinciae* (for the meaning of this term see pp. 28–9) Sicily, Corsica, Sardinia and Spain. No Roman magistrates were regularly installed in the eastern Mediterranean until 148–7. Instead, commanders were sent, when and where necessary, to fight wars and to organise peoples who had voluntarily become allies or succumbed to Roman power. A characteristic pattern of behaviour developed. Foreign embassies would come to Rome to spend the winter lobbying magistrates and senators: 'they met the leading men and by greeting them at their levées won them over and they made their own patrons look after the interests of Abdera' – so runs a text in which Abdera honoured the diplomats of its mother-city Teos.[8] In response the following spring embassies would set out from Rome to publicise Roman policy, reconcile friends and spy on potential enemies.

Such indirect control was possible because the Romans were dealing either with monarchs or with well-established local institutions in the form of a city (*polis*) or a non-urban political community (*ethnos*), which they could on the whole manipulate to achieve stability in their own interests (they preferred to deal with oligarchic groups of powerful men). However, while the public presence of Rome was often minimal, there seems to have been a significant, if unquantifiable, increase in the number of Romans and Italians who held property and undertook business enterprises abroad (men called in Latin *negotiatores*). These men could be used as channels of political influence as well as sources of information. The Roman *negotiatores*, both residents and visitors, on the island of Chios about 200 BC are attested in an inscription, which honours a man who put on an entertainment for them and set up a monument to Rome, which commemorated the descent of the Romans from Romulus and Remus. I have already mentioned the family of the Rammii established in Thessaly in the mid-third century BC. It was without doubt a connection of theirs whom we find entertaining Roman magistrates and Greek embassies to Rome at Brundisium in 172.[9] The Roman decision to make Delos a free port after it was transferred to the jurisdiction of Athens in 165 led to a great increase in the number of Romans and Italians attested there, who seem to a considerable extent to have been involved with the slave-trade. It has been plausibly argued that the '*agora* of the Italians' there is in fact a slave-market.[10] Such emigration also helped to confirm Roman influence in Sicily and Spain.

According to Polybius,[11] before the Third Macedonian War Rome was regarded as comparatively tolerant of rival powers whom she had defeated: she allowed them to exist and prosper, provided that they posed no serious threat to her security. The Third Macedonian War and the final elimination of the kingdom there marked a change in this policy, and the new hard line came even more into evidence about 150 BC. Carthage, which had remained a free city, though stripped of much of her territory, after considerable provocation attacked the neighbouring king of Numidia, Masinissa, contrary to her treaty with Rome. The attack was a failure. Moreover, the Romans who had become suspicious of Carthage's economic recovery in the last fifty years, required them to make an unconditional surrender, if they wished to avoid a new war with Rome. Although originally prepared to submit, the Carthaginians refused to obey when instructed to abandon their city and after a siege lasting three years were overwhelmed in 146, their city being razed to the ground and their territory confiscated to become a province. In Macedonia a pretender to the throne, Andriscus, led an uprising in 148 and his defeat led to the Macedonians, previously organised in four self-governing regions with their constituent cities, receiving a Roman governor for the first time. In 147 BC the Achaean League, which had helped to protect Thessaly against Andriscus, was required by the Romans after a dispute with Sparta not only to release Sparta from the League but to strip itself of other members of the federation, including Corinth and Argos. It refused to give up hostilities against Sparta or to obey other

Roman commands and was defeated after a short campaign in 146. Corinth was razed to the ground; other cities who had opposed Rome lost at least temporarily their liberty; territory, including that belonging to Corinth and the island of Euboea, was confiscated and parts of Greee became an adjunct of the province of Macedonia.[12]

Rome thus acquired new provinces in Africa and the East. During the next fifty years, before Italy was thrown into chaos by the war between Rome and her Italian allies and the ensuing first civil war, the Romans consolidated their hold on Cisalpine Gaul as far as the Alps, establishing also for the first time a permanent military presence and administration in southern Transalpine Gaul (Provence is a major part of the original Roman *provincia*). Here the soldiers moved into an area probably already visited by Roman businessmen, and their presence in turn encouraged settlement and the acquisition of land by private citizens. Although Roman control in Transalpine and Cisalpine Gaul was badly shaken by the invasions of Germanic tribes in the last decades of the second century BC, thanks to the generalship of C. Marius and his colleagues Rome was able to reassert her supremacy. In Africa the war with the Numidian prince Jugurtha (111–105 BC) does not seem to have disturbed the settlement of Romans in what is now Tunisia, whether they had free grants of land from the state or had acquired it by purchase. In fact, after Marius' victory some of his discharged soldiers were assigned land there.[13] In the east the number of Roman and Italian settlers also increased, partly because of new political developments. After the last king of Pergamum died in 133, leaving the Roman people heir to his kingdom, Roman magistrates and soldiers moved into Asia, meeting with initial resistance from a nationalist revolt. Once established in western Asia Minor they began to spread Roman physical power eastwards. Greater Phrygia and Lycaonia, originally ceded to allied kings, were reattached to the new province. Then campaigning against the pirates in southern Asia Minor led to the creation of a new *provincia* in Cilicia.[14]

Roman advance in this region was contemporary with the effective collapse of the Seleucid kingdom before the new rulers of what had been once the Persian empire – the Parthians. They had taken Babylon *c.* 120 BC and were on the Euphrates border of northern Syria in 96–5 BC, where they had their first diplomatic contact with a Roman, the proconsul Sulla. However, Roman interests clashed more immediately with Mithridates VI of Pontus, who wanted, as they did, to dominate the rulers of the other kingdoms in Asia Minor.

Mithridates received unjustified and foolhardy provocation from the Romans and the Bithynian king after his own dynastic intervention in Bithynia and took his chance, when the Romans were preoccupied by wars with their Italian allies and each other. In 89–8 BC he conquered western Asia Minor, slaughtering a great number of Romans and Italians, and invaded Greece, where Athens under two successive philosopher–dictators voluntarily took his side. However, Sulla twice defeated Mithridates' forces in Greece, while a commander of Marian allegiance, Fimbria, threatened the king's Asiatic conquests. In 85 the king was persuaded to abandon his gains, and it was over 300 years before Roman rule in Greece was threatened again. At the beginning of the last century BC both Cyrene and Egypt were left to Rome in the wills of kings, but for the time being neither offer was accepted.[15]

Sulla's victory in the civil wars and his establishment of a new political order in 81 was the prelude to a last burst of imperial expansion under Republican institutions, associated above all with Pompey and Caesar. Wars were usually originated as responses to provocation but rapidly developed a powerful momentum of their own. About 100 BC Rome had tried to suppress systematically for the first time the pirates operating in the eastern Mediterranean, especially those based in Cilicia, but the civil wars had allowed the raiders fresh scope and now they were offered political co-operation by Mithridates. Similar help was given to the pirates in the west by the Roman rebel in Spain, Sertorius. Mithridates was suspicious of Roman attempts to recover and expand their political dominance in Asia Minor, and took the opportunity provided by the death of the king of Bithynia in 75 to mount a new expedition westwards. The Roman frontier in Gaul came under threat from Gallic and Germanic tribes. The Roman response to these challenges involved more thoroughgoing annexation than ever before. In the east, after almost ten years of campaigning first by Lucullus and later by Pompey, the province of Cilicia was expanded, two new provinces, Bithynia and Syria, were created and Rome, through a series of friendly kings and dynasts, came to exercise power effectively as far as the Jordan, the Euphrates, the Causasus and the Crimea. Cyrene was made a province in 75, Crete in 66, Cyprus in 58; Palestine became an adjunct of Syria, while Egypt only remained free from annexation through internal political divisions at Rome. In the west in his nine years as proconsul of Gaul Julius Caesar used the pretext of Helvetian and German incursions to overrun an area comprising modern France, Belgium and Germany west of the Rhine. He also invaded southern Britain and demanded submission from the chiefs there.[16]

By the time Caesar crossed the Rubicon in 49 Rome had few serious foreign enemies. Principal among these were the Parthians. They had crushed M. Crassus in 53, when he had attempted to expand the Roman empire into Mesopotamia, and had subsequently invaded Syria, but in general they were not the first to use military force. Near the lower Danube a Dacian chief Burebista, later to be commemorated in Jordanes' *History of the Getae*, had a formidable reputation but in fact did nothing to threaten Rome, though Pompey considered getting his aid in the civil war.[17] The Germanic peoples offered little opposition to Caesar after Ariovistus' defeat west of the Rhine in 58.

This empire survived almost twenty years of Roman civil war remarkably intact. There was one major, but temporary, exception. In 40 BC Q. Labienus, a Roman who had been sent by the tyrannicides, Brutus and Cassius, to enlist Parthian help, invaded Syria and Asia Minor at the head of a Parthian army with the Parthian prince Pacorus as his colleague. Two years too late to revive the Republican cause, he nevertheless led the Parthians across Asia Minor to the Aegean – further than they had ever gone before or were subsequently to go.[18] However, he was defeated in 39 by Mark Antony's subordinate, Ventidius Bassus. Antony's own counter-invasion of Armenia and Media proved ultimately fruitless. However, the civil wars brought new gains to the empire with the extension of provincial territory beyond the original province of Africa and finally, after the deaths of Antony and Cleopatra, with the acquisition of Egypt.

The new master of the Roman world, Caesar Augustus, had no wish to rest on other people's laurels. He claimed to have expanded the empire, wherever it bordered on unsubjected peoples.[19] In Africa this involved the extension of Roman power in the Maghreb, Cyrenaica and southern Egypt; in the east the invasion of Arabia. However, it was not so much a question in these regions of territorial acquisition as the establishment of a psychological ascendancy over peoples living at the fringe of the desert or wandering from the desert into cultivated areas. The main theatre of campaigning was the northern European frontier. These wars seem to owe their origin chiefly to Augustus' desire not to fall short of the great conquerors of the late Republic and to assert that the proper use of Roman arms was to humble barbarians, not to cut other Romans' throats. However, there was also the traditional fear of Celtic and Germanic peoples – whom the

12

Romans at that time did not clearly distinguish.[20] Military and political logic (though we cannot be sure that such considerations were actually present in the minds of Augustus and his advisers) would have suggested that the northern frontier should be moved away from the Mediterranean near the head of the Adriatic, where east–west communication was currently most difficult and the empire could most easily be cut in two.[21] The conquest of the Alps, Raetia, Noricum, Pannonia, Illyricum, Moesia and Thrace (that is, Switzerland, Austria, south-western Hungary, Yugoslavia and Bulgaria) not only subdued areas potentially hostile to Rome but allowed the Romans to use the east–west communications provided by the Danube plain.

Julius Caesar's Gaul had been bounded on the east by the Rhine. Augustus was originally not satisfied with this, and his armies advanced eastwards to the Elbe and northwards over the Danube both into Bohemia and to the east into Dacia (modern Rumania). From about 6 BC to 9 AD Germany was being treated like a province, even if Roman control was far from complete. However, in 6 AD the Pannonian revolt, which spread into Illyricum, required a massive concentration of military strength for three years to suppress it, and in its aftermath the German chief Arminius seceded from the empire and ambushed three Roman legions in the Teutoburgerwald between the rivers Ems and Weser. The Romans had to abandon Germany beyond the Rhine through lack of resources, and, although they subsequently campaigned there and maintained some forts along routes leading into the heart of Germany, the province was never recovered – except for one district. The emperor Domitian brought the region of the Black Forest into the empire by developing a new frontier line along the Neckar and between this river and the Danube.

The emperors of the first and second centuries AD strove to maintain influence beyond the Rhine and the Danube, by supporting and subsidising local chiefs (as they did also on the fringes of the Sahara and the Arabian desert). A more aggressive policy, in part a response to trouble on the Danube frontier under Domitian, was developed by Trajan when he attacked the Dacian prince Decebalus in 101–2 and 105–6. (This contrasted with Domitian's final decision to supply Decebalus with money and technical assistance.) In consequence part of Dacia (Romania) became a Roman province. In the east a province was created called Arabia in what is now the kingdom of Jordan. Furthermore, Trajan tried to add Mesopotamia to the empire but had to surrender most of it in face of revolt and Parthian reprisals. Later campaigns by Lucius Verus and Septimius Severus led to the establishment of a Roman defensive system in the north of Mesopotamia. One further item of expansion must be noted, the acquisition of Britannia between 43 and 84 AD. Direct control was established in England and Wales, while in Scotland suzerainty was most of the time only nominal, when no armies were present, though power was exercised, where possible, through local chiefs.

Thus the Roman empire during the Principate remained territorially much what it had been at Augustus' death. At times it may have seemed in effect infinite since there was little serious opposition outside. However, the Germanic and Scythian tribes were a continual threat and limitation from the mid-second century AD onwards, while in the east the new Sassanian Persian dynasty, who took over the Parthian empire shortly before 230, proved much tougher opposition than the Parthians had been. The Romans could never quite forget the empire without end, which Jupiter claims to have given them in Vergil's *Aeneid*, and they remained a nation devoted to military glory, as the monuments of the imperial city show.[22] Yet in practice after Augustus', and again after Trajan's, death annexation dwindled in face of the problem of finding and funding the troops required to maintain wider frontiers. The concept of the empire changed from that of an inexorably expanding community – implicit not only in Vergil but in Augustus' *Res Gestae* and Claudius' speech on the admission of Gallic senators – to an image of a fortress of civilisation, whose grandeur dominated even what lay beyond its walls.[23]

Roman success in empire-building was founded on the phenomenal achievements of their army. However, this topic lies for the most part outside the scope of this book. Other important works are devoted to Roman strategy, military techniques and the vast reservoir of Italian manpower which won the empire in the first place, later augmented and ultimately replaced by the manpower of the Roman provinces and frontiers. Nor can we discuss what impressed Polybius, the constitutional stability and political coherence which sustained Rome in the early centuries of expansion. We are concerned here with the methods, largely those of peace, by which the empire was held. It may well be thought that Roman methods of organisation and government fell short of their military ability and that in peace mismanagement and corruption went far towards subverting the gains of war. Yet Roman administration because of its very flexibility and its readiness to work through existing institutions deserves study, not least because the Romans themselves believed that by offering their subjects

Roman law and political control they were providing something genuinely new and valuable. On the other side it is clear that the empire was not held down merely by military force and that Roman rule, even if at many points unjust and inefficient, was not only tolerated but appreciated by many of its subjects.

2

ELEMENTS OF EMPIRE

THE ROMAN BACKGROUND

Probably from her earliest times as a city Rome was a member of an alliance of kindred peoples, the Latin name (*nomen Latinum*), a League, whose chief functions were to wage wars in common and to hold common religious ceremonies. This league was eventually regulated by a treaty (*foedus*), texts of which were still available to be read in the late Republic, though the exact date of the treaty (or treaties) to which the texts referred is not certain.[1] What we know of it concerns military leadership, distribution of booty gained in common wars and the settlement of disputes between member-states. Even after the reformation of the league under her own leadership in 338 Rome exploited the concept of the Latin name to link herself with strategically placed colonies, which she founded as cities in their own right throughout Italy.[2]

Rome's treaty relationships with her Italian allies were never so close, though they resembled the Latin treaty in one respect through having a fundamentally military function. We can only reconstruct what these were like from the formulae used in later treaties with communities abroad, for the most part preserved in inscriptions, which are clearly primitive in form. They resembled a Greek *summachia* of the classical period, being comprised of a series of reciprocal engagements to refrain from giving assistance to enemies of the partner and to provide military aid when the partner or allies of the partner were attacked.[3] In Italian treaties there were probably more precise provisions regarding the quantity of military aid to be supplied to Rome or at least a reference to the *formula togatorum*, the list of allies which was the basis for raising armies.[4] Such was what the Romans termed a *foedus aequum*, a reciprocal agreement in which the

16

contracting parties appeared to be on the same level, even if the interests of the greater power, Rome, would tend to prevail.

Other treaties, like that later imposed on the Aetolians in 189, were more one-sided: they imposed obligations on Rome's partner without necessarily corresponding obligations for Rome on each point and included a clause requiring the ally to act to preserve the empire and majesty of the Roman people without deceit.[5] There were generally two situations in which a treaty might take such a form. Either Rome made a settlement with a defeated enemy establishing peace and an alliance for the future, or a people not currently at war with Rome, but perhaps in conflict with another power, applied for a military alliance in its own interest. In both cases the quasi-legal ritual *deditio* was required by Rome, in which the other community placed itself unreservedly under Roman authority. A simple form of surrender is recorded on a bronze tablet from Spain set up in 104 BC.

> The Seanoc . . . people surrendered itself to L. Caesius the commander. L. Caesius the commander, after he had received the surrender, referred to his council the question of what demands he should make of them. On the council's suggestion he demanded that they should give back the captives, horses and mares, which they had taken. They surrendered them all. Then L. Caesius ordered them to have existence (in their own right); he returned to them their lands and buildings, their laws and everything else which had been theirs and was in existence the day before they surrendered, provided that the Roman people (and the senate) approved. Concerning that point he instructed them to go (to Rome).[6]

This procedure was also termed *deditio in fidem* or *venire in fidem*, where the *fides*, into which the other community was surrendering itself, has the moral significance of good faith, and the practical significance of protection.[7] Although this terminology appears in the historical sources, especially Polybius and Livy, which describe such surrenders, there is no evidence that the word *fides* itself had some technical quasi-legal significance. Polybius and Livy indeed assert that a surrender *in fidem* was for the Romans a total surrender into their discretion and this the Aetolians failed to recognise to their own discomfort. However, the concept of good faith (*fides* = Greek *pistis*) was not unknown to Greeks in such situations, where a weaker power put itself into the hands of a stronger power.[8] The Romans, moreover, accepted that they had a moral obligation as the receivers of a surrender, provided that this was made before any Roman assault on the town of Rome's enemies, not to kill or enslave those surrendering and to create a peaceful settlement appropriate to the circumstances.[9] Nevertheless, a *deditio* was a total surrender with no specific conditions, one in which those who yielded lost, though usually only for a short time, their status as an independent community and any legal rights as such. They were *in dicione* of the Romans, subject to their absolute discretion.

If a community, with whom Rome was not at war, was seeking protection, a treaty soon followed in which it was revived as a separate political entity. The procedure did, however, allow the Romans discretion over the treaty terms and in the meantime made it possible for them to fight on behalf of those who had surrendered without further ado, since the other community's territory was now under Roman sovereignty. A defeated enemy, on the other hand, could not necessarily expect to be restored to independence immediately. Under the Principate certain peoples (probably non-Greek and with little political culture) seem to have been left as *dediticii*, in a state of permanent surrender. Under the Republic we hear of those in *arbitratu dicione potestate*, under the sovereignty, dominion and power, of the Roman people.[10]

These in some respects crude practices formed the native tradition to which the Romans might have recourse when defining their relationships with friends and defeated enemies abroad. It should be added, however, that they also had a tradition of incorporating entire foreign communities in their body politic, whether as citizens with full rights or citizens without the vote – something of which there were only rare instances in the Greek world, one being the grant of Athenian citizenship to the Samians in 405–4 BC.[11] Although whole-sale grants of Roman citizenship only occurred within Italy and Cisalpine Gaul during the period of expansion under the Republic, in the long run this principle was to make an important contribution to the unification of the empire (see further Chapter 10).

THE FOREIGN BACKGROUND

The regular form of linking two sovereign communities in the Greek world had been the military *summachia*, an agreement for reciprocal military support which was similar to (and perhaps the parent of) Roman treaties. In the late sixth and fifth centuries this form had been elaborated by Sparta into the Peloponnesian League and by

Athens into the Delian League, organisations in which a greater number of communities became military allies under a *hegemon* (leader) with some provision for joint consultation. Discussion over policy and the contributions to be made to common enterprises remained a feature of the Peloponnesian League during the fifth century, though it then lapsed; in the Delian League it had ceased by 431, but was revived in Athens second confederacy in 377. By contrast Rome's alliance with her Italian associates was in fact a number of separate agreements. So there were no joint institutions, such as had existed in the Latin League until 338 BC. Nor were there in Italy any equivalents to the 'Common Peace' treaties characteristic of fourth-century Greece. These agreements were in theory intended to eliminate war and were defensive, though they might be exploited as a means of assembling military support against a dissident Greek or a foreign power, as the League of Corinth was used by Philip II of Macedon against Persia.[12]

However, the fourth-century treaties had one aspect which was to be a legacy to the Hellenistic world and later to Rome – the concept of a free city within an alliance. Because they were intended to avoid the mistakes made by earlier Athenian and Spartan hegemonies, stress was laid on abstention from interference in the internal affairs of the constituent communities. Members of the alliances were to be free and autonomous, not subject to exactions of tribute and other forms of exploitation by the leading power. Ironically, intervention was allowed to suppress a political revolution (the constitution of the League of Corinth is a classic example) on the ground that it might affect the city's external alignment.[13] Moreover, in practice leading states could not resist trying to impose their political will on their allies over domestic issues. However, a principle, or at least something more than a mere slogan, had been established, and the successors to Alexander the Great, fighting over his legacy of empire in Greece, the Aegean and Asia, made solemn declarations that guaranteed this freedom to the members of the leagues that they formed, associating it in particular with freedom from tribute and billeting. Such freedom became a privilege in the Hellenistic period which the kings who dominated the Greek cities did not automatically confer, and it must be distinguished from the *de facto* local autonomy, which kings had perforce to delegate, because they did not have the interest or the officials to replace it. In fact, when a city was not declared free, the king might well appoint a curator or supervisor from time to time.[14]

The free city also emerged from a different political context in Sicily, where it probably had an earlier impact on Roman thinking. About 339–8 BC Timoleon, the Corinthian who had liberated Syracuse from Dionysius II's tyranny and the threat of Punic conquest, made an agreement with Carthage, whereby the river Halykos was to be the boundary between the zones of influence of Carthage and of Syracuse and in both zones all Greek cities were to be free.[15] The cities in the Greek zone came later to be dominated by Syracuse, but those in the Punic zone probably fared better: it is siginificant that after being 'liberated' by Pyrrhus about 278 BC they broke away from him and returned to their Punic allegiance.[16]

By the Hellenistic period the non-urban political community (*ethnos*) in Greece had developed many of the features of cities in possessing political centres, regular magistrates and assemblies. What has been said about the cities in the government of the Hellenistic world may apply equally well to them. Other peoples, called *nationes* by the Romans, were ruled by individual kings or chiefs or jointly by an aristocracy. In Celtic Gaul and in Iberian and Celtiberian Spain the majority of the people were probably bound as dependants to the aristocrats. The most detailed picture of this is provided by our sources on Gaul – Caesar in the sixth book of the *Gallic War* and Poseidonius[17] – but the relation of Spanish communities to powerful men is shown by the later tablets recording the appointment of patrons, a procedure where non-Roman and Roman elements seem to have fused.[18] The Romans well understood the operation of patronage and were happy to make use of existing vertical social links in order to control societies that may have been less susceptible to other forms of management. Nor was this incompatible in the long run with urbanisation.

The administration of the subjects of Hellenistic kings outside their homelands was carried out by generals and other military commanders. The same was true of Carthage, whose generals were sent out as viceroys for long periods with immense discretionary powers, especially tbe Barcids in Spain. The Roman consul or praetor at the head of an army fitted easily into this world of military authority sustained by a social and economic platform of city life, and it is not surprising that the Romans adapted rapidly to it.

Socially and economically the world of kings and cities was as hierarchical as it tended to be politically. The Hellenistic general and regional commander was, even before he retired, a great landowner, gifted with estates by his king.[19] Class divisions had been accentuated in the cities, partly because external owners tended to boost the status of leading citizens who would serve their turn, partly through the pressure on the poorer citizens caused by the political and economic decline of the cities *vis-à-vis* the great powers.[20] Ex-soldiers settled by the direct or indirect intervention of the kings formed a special class in city society.[21] Even cities which were nominally democracies, like Athens, were socially oligarchic[22] and it was especially 'the few' that the Romans learnt to draw into their orbit. The debt of the Romans to Hellenistic practices in their organisation and administration of empire will be apparent at many points later. It is symptomatic that the formula used to open official Roman letters, 'If you are well, it is well. I and the army are well', derives from the letters of the kings of Syria and Pergamum and in embryo from Ptolemaic officials in Egypt.[23]

3

THE ORGANISATION OF EMPIRE

We tend to envisage empires in terms of territories of a certain colour on a map and their rulers as landlords. The Roman people certainly regarded itself also as a landlord in particular contexts, but this was not the root idea of *imperium*. The essential notion was rather the giving of commands by a general (*imperator*). In the second century BC Polybius correctly understood the Roman aim in their greatest bout of imperial expansion as one of exacting obedience, compelling other peoples to obey orders.[1] The emperor Augustus later stated in his official autobiography that his army had forced even the Dacians beyond the Danube to *perferre Romana imperia*, submit to Roman instructions.[2] At the time when Polybius wrote, in many parts of the world which he held that Rome dominated these orders were intermittent (notably in Asia Minor) and the Romans were at times far from zealous in punishing disobedience.[3] As the empire grew older, Rome grew more exacting: under the Principate we find detailed regulations in imperial edicts which would have been unthinkable under the Republic. Yet it remained true that being subject to Rome was not a perpetual discipline. Provided that the communities reacted to specific orders they were left a considerable degree of liberty or self-regulation.

PROVINCIAE

The term that the Romans came to use for the areas directly administered by their officials was *provincia*. The basic meaning of this word was 'appointment' or 'task'. Thus one of the quaestors in Italy had the treasury as his *provincia*.[4] Overseas a *provincia* was originally the field of operations assigned to a magistrate. Some of these of course had clear natural geographical limits; for example,

Sicily or Corsica and Sardinia which became the first permanent *provinciae* overseas in 241 and 227 BC respectively. However, the first evidence of an attempt to draw geographical boundaries over a large land mass relates to the year 197 BC, when two new praetors were created to be the regular governors of two Spanish *provinciae* and the first appointees were sent out with instructions to place boundary stones in order to maintain the distinction between Further and Nearer Spain (Hispania Ulterior and Citerior). This boundary later ran south of New Carthage and the source of the river Baetis.[5] Nevertheless, this division was not strictly observed by governors for a number of years and it is hard to see how a precise line could be drawn in the interior of Spain where Roman power was insecure. At best there may have been stones on major roads or on high ground.

The earliest contemporary evidence for the existence of a technical term for a geographical area ruled by Rome comes with the creation of the province of Macedonia in 148–7 and its Greek annexes in 146–5. In a letter of a magistrate (probably the conqueror L. Mummius) to the guild of Dionysiac Artists we find a reference to the *eparcheia* of the Romans. Greece is likewise referred to in these terms in an inscription recording the judgement of Milesians on a land-dispute in Messenia *c.* 140 BC – 'when L. Mummius was in this *eparcheia*' – while we find the province of Asia called an *eparcheia* in the Claros texts of the late second century.[6] By contrast, in that part of the agrarian law of 111 BC preserved on bronze, which deals with Africa and other Roman overseas possessions, there is no mention of the word *provincia* in the surviving text. Within a few years the Greek translation at Delphi and Cnidos of a Roman document, the law about the provinces of 101–100 BC, shows the word *eparcheia* (= *provincia*) in three senses – the traditional one, that is, a sphere of operations assigned to a magistrate; an existing territorial division of Roman administration, such as Asia and Macedonia; a new territory added to these, such as Lycaonia and the Caenic Chersonnesos. In the first sense the word occurs in a repetition of one of the provisions of a *lex Porcia* passed shortly before it, which forbad a magistrate or pro-magistrate leaving his province without permission from the senate or people, except for purposes of transit and expeditions in the public interest (*rei publicae causa*) – a provision which was to reappear later in Sulla's *lex Cornelia de maiestate* and Caesar's *lex Iulia de repetundis*.[7] This clause shows that by 101 BC the spatial concept of a *provincia* was firmly established, though only in the context of assigning specific functions to magistrates.

23

However, we should not infer that the Romans were thinking in terms of absolutely precise boundaries. The governor of Macedonia had direct responsibility for portions of peninsular Greece – Boeotia, Euboea and parts of the Peloponnese. To reach them his land route lay through Thessaly, which remained a union of free cities until the end of the Republic. Furthermore, the permission to make expeditions *rei publicae causa* gave governors additional scope. The most frequently recorded actions of magistrates in Macedonia are campaigns against tribes in Thrace and Illyria, which tended to take the armies over any nominal northern boundary to Macedonia. For example, in the 70s BC Appius Claudius, C. Scribonius Curio and M. Lucullus all campaigned beyond the border, as did Cicero's enemy L. Piso later.[8] Although Cicero does not mention the exception, *rei publicae causa*, as existing under the *lex Cornelia* and *lex Iulia* then in force, this is surely because he is putting the worst possible construction on Piso's actions: he never says in so many words that Piso broke the law by entering Thrace. Moreover, Gabinius' defence of his invasion of Egypt as *rei publicae causa* (see p. 27) suggests that this exception was still valid.[9]

The flexibility of the concept of *provincia* even in the late Republic is illustrated by Cicero's own activities in Cilicia. Syme, when discussing the early history of that province, took it as a classic example of the word retaining its original sense of official duty. However, we need not deny the territorial sense, provided that is not interpreted too rigidly. Levick comments that 'the province will extend as far as the proconsul is led in the course of carrying out the duties of his office and as far as is necessary for their efficient performance'.[10] Cicero's Cilicia was a curious amalgam, stretching from Laodicea in southern Phrygia to the west through Lycaonia and Isauria and crossing the Taurus mountains into Rough Cilicia and Cilicia of the Plain. Its backbone was the main road, one of the two chief routes to the east, which was the axis of Cicero's activity. However, this route passed through land assigned to Cappadocia by Pompey after the Mithridatic Wars, which had previously belonged to the province. In order to reach the eastern end of his province by road Cicero had no alternative to entering this kingdom, except to enter another kingdom, that of Antipater of Derbe.[11] But he did not merely enter Cappadocia for the sake of transit, as the *lex Porcia* envisaged: he also made contact with Ariobarzanes of Cappadocia and gave him diplomatic support.[12] It may be that he had some special mandate to do this from the senate, but his letter to the senate and the people makes no mention of this: it merely assumes that this was a job to be done in order to protect the security of Roman interests in the east (that is, *rei publicae causa*). Cicero also had close contact with king Deiotarus of Galatia, who provided him with considerable auxiliary forces and entertained his son and nephew, and he visited Antipater of Derbe.[13] The governor of Cilicia, therefore, had under the Republic a sphere of activity and responsibility which went beyond the area he administered directly.

The province of Syria created by Pompey is another example of one with which allied kingdoms were integrated. After the death of Herod the Great in 4 BC, when Gaza and its surrounding territory were once more made part of Syria, it stretched from the *mons Amanus* at the south-eastern end of Cilicia in the north as far as Egypt in the south. This included a number of tetrarchies and petty kingdoms, including Apamea, which a recently discovered inscription has shown to have been the possession of one Dexandros (he combined his position there with that of being the first *flamen*, provincial high-priest, of the cult of Rome and Augustus in Syria).[14] The former kingdom of the Jews was placed in a similar category by Pompey's settlement of 63 BC: the ethnarchs and high-priests were ultimately subject to the governor of Syria, however much discretion they were allowed. Even Herod, the 'lover of Rome and of Caesar', who was granted the title of king and considerable latitude in his activities by Mark Antony and Augustus, was closely associated with the Roman administration, as is shown by his appointment to be a leading imperial procurator in Syria *c.* 20 BC.[15]

Caesar's extension by conquest of the Transalpine Gallic province to include all 'Long-haired Gaul' has been taken as an example of a proconsul breaching the rules which bound Republican governors,[16] but in fact it may simply be yet another illustration of the flexibility of the concept of *provincia*. Ironically, Caesar's own commentaries may be used as testimony against him. Caesar states that in 58 BC Tolosa (Toulouse) was inside the province, while the Santones north of the Gironde were outside; in the east the Allobroges were inside but the Sequani north of the Rhône were not; as for the Arverni and Ruteni in the Massif Central and the Cevennes, although they had been conquered (*c.* 119 BC), they had been pardoned and so not subjected to tribute or made part of the *provincia*. The context of this last remark is important. Caesar is replying to Ariovistus' claim during the negotiations before the battle of Vesontio that Roman armies had never left the boundary of *provincia Gallia*.[17] He is arguing that the territory which the Romans deliberately refused to make part of their *provincia* is nevertheless under their protection. He has previously said that in his judgement Gaul belongs no more to Ariovistus than to the Romans and now continues his argument by applying the decision taken in 119 BC, to leave the Arverni and Ruteni free, to the whole of Gaul: 'if the judgement of the senate should be respected, Gaul ought to be free, since the senate has wished it to be autonomous after conquest in war'. Here he tendentiously asserts the patronage of the Roman people over all Transalpine Gaul, perhaps on the ground that the father of the Arvernian chief Bituitus, whom they vanquished, had claimed the leadership of all the Gallic peoples.[18]

We may well wonder how far other Romans would have shared Caesar's view of Gaul. Yet it is clear that the Arverni and Ruteni were, both in the Roman view and their own, part of the *imperium Romanum* before Caesar's governorship, since they revolted in 53 without any prior intervention by Caesar in their territory. Moreover, the *senatus consultum* of 61 BC, which Caesar quoted, urging the governors of *Gallia provincia* to protect the Aedui and the other friends of the Roman people, did in fact give him a commission to leave the land directly ruled by Rome in order to defend not only the Aedui but also the Arverni, Ruteni and any other Gallic peoples who had been addressed as friends in diplomatic relations in the past.[19]

Therefore any impression given by the Cnidos text of the law about the provinces that through the *lex Porcia* a province had become something neatly defined is an illusion. The public interest required that magistrates acted outside the borders of the territory directly under their authority in order to sustain and reconcile friends and to impress barbarian neighbours with Roman power. Roman military strategy in the Republic and early Principate was not based on holding a defensive line but on retaliatory and sometimes on pre-emptive strikes.[20] Hence the escape clause allowing sorties *rei publicae causa*. The loophole thus left for indiscriminate aggression could not easily be closed without sacrificing military effectiveness, and it is arguable that most Roman senators, habituated to the expansion of the empire by intervention outside Rome's sphere of immediate interest, were not much concerned to do so. What M. Porcius Cato, the great-grandson of Cato the Censor,[21] had probably sought to achieve by his law was simply that magistrates should not interfere in each other's provinces – like C. Cassius (cos. 171 BC), who, because he could not find a satisfactory war in Cisalpine Gaul, set out through Illyricum for Macedonia in order to join in the Third Macedonian War.[22]

The classic example of a magistrate being prosecuted for going beyond his province is that of A. Gabinius (cos. 58 BC), the *bête noire* of Cicero after his hostility at the time of Cicero's exile, and of the Roman tax-collectors for cutting down the tax burdens (probably arrears) of the provincials. During his term in Syria he intervened in Palestine – something about which Cicero rightly made no complaint because it was part of the Syrian *provincia* – he also planned a Parthian war and he actually marched into Egypt to restore Ptolemy XII to the throne.[23] In Cicero's view this last act was contrary to the clauses in the *lex Cornelia de maiestate* and the *lex Iulia de repetundis* which forbad a magistrate to leave his province, and contrary to the senate's ruling that Ptolemy was not to be restored with an army.[24] Gabinius was in fact acquitted when charged *de maiestate* in October 54, according to Cicero through corruption and fear of the senate. Yet Domitius Calvinus and the self-consciously upright Cato acquitted, which might suggest, whatever their actual motives, that Gabinius had a case according to one interpretation of the law. Cicero admitted that Gabinius had claimed his invasion of Egypt to have been *rei publicae causa*.[25] We should not be too ready to take Cicero's word that acquittals in hotly contested cases were corrupt. It is better to concede that the installation of a friend and ally in his kingdom, even by methods breaching a two-year-old decree of the senate, was in principle defensible as an act in the best interests of Rome.

The *provincia* in the late Republic had become more closely defined geographically but its borders, especially with hostile peoples, were imprecise, and it might be interspersed with districts belonging to free cities or the possessions of allied kings and dynasts. However, the essential ambiguity of the concept lay elsewhere. The magistrate had a penumbra of responsibility outside the area he ruled directly; his assignment was up to a point open-ended, provided that he did not trespass on a fellow magistrate's preserves. As we shall see, opportunities for initiatives beyond the frontiers became more restricted under the Principate through closer supervision of magistrates by the emperor. Yet Agricola's conquest of southern Scotland, for example, may have owed less to Flavian policies than to a revival of a long-standing tradition.

A constitution for the *provincia*

As a military assignment a *provincia* might be ill-defined. This was not admissible when it came to administration, justice and the collection of taxes. Yet even here a greater stability of organisation is sometimes assumed than is warranted by the evidence. At the heart of the problem is the so-called *lex provinciae*, an institution supposed by modern scholars to have defined the *provincia* politically and juridically, being a body of law which turned into a permanent peaceful province what before had been a sphere of military operations. Obviously this sort of transition took place, but it did not happen always at one point in the province's history nor was the *lex provinciae* necessarily the instrument.

There are three, or perhaps four, examples of bodies of law regulating provinces named after Roman commanders. About 110 AD the younger Pliny could still refer to the *lex Pompeia* in Bithynia, which must have been created by Pompey about 63 BC;[26] Cicero mentions the decree of Rupilius, 'which the Sicilians calls the *lex Rupilia*' – one drafted according to the advice of a ten-man commission and given to the Sicilians by the consul of 132 BC – and the law which P. Lentulus Spinther gave to Cyprus, probably in 57 BC. We have also references to a *lex Cornelia* regulating elections in the province of Asia in the Augustan period, which may be part of a more general provincial ordinance.[27] These *leges* were certainly used to bring order to a province either after annexation (Bithynia, Cyprus) or a great upheaval like the first slave-revolt in Sicily. However, they are not strong enough evidence for a uniform regular procedure for establishing Roman rule.

Using a commission of advisers seems standard Roman practice. Yet neither Pompey nor, as it appears, Lentulus Spinther employed one. Such commissions were, however, customarily sent to make a settlement after a victory, when no territory was annexed to Rome, for instance in 196, when Flamininus declared Greece free, and in 189 for Manlius Vulso's organisation of Asia.[28] Settlements of this kind, which provide a useful comparison to the organisation of a province, were made in Macedonia and Illyricum at the close of the Third Macedonian War (167). Neither of the two areas were permanently subjected to a governor and Macedonia was divided into four independent regions. The basic schemes of the settlement there are called *formulae* (schedules) by Livy.[29] These were lists of the communities involved according to their geographical divisions, with notes of the tribute they had to pay (similar to the assessments of the Athenian fifth-century empire). We hear later from the elder Pliny how the emperor Galba added two Alpine communes to the *formula* of Gallia Narbonensis.[30] Apart from the *formulae*, Aemilius Paulus laid down detailed constitutions for the four regions (*merē*) in Macedonia and the cities within them. Although the settlements of Macedonia and Illyricum in 167 did not create provinces, they provide a plausible pattern for provincial settlements – a register of communities with their tax assessments, supplemented by a number of more detailed regulations relating to communities or groups of communities.

Yet, though a *formula* would be essential when a province was created, the articulation of detailed constitutions and regulations might just as plausibly have developed over a period. As we have seen, the initial definition of two Spanish provinces occurred in 197. However, until the praetorship of Tiberius Gracchus (father of the famous tribune) in 180–8 there seems to have been no fixed schedule of tax assessments: magistrates exacted what they could in cash and grain. Thus Q. Fulvius Flaccus was able to tell the senate in 180 that in this year sufficient taxation had been obtained to make further subventions from Rome unnecessary. In practice Gracchus' tax system was disregarded and had to be reimposed by M. Marcellus in 152–1, and even this would have required revision after Scipio Aemilianus' capture of Numantia and the end of the war with Viriathus in 132.[31]

Although part of Cicero's province of Cilicia, Cyprus, had received a *lex* from Lentulus Spinther in 57, Cicero never refers to anything similar affecting his mainland assignment, even where this might be most expected – in the discussion of his provincial edict. He had drafted this on the model of the edict propounded for Asia by Q. Mucius Scaevola (cos. 95), which apparently had been recommended as a standard for subsequent governors by a senate decree.[32] It was the result of Scaevola's precedent, not of any *lex provinciae*, that Cicero gave the Greeks freedom to sue one another according to the laws of their own cities before Greek judges. In fact Lycaonia and the three Phrygian dioceses now in Cilicia had once been part of the province of Asia. Cicero was thus transferring to Cilicia what had no doubt been customary in these regions. However, the implication for both Asia and Cilicia is that the juridical framework of these provinces was allowed to develop over a period. By contrast, the elaborate system in Sicily attested at the time of Verres' governorship (73–1 BC) was indeed the product of a single act, Rupilius' decree of 132.

However, this had come long after the original registration of the communities in the Sicilian province, which must have occurred soon after 241, and the organisation of their taxation, which probably stemmed from the settlement in 211–10 after the revolt of Syracuse and other allies during the Second Punic War (the list of cities either with treaties or immunity from taxation reflects the situation at that time).[33]

Perhaps the most direct evidence we have of a provincial settlement is that provided by the *lex agraria* of 111 BC, preserved in part on fragments of bronze, which has a section dealing with Africa.[34] We know from the elder Pliny that in 146 Scipio Aemilianus created the *fossa regia*, a trench modelled on the earlier 'Punic trenches' which separated the previously Carthaginian territory he had assigned to Rome from that conceded to the kings of Numidia. Corresponding to this, we find in the agrarian law a reference to land conceded by someone in the singular (his name is lost) to the children of king Masinissa. Also mentioned in the same line is land granted by the ten men appointed under the *lex Livia* to the city of Utica (that is, in addition to the original territory of Utica mentioned earlier in the law). This ten-man commission must be identical with that which, according to Appian, was sent by the senate to assist Scipio in Africa and assigned to Utica all the land stretching from Carthage to Hippo Diarrhytus (Bizerta).[35] Appian is clearly wrong in suggesting that the senate sent this commission itself, as usually happened; perhaps the law was passed after a *senatus consultum*. Nevertheless, the outline of the procedure is clear. It began with the conquering general in effect setting the geographical limits of the province according to his own initiative and continued with a commission operating under the terms of a law or plebiscite. This may have been passed in order to give greater authority to the commission's activities, especially if it were to find it necessary to overrule Scipio at any point. In fact the commission gave recognition to a number of free cities in Africa, imposed tribute (*stipendium*) on the rest of the local peoples and probably began the first massive grid of centuriation, largely reconstructed by archaeologists through air-photography, which was to be the basis of land-assignation in the province.[36]

M'. Aquillius carried out a settlement with the aid of ten *legati* in the province of Asia created from the old kingdom of Pergamum, left to Rome by the will of Attalus III in 133 BC. This settlement is mentioned in the *senatus consultum* concerning Pergamene territory (whether prospectively, if the decree is of early 129, as is normally held, or retrospectively, if the decree is of 101, as is powerfully argued by H. B. Mattingly). According to Strabo, Aquillius organised the province into the form which still survived in his own day (under Augustus).[37] Strabo seems to be referring to the *formula* detailing the composition of the province. Nevertheless, the outlines of the settlement were still the subject of debate after Aquillius had returned to Rome in 126. In 124 or 123 C. Gracchus spoke against a *lex Aufeia*, which apportioned land previously Pergamene to the kings of Bithynia and of Pontus, Nicomedes II and Mithridates V. This bill must by the same token have defined the area to be directly ruled by Rome and probably also the status of the communities inside it, since C. Gracchus is concerned with the effect on Roman revenues. The bill seems to have failed and C. Gracchus himself later passed a law laying down the procedure for collecting taxation in Asia, which was to depend on auctions among the *societates* of *publicani* at Rome.[38] The law is unlikely to have been confined to the matter of auctions alone, but probably defined the nature of taxation in the province and was thus a major contribution to the provincial settlement. Here, as in Africa, important parts of the provincial settlement depended on a law passed by a popular assembly at Rome, which followed the original delimitation of the province.

On the other hand, the Romans might subject territory to direct rule without clearly defining a province or even achieving a complete pacification. This, as we have seen, was the position during the early years of Roman rule in Spain. The boundaries of Illyricum also remained uncertain during the Republic in spite of the original *formula* drawn up in 167–6, when its southern section, the former kingdom of Gentius, had been organised and subjected to tribute.[39] Much later, under Augustus, it was assumed that, when Tiberius returned to Rome in 8 BC for his second triumph and consulship, he had reduced Germany more or less into the form of a tax-paying province. The unwary Quinctilius Varus was exacting tribute and holding assizes there in AD 9 as if in a pacified province – so a contemporary historian complained. Indeed it is suggested elsewhere that the Germans were being introduced to urban life.[40] The slaughter in the Teutoburgerwald showed how this superficial control could be dissolved at one stroke.

We cannot therefore presume that there was a single enact-ment regulating each province, which had been passed shortly after its incorporation into Roman territory, nor use this as a criterion for its being an organised sphere of administration rather than the assignment of a military commander. The point when the senate or people decided to send a magistrate regularly to the area was an important date in its history. So was the moment (often the same) when the land itself was claimed to be Roman (it is significant that the agrarian law of 111 BC assumed that ultimately even the land of the free cities in Africa was at the disposal of the Roman people). Following the definition of the territory in the *formula*, there might be a long series of enactments by the assembly, the senate or individual governors which determined the political conditions under which the provincials should live. Nevertheless, Roman magistrates might exercise political authority without a closely defined area of operations and, conversely, there could be precise definition of a territory without direct Roman rule.

ALLIED KINGS

The Roman titles for those who are conventionally called by modern historians 'client-kings' are 'kings and friends of the Roman people' or 'kings, allies and friends of the Roman people'. Paradoxically, although the Roman Republic had arisen after the expulsion of kings, it conferred on its allies the traditional regal insignia of Etruscan origin – an ivory sceptre and embroidered toga, perhaps also a tunic decorated with palms – as well as the insignia of magistrates – a *toga praetextata* and a curule chair.[41] Kings were not necessarily bound to Rome by treaties of alliance. Defeated enemies, such as the kings of Macedon and of Syria, had a peace-treaty but were not granted a *foedus* of alliance, though they were called *amici* and even *socii*. Other kings, like Masinissa of Numidia, received the title without any treaty at all.[42] There is currently a complex debate about the distinction between 'friends' and 'allies' in the language of Roman diplomacy of the late third and early second centuries. On occasions, certainly, friendship (*amicitia*) excluded any formal alliance while alliance (*societas*) was something created by treaty. However, there was also a looser usage, whereby all *amici* were also *socii*, especially if, like the Achaeans in the early 190s, they were actually partners in a war, whether they had a treaty or not.[43]

These allied kings, then, seem to have derived their status either from a peace or simply from nomination by the senate. This act was probably recorded in a *formula*. We hear of a *formula sociorum* and one of *amicorum*, in which friendly cities and individuals were registered and it is likely that the kings found their place in one of these.[44] Furthermore, they publicised their relationship by inscribing dedications to the Roman people, presumably after receiving permission to do so from the Roman senate.[45] For we find on the Capitol at Rome dedications to Juppiter Capitolinus and the *populus Romanus* from kings of Pontus, Cappadocia and Nabataea as well as from *nationes* like the Lycians and cities like Ephesus. It was on the Capitol too that the king or his representatives made a sacrifice on the occasion of his formal recognition.[46]

The relationship between Rome and her allies is in one or two ancient texts interpreted as being between a patron and clients; the term 'client-king', however, is an invention of post-Renaissance scholarship.[47] It may seem unexceptionable as a metaphor, especially since the concept of patronage is widely used today by anthropologists and historians to explain positions of authority and dependence which are not defined by law or contract. Yet this vocabulary may be misleading in Roman international relations, in that it suggests a more precisely defined status for allied kings than they had in fact, that they were clients of the Roman people on the same terms as an individual Roman was the client of another Roman and his family. It is indeed clear that allied kings and communities had links with leading Roman senators, which resembled closely the patron–client relationships in Roman society. Q. Oppius, in a newly published letter to the people of Aphrodisias in Caria, promises to accede to their request and be their patron.[48] Other inscriptions show foreign ambassadors behaving like clients at the houses of Roman senators, probably during the winter that preceded their being heard officially by the senate. In the mid-second century BC Abdera honoured ambassadors sent to Rome from her mother-city Teos who had pleaded on Abdera's behalf for territory also claimed by Cotys, king of Thrace. They had met the Roman *principes* and by performing *salutatio* had won them over; then they had persuaded their own patrons to look after Abdera's interests. Another document from Aphrodisias claims that some ambassadors of theirs had lobbied the *principes* on all occasions and there is a similar decree from Alabanda.[49] We know that the Numidian royal house regarded themselves as clients of the Scipio family and indeed sought wider contacts, as is shown by young Jugurtha's behaviour in the army of Scipio Aemilianus in Spain.[50] Yet this did not define the relationship of any king or city with the Roman people.

The kings were in the *amicitia* of the Roman people and also in their *fides* (the protection to which they have entrusted themselves)[51] without this necessarily implying the dependence characteristic of a Roman client. To call them client-kings suggests a greater theoretical inferiority than the official term, 'friends and allies' warrants, though it may not exaggerate their dependence in fact. Moreover, the client metaphor may deceptively suggest that the relationship was characterised by strict moral obligations, whereas Rome treated her vassals no differently than other dominant powers did, allowing, as Polybius saw, the pursuit of self-interest to override considerations of justice.[52]

Some of the earliest kings to be recognised as friends and allies – Ptolemy II Philadelphus, Attalus I of Pergamum, Hiero II of Syracuse (though he had a formal treaty) – were not treated as inferiors. Soon, however, Rome was responsible for putting kings in power, like Demetrios of Pharos and Masinissa.[53] Then two of the principal royal houses in the eastern Mediterranean, those of Macedon and Syria, were defeated and forced into dependence and Roman success began to affect generally the atittudes of other kings. In 189 Eumenes II of Pergamum was reluctant to assert his claims for reward after the defeat of Antiochus III until he was positively urged to do so by the senate.[54] After the Roman victory in the Third Macedonian War the brusque diplomatic rebuff given to Antiochus IV of Syria, when he tried to invade Egypt, showed Rome's perception of her position, as did her humiliation of Eumenes II and the attempt to replace him prematurely by his brother Attalus. At this time Prusias of Bithynia tried to display his recognition of his current standing *vis-à-vis* Rome by presenting himself in the senate in a freedman's cap, as someone who owed his liberty to the Romans and was by Roman rules automatically their client.[55]

Sallust in a speech assigned to the Numidian prince Adherbal, whose dramatic date is *c.* 115 BC but was written about seventy-five years later, made the king claim that he was merely a bailiff (*procurator*) of the Roman people, who were the ultimate sovereigns of his land. This is the developed concept of the allied kingdom implicit in Augustus' tendentious statement in his *Res Gestae*: 'Although I could have made Greater Armenia a province, I preferred to hand it over as a kingdom to Tigranes, following the precendent of our ancestors.' According to Suetonius, Augustus placed most conquered kingdoms under either their old rulers or new appointees and took care of them as parts of the empire by appointing instructors for monarchs who had not the intellectual capacity. The same view can still be found in a historian of the early third century AD, Cassius Dio, who ascribes to Julius Caesar (the speech is Dio's own composition full of Thucydidean echoes) the following comment on Roman conquests: 'Although we did not even know their names properly before, we rule some of these lands ourselves, the rest we have handed over to others, so that we have received from them income, military power, honour and alliance.'[56]

Under the Republic the only good evidence for regular taxation of a territory akin to a kingdom concerns Judaea. Under Pompey's settlement of 64 BC the Jews, now ruled by the high-priest Hyrcanus, were not only subject to the governor of Syria but paid tribute for Jerusalem and its surrounding territory. This may have continued under Augustus: we have already seen that Herod the Great was a Roman procurator.[57] Military co-operation was also expected. Caesar in 47 BC respected the status of the Syrian kings he received into submission on condition that they helped to protect the province.[58] If a ruler was not obliged to make payments to the Roman people as an indemnity for the military losses he had caused or the price of his throne, he may have paid as much or more to the man who freed him from his obligation. This perhaps explains by Ariobarzanes of Cappadocia owed so much to Pompey by 50 BC that the interest exceeded 33 talents a month (200,000 *denarii*).[59]

In Augustus' time Roman colonies were to be found in the kingdom of Mauretania ruled by Juba II (later the provinces of Mauretania Caesariensis and Tingitana), for example, Tingi and Zulil. Even if they were actually founded between 37 and 25 BC when there was no king of Mauretania, their continued presence showed that royal sovereignty was incomplete.[60] We know of nothing similar under the Republic. It is true that there is an imperial dedication to Marius as the founder of the colony at Thuburnica, in his time part of the Numidian kingdom, and the appearance of many Marii in eastern Numidia suggests that Marius had settled men there.[61] However, it is not likely that these were Romans, who would more probably have been given land within the centuriated area in the province. In fact, we know that Caesar encountered in 46 BC some aristocratic cavalry, then members of the Numidian royal guard, who were descended from men who had served under Marius and had been given estates by him. A Marius Gaetulicus has recently appeared on an imperial inscription at Theveste.[62] It seems, therefore, that Marius, when he gave the Numidian kingdom to Gauda in 105, provided him with the nucleus of an army from these ex-soldiers of his by giving them land in eastern Numidia. He thus simultaneously protected Gauda and secured his loyalty to Rome.

Under the Republic, even after the *lex Porcia* and its successors which regulated the conduct of governors, a Roman magistrate was entitled to enter an allied kingdom, if this was in the interests of Rome. Under the Principate the rules became somewhat different. This is revealed by the prosecution of M. Primus in 23 or 22 BC for making war on an allied people, the Thracian Odrysae, without authority.[63] In his defence he alleged that this had been recommended by Augustus and Marcellus, but Augustus presented himself as a witness 'in the public interest' and denied it. Clearly both Primus and Augustus thought that the *princeps'* authority was already sufficient justification for a provincial governor, who was not the *princeps'* direct subordinate, to leave his province and make war on Roman allies. As a corollary, without such approval military operations of this kind became hard to justify. Indeed it became accepted that the kingdoms were all part of Augustus' *provincia*.[64] So imperial legates and even procurators readily intervened. For example, in Britain Ostorius Scapula forcibly disarmed the Iceni under Prasutagus. Later, when Prasutagus died, a centurion and the procurator's slaves took the kingdom from Boudicca. The quarrel of Cartimandua, queen of the Brigantes, with her husband Venutius led to direct Roman rule.[65] More fortunate was Cogidubnus, king of the Regnenses – 'a great king of Britain' as he is styled in an inscription – who was given a number of tribes to rule. Tacitus' comment on this is: 'It was an ancient and long-accepted tradition of the Roman people to have even kings as instruments of subjection.'[66]

FREE CITIES

We have already considered how the concept of the 'free city' developed in the Hellenistic world both under Alexander the Great's successors and also probably in Sicily. Among the free cities in Sicily under the late Republic were three from the former Punic district – Segesta, Halicyae and Panormus.[67] It is in my view likely that they had been in this state since Sicily first passed into Roman control during the First Punic War. In Greece and Asia Minor the story begins with Titus Flamininus' famous declaration at the Isthmus in 196, following a *senatus consultum* the previous winter, that the Greek cities were to be free (*eleutheroi*), in possession of their own laws (*autonomoi*), free from garrisons (*aphrouretoi*) and from tribute (*aphorologetoi*).[68] Such declarations had been formerly made about individual cities by Antiochus II and III and by Philip V (different vocabulary but to similar effect had been used by Ptolemy II and by Alexander the Great himself).[69] General declarations of Greek freedom, as we have seen (see p. 19), had also a long history stretching back through Alexander's successors to the King's Peace of 387–6.

This Roman declaration was remarkable for simultaneously being general and conferring precise privileges. At the time it may have de facto involved a greater degree of genuine independence than previous declarations by Hellenistic kings, since in the immediate aftermath the Romans were cautious about direct intervention in Greek affairs. However, the freedom was conditional on the Greeks' continued friendship with Rome. Moreover, any freedom granted by a dominant power has implicitly an element of dependence, and most Greeks had no doubt that they were still subject to a dominant power (*hegemon*). Indeed the constitutions of the free Thessalian cities were created by Flamininus and he ruthlessly tried to instal pro-Roman factions in authority in Boeotia.[70]

There is not the space here to rehearse and document in detail the story of this 'freedom' in the years immediately following – how it was regarded by some (notably the Aetolians) as a tyranny, while others offended the Romans by interpreting it too generously, until the Achaean statesman Callicrates advised the Romans to stop pussyfooting in the relations between Greek communities and in their internal politics: they should make their wishes clearly known.[71] The free Greeks felt more Roman weight at the time of the Third Macedonian War (171–67), which led *inter alia* to the political detention of Polybius, and again in 147–6, when the refusal of the Achaeans and Boeotians to accept Roman demands led to their defeat and subjection. After 146 many cities in Greece – for example, Athens, Sparta and the Thessalian cities – remained free, while the rest of Greece was attached as provincial territory to Macedonia (see p. 10). But this freedom must have seemed more cramped.

It is interesting to compare how the cities were treated in the contemporary settlement of Africa after the destruction of Carthage, as it is documented in the agrarian law of 111 BC (lines 75–7, 85). Rome acknowledged the freedom of those cities which had supported her in the war against Carthage, such as Utica and Thapsus, and granted them their own land. Yet the land in Africa as a whole is viewed as in principle at Rome's disposal, as can be seen in the clauses exempting the cities' land from taxation and providing for compensation when the land had been improperly sold to Roman citizens. Perhaps the most striking anomaly in the African province in this period was that Utica, while remaining a free city, became the residence of the Roman governor.[72]

In the period after Sulla a free city was one which had recieved a special privilege from Rome. The *lex Antonia*, probably of 68 BC,[73] restored to Termessus Maior in Pisidia the position that it had held before the First Mithridatic War. It provided that the people should be 'free friends and allies of the Roman people' and that 'they should be allowed to enjoy all their own laws, in so far as this may not be contrary to this law' (Bruns[7], 14, I, 7ff.). The status and autonomy of Termessus are thus defined by a resolution of the Roman people. Later in the law (ibid., II, 6ff.) the people of Termessus are exempted from billeting and providing food and hospitality to Roman officials beyond what is allowed by the *lex Porcia* (i.e., the law of 101–100 which regulated the behaviour of provincial governors, see p. 23). Permission is also given for them to exact their own transit dues (*portoria*), except on the proceeds of tax-collection by Roman *publicani* (ibid., II, 31ff.). These privileges are thus a variant on those granted to Greece by Flamininus, but not quite so comprehensive and certainly not automatic following the grant of autonomy, as the careful enumeration shows. Indeed the impression given by this law, unlike the declaration of Flamininus, is that generous, but precise, upper limits are being set to the city's freedom. A similar impression is given by the *senatus consultum* of 39 BC, inspired by Octavian, which made an equally generous grant to Aphrodisias in Caria (Reynolds 1982, no. 8, *RDGE* 28), where we find specified in conjunction with freedom and autonomy immunity from tribute and asylum status for their precinct of Aphrodite.[74]

While autonomy in some sense was the norm among cities of the empire in the late Republic, freedom from tribute was not. In Sicily there were three cities with treaties and five declared free and immune from tribute and other exactions, but the rest paid tithes, even though they were allowed to enjoy their own laws.[75] The free cities as well as those with treaties (Tauromenium excepted) were required to give military aid in the form of ships and crews. A recently discovered inscription shows Halaesans among the sailors serving under Caninius Niger.[76] In Greece Gytheion, a free city in Lakonia, was liable to furnish supplies and billets, while Epidauros not only provided troops but was also subject to billeting *c.* 73 BC after concluding a treaty with Rome in 112 BC.[77]

Those cities in Sicily with treaties possessed them through the special circumstances of their association with Rome – the beginning of the First Punic War in Messana's case, loyalty to Rome in the Second Punic War in that of Tauromenium and probably Neaeton. We find a number of cities elsewhere holding treaties, which we might otherwise have expected to have the status of a free city. Such an agreement should have been ratified by the Roman people in an assembly, but Gades' treaty, known to us from Cicero's *pro Balbo* (34), had only been approved by the senate and in the treaties known to us from inscriptions there is no clear reference to any law and frequently some allusion to senatorial activity.[78] It seems that these treaties were granted occasionally and for tactical reasons – either as a special reward or to secure the loyalty of small communities which were in positions of strategic (e.g., Maroneia, Callatis) or political influence (e.g., Elaea). It may be that the old-fashioned formal treaty with its stress on military obligations (above p. 16) was also considered appropriate where Rome wished to emphasise her need for military contributions from her friends. Against this argument, however, we must set the long period before 167 where Rhodes, a military ally of vital importance, is said to have had no treaty relationship with Rome.[79]

Cities with treaties and free cities were eventually alike in having their status in effect regulated by Rome, involving similar privileges and in some cases duties, though differing in detail from city to city. They and their citizens should not be regarded as automatically reserved from the authority and jurisdiction of a Roman magistrate, especially when they were in dispute with people from outside their citizen body. Two honorific decrees from Claros relating to citizens of Colophon praise their efforts in protecting Colophonians from the justice of a Roman court by claiming the city's autonomy. In one case a Colophonian accused of an offence against a Roman was actually summoned to Rome for trial. Though the Romans were persuaded to make a formal declaration of Colophon's autonomy, it seems clear that only protests made them desist from exercising authority and it would be unwise to assume that they exercised the same restraint with every other free city. Later Cicero had to console his friend Atticus over a rider added to a *senatus consultum* of 60 BC, which forbad a Roman magistrate exercising jurisdiction in disputes arising from loans made to a citizen of a free city, and this provision was repeated next year in Caesar's *lex Iulia de repetundis*.[80] However, this implies that Roman magistrates had not previously been limited in such matters. A similar inference may be drawn from a *senatus consultum* of 80 BC, mentioned in a letter of a proconsul of Augustus' time to Chios (EJ, 317, *RDGE*, 70). This decree reaffirmed the freedom of the Chians and required that the Romans resident on Chios should obey Chian laws (presumably in their relations with the Greeks and other Romans on the island). It is not surprising that the Romans, belonging in their view to a new master race, were reluctant to submit to the laws of their host city. Cicero's writings, especially his correspondence, bear ample testimony to requests for the intervention of Roman magistrates in Greek communities, to protect Roman interests, both before and after Caesar's law of 59.[81]

COMMUNITIES LACKING SPECIAL STATUS

Communities with no special status to limit the governor's authority there and no immunity from taxation and corvées were called *stipendiariae*, payers of *stipendium*.[82] Those in this position were not, however, without rights or a degree of local autonomy. The majority of the cities in Sicily and the Asiatic province, which for the most part had existed before the advent of Roman rule, had this status. Yet each maintained an identity, a citizenship and a local jurisdiction of their own. Cicero's own Sicilian clients and the Asiatic clients of his opponent in the *pro Flacco* are all identified by their local city. Nor was respect for local self-government confined to the Hellenised provinces. The important new evidence from Contrebia in Spain shows a dispute over land- and water-rights in 87 BC between two subjected peoples being first formulated according to Roman principles by a Roman governor but then entrusted to the local senate of Contrebia for the actual judicial decision.[83] The Romans not only made use of existing towns and communes in Spain but actually created urban settlements for the provincials from the second century BC onwards. Ti. Gracchus (pr. 180–79) founded Gracchuris and Iliturgi, D. Brutus (cos. 138) Brutobriga – this apart from those towns founded wholly or in part for Romans or those of mixed descent.[84]

Useful evidence of how the Romans handled pre-existing communities at an early stage in their conquest is provided by Caesar's commentaries on his Gallic War. In some areas we hear only of chiefs who received the title 'friend of the Roman people'.[85] However, among the Aedui Caesar tried to operate through the *vergobreta*, the annual magistrate elected with supreme powers.[86] He also frequently summoned the traditional council of chiefs, the *concilium Galliae*,[87] which was a precedent for the later provincial council in Gaul under the Principate.

Elsewhere in the empire the Romans profited from the existence of some union or council of communities and it seems likely that they actually encouraged their development. A *commune Siciliae* met at Syracuse in Verres' time.[88] In the east the Achaean League was allowed to revive not long after its defeat in 146,[89] while the *koinon* of Asia, which seems to have existed in embryo *c.* 94 BC during the proconsulship of Q. Mucius Scaevola, is shown to be an established organisation in the late Republic: it co-ordinated the dispatch of embassies to Rome and was also used as a channel of information downwards by the Roman authorities.[90]

Some people, however, appear to have had no civic identity. The agrarian law of 111 BC, in the section dealing with Africa, refers to the free cities by name but lumps together the fully subject provincials as *stipendiarii* when it provides for their compensation for any land taken from them improperly and given to Roman citizens.[91] Nor is there any archaeological evidence for towns in the Republican era of the province apart from the free cities. It is possible that some form of local organisation existed in *pagi* – territorial divisions inherited i n some cases from Punic and Numidian administration. The *pagus Tuscae* stretching north from Mactar was formerly 'RST TŠKT under king Mikipsa.[92] However, it does not follow that these districts provided their inhabitants with a local citizenship and political organisation. These people may have been the equivalent of the *dediticii* under the Principate, non-Romans who had not been incorporated or reincorporated into a local community and who were incapable of attaining Roman citizenship.[93]

THE BOUNDARIES OF THE EMPIRE

Such are the forms by which the Romans defined their relationship with those whom they regarded as their subordinates (even if they generally termed them friends and allies). The multiplicity of the typology is confusing and tends to obscure the fundamental homogeneity in the *imperium Romanum* – the fact that the Romans expected their commands to be obeyed, even when they allowed a great deal of *de facto* autonomy and frequently exercised power by indirect means. The lack of internal uniformity and sometimes of coherence was matched by a vagueness in the circumscription of the empire, which in some areas lasted until well into the Principate.

The word which the Romans later used for a frontier, *limes*, meant in the context of land-distribution a road which separated one terrain from another. In the history of the empire it is first used, not for roads marking a frontier, but for routes of penetration into enemy territory.[94] Tacitus still uses the word with this meaning, but also provides the earliest clear instances of the meaning 'frontier of the empire'. The first surviving inscription in which *limes* means precisely a fortified frontier comes from the reign of Caracalla.[95] The term *fines* is used even more loosely. In his *Res Gestae* Augustus claimed that he had placed the *fines Illyrici* on the Danube, but goes on to claim in the same chapter that his army had forced the Dacians beyond the Danube to submit to Roman *imperia*.[96]

The development of a dense military screen along the frontier is a characteristic of imperial policy from Hadrian onwards. However, before this time any road or chain of forts and signal-stations in a frontier area should not be considered so much a border as a control line and a base for future advances.[97] This was clearly true of Agricola's Stanegate line between the Tyne and Solway and perhaps of the Fosse Way earlier in the 40s AD.[98] Even after Hadrian the *limes* is less a demarcation line than a frontier zone. For example, in the Syrian desert we find a network of roads and forts first created in the second century AD along a lateral axis of high ground between the Lebanon and the Euphrates, which penetrated into the desert to the south-east while screening the cultivated areas of Syria to the north-west.[99] The *Fossatum Africae*, originally detected like the Syrian frontier by air-photography and probably dating from the same period, is not a linear frontier but a series of defence lines and individual forts which protect civilian settlements, control oases and channel movement from the desert along defined routes.[100] The empire thus remained for centuries open-ended geographically as well as conceptually, and, even when in the second century AD it tended to become a fortress, remained permeable to outside influences. Indeed the frontier could be viewed as a controlled environment in which contact with the outside world could be facilitated.

4

GOVERNMENT AND THE GOVERNOR

The practice established under the Republic

THE GOVERNOR AND ROME

One implication of the previous chapter is that it will be hard to apply a single concept of government throughout the Roman empire. Moreover, even if we disregard the allied kingdoms and free cities, those peoples directly subject to a Roman magistrate were not administered or controlled in the continuous all-pervasive way that recent colonial experience might lead us to assume. The nature of Roman government in the empire principally depended on the governor, the Roman magistrate in the field, and it is with him that this chapter will be primarily concerned. However, administration can only be understood in the light of major policy decisions. Roman governors were notorious in the Republic and even under the Principate for taking important decisions themselves. Yet they were not only in theory answerable to the senate and Roman people but in fact increasingly subject to instructions from them in the Republic, and under the Principate both answerable and subject to emperor and senate.

During the great period of overseas growth under the Republic the people meeting in assemblies under the presidency of a magistrate were constitutionally the body which authorised the declaration of major wars and the conclusion of peace or a treaty.[1] This prerogative was apparently eroded during the second century BC. We do not know if the people were consulted before the wars against Macedon and Achaia in the 140s, and, even when our sources talk of war votes before the Third Punic War and later the First Mithridatic War, they do not make it clear who voted.[2] Peace and treaties of alliance traditionally required the authorisation of the people but, as has been already explained (see p. 39), this principle also came to be neglected in the second century BC and the senate's authority was regarded as

43

sufficient. The senate, sometimes enlisting the co-operation of the tribunes and the assembly, also tried to exercise a basic control over the activities of magistrates abroad. There is the saga of M. Popillius Laenas and the Statellates in 173-2 BC, when Laenas was ultimately forced to make reparations for measures he had taken in a war against loyal allies.[3] Two years later the consul C. Cassius had to be restrained by an embassy sent by the senate from leaving his province, Gaul, in order to march through Illyricum and join in the Third Macedonian War.[4]

The settlement of areas which became subject to Roman power as a result of the successful conclusion of a war were usually undertaken by a magistrate with *imperium*, assisted by a senatorial commission but following, at least in broad outline, instructions given in Rome. For Greece after the Second and Third Macedonian Wars these instructions came from the senate.[5] In Africa in 146 Scipio Aemilianus had a commission established by the people through a law, one perhaps passed *ex senatus consulto*. Aquillius' initial settlement of Asia in 129-6 seems to have followed lines laid down by the senate, but was then altered by C. Gracchus' law, which was itself a substitute for a *lex Aufeia* (see pp. 30-1).

From early in the second century BC we hear of specific instructions given to governors by the senate about the letting of tax contracts in Spain and the requisitioning of grain. There seem also to have been regulations forbidding Roman officials and their soldiers using their positions to acquire land and slaves in the provinces.[6] Probably the first general attempt to define the governor's activities legally was the *lex Porcia* of 101-100 BC,[7] which prescribed that he should not move himself or his army outside his province without good reason and which put a limit on what he could legitimately requisition. To some extent also the *leges de repetundis*, in providing for the recovery of the ill-gotten gains of Roman officials, created general distinctions between legal and illegal activities, especially when they deal with gifts which the giver did not seek to recover but were not in the public interest because they were bribes or kickbacks (see pp. 100-7).

Nevertheless, there was no question of a Roman magistrate in the Republic being supplied with a handbook of standing orders. He had to take note of the limit of the *provincia* assigned him, whether this was more a territorial *provincia* defined by a *formula* or a task circumscribed in some other way. He was in theory bound to respect agreements concluded by the senate and people with Rome's friends and allies as well as arrangements for administering his *provincia* which stemmed from the senate or people. But this did not mean that he had to follow every precedent set by earlier magistrates in the area. It is a nice point whether Verres might have defended himself against Cicero's charges that he had breached the *lex Rupilia*,[8] on the ground that this was simply an arrangement concluded by a governor and his advisers on the spot, which was not legally binding on his successors, but only a model which need not be slavishly imitated. For it is not clear that the *lex Rupilia* had been approved in detail by the senate and people. Each governor under the Republic, like the praetors at Rome, produced his own edict, a document in many points inherited from predecessors but one in which his own views on justice and judicial procedure could be given scope. For example, Cicero's adoption of a clause in Scaevola's edict, in which he made an exception for contracts which should not in good faith be adhered to, was from one point of view respect for precedent, from another an instance of Cicero's imposing his own view of justice in the province. Bibulus had done something similar, but without using the form of words inherited from Scaevola, and that was completely within his discretion.[9] Other governors, as Atticus and other *equites* clearly hoped, might not have included such a clause at all.

How far could decisions be taken over the head of a magistrate or a governor, while he was in a province? A recognised procedure for appeal in judicial matters existed under the Principate, but there is little sign of this under the Republic, except in Cisalpine Gaul after the Social War and the unification of Italy. When P. Scandilius, a Roman citizen, demanded that Verres should refer his civil lawsuit, in which Verres himself was the defendant, to Rome, Verres refused and Scandilius was powerless.[10] Sthenius of Thermae escaped a criminal prosecution organised by Verres by escaping to Rome, where the tribunes gave him their protection and the senate passed a decree in his favour, but he still did not dare to go back to Sicily.[11]

Nevertheless, some problems were referred to the senate and decided there. Even before regular governors were sent to an area, the senate had acted as an arbitrator in disputes between communities allied to her, for example, those between Samos and Priene and between Itanos and Hierapytna.[12] Nor did these arbitrations cease when a governor was installed in the neighbourhood of the communities in dispute. The dispute might be so troublesome that the governor was happy to see it referred to Rome. Alternatively, the communities themselves might decide to take their case there. Free cities in particular might consider a direct approach to the senate more consonant with their status – for example, two small towns in Thessaly, Narthakion and Melitaea, who approached the senate about 140 BC, shortly after governors first began to be appointed to Macedonia and Greece.[13] An immensely difficult dispute, akin to one between cities, was that between two associations of Dionysiac artists, one based at the Isthmus, the other at Athens: this was eventually referred to the senate in 112 BC after successive governors of Macedonia could not settle it.[14]

The senate also listened to cries for help against injustice, for instance, the protest in the 70s BC by the *koinon* of Asia, led by Aphrodisias, about the tax burdens imposed by Sulla or the appeal by Oropos in 73 BC against the attempt to collect taxes from the shrine of Amphiaraus.[15] There is a political point here: the large tax companies were very influential and a governor might be reluctant to move against them without backing. Indeed, it may well have been that in both these cases the respective governors encouraged the embassies, in order to shift the burden of decision from their shoulders. On other occasions the cry for help was precisely because of the injustice of a governor and led to the prosecution of that man *de repetundis*.[16] Such protests, however, usually only took place after he had left the province. Like most of the measures against governors, they did not so much control as correct his behaviour after the event (see below, Chapter 6).

THE APPOINTMENT OF GOVERNORS

In the period before Sulla's dictatorship provinces were regularly governed by magistrates in their years of office. This term was sometimes extended for further years by prorogation. Routine provincial tasks were mainly for praetors and ex-praetors (four praetorships had been originally created specifically for Sicily, Sardinia and the two parts of Spain in 227 and 197 BC).[17] Before the Social War consuls tended to be reserved for major wars which they went out to fight early in their year of office. Between Sulla's dictatorship and 52 BC the praetors, now increased in number to eight, were kept at Rome during their year of office and did not in fact receive their external appointments until they were ex-praetors the following year.[18] The consuls, meanwhile, had provinces promised to them before their year of office,[19] but did not usually go out to them until late in the year, unless there was an emergency (Lepidus had to leave Rome for Etruria in summer 78 BC; the consuls of 60 were expected to go out swiftly to meet the threat of Ariovistus). Whether there was prorogation or not, a governor had the right to remain in his province until a successor arrived, but then was required to leave within thirty days, according to the *lex Cornelia de maiestate*.[20] By a *lex Pompeia* of 52 BC a five-year interval was imposed between magistracies in the city and provincial governorships,[21] so that ex-magistrates who had not previously gone to provinces had to be recruited to fill the posts. This reform lasted for little over two years until the civil war; it was abandoned under Caesar's dictatorship and the triumvirate and reappeared, more *de facto* than *de iure*, only in the separation between consulships and the major proconsulships of Africa and Asia under the Principate.

The posts in *provinciae* to be filled were traditionally selected by the senate. In the late Republic some special appointments were made by plebiscite; that of Marius to the Jugurthine War in 107, for instance, or the long-term commands granted to Pompey by the *leges Gabinia* and *Manilia* against the pirates and Mithridates. (In fact there was one early precedent, the selection by the people at the senate's request of commanders for Spain in 211 and from 204 to 198. The first was P. Scipio, later Africanus.)[22] In the early second century BC decisions about provincial posts were usually made immediately the magistrates took up office on the Ides of March. Consular and praetorian provinces were selected; the consul and praetors were then required to draw lots, although on occasions the consuls might arrange things between them (*comparare inter se*), as much later Cicero allowed his colleague C. Antonius to take Macedonia.[23] This procedure continued after the start of the official year was moved to 1 January in 153 BC, but was modified in 123 or 122 when C. Gracchus enacted that the consular provinces should be chosen before the consular elections,[24] a reform which remained in force until rendered otiose by the *lex Pompeia* of 52.

A formal procedure before the lictors, who represented the obsolete *comitia curiata*, seems to have been in theory required for a magistrate who was not a consul or praetor in office, if he was to hold the auspices while in his province and thus have the right to claim a triumph on his return (proper *sortitio* may also have been needed for a commander to be able to claim divine approval for his appointment). We know of one occasion when these requirements were ignored by Appius Claudius and Domitius Ahenobarbus in 54 BC. There was no doubt that they could go out as consuls with *imperium* and retain this until they returned to the city – according to the *lex*

Cornelia de maiestate, in this respect following the precedent of the *lex de provinciis* of 101–100. It is possible, however, that a *lex curiata* was customarily required before the senate voted a magistrate his expenses, apart from any religious requirement.[25]

FUNDING

Giving a magistrate the funds necessary to conduct his business was known as *ornare provinciam.* We know very little about the mechanics of this. No money was drawn from the treasury in the late Republic without senatorial sanction, although a consul may have had a traditional right to do so.[26] Originally a Roman magistrate would have set out for his province with chests full of silver and bronze to pay his staff, troops and those from whom he had to make purchases. We have an indication that this still happened in 59 BC when we hear of supplementary funds in coin being sent to Quintus Cicero for a new year of his governorship of Asia.[27] His brother was worried that the quaestors might only pay out in the silver *cistophori* brought back as booty by Pompey and not in Roman *denarii.*

A number of points arise from this. First, the Roman Republic did not impose a uniform silver currency throughout the empire. For example, in Asia the issue of silver tetradrachms bearing the design of the *cista mystica,* bow-case and coiled serpent, was maintained by the Romans after the end of Attalid dynasty, which had invented them, until the beginning of the Principate. In Macedonia the coinage of the Antigonid kings, with a Macedonian shield on the obverse and wreath and club on the reverse, was adapted by the Romans, Artemis' head being substituted for that of the kings, while in Greece the new-style wide-flan Athenian tetradrachms became dominant to the extent that a law from Delphi made them the basis of financial calculations.[28] In Spain *c.* 200–150 BC a new coinage emerged of the same weight as the *denarius* and bearing its identifying sign ($\bar{X}$), but with local Celtic types (young male head/horseman with spear) and Iberian legends. These coinages circulated in their own areas, while Roman *denarii,* though present in Spain, Sicily and the north of Italy, are rarely found in Greece before the late Republic.[29]

There must have been a natural tendency for magistrates to use local coinages, which were in any case the medium of local taxation. As early as 180 BC Q. Fulvius Flaccus wrote to the senate from Spain that there was no need for grain and cash to be sent from Rome, since enough had been raised locally.[30] Money from tribute was probably kept in provincial treasuries (known as *fisci*, chests), when it was going to be required for Roman expenses in the area. So we find Pompey being empowered under the *lex Gabinia* to draw money from provincial *fisci* and also from the overseas deposits of the *societates* of tax-collectors.[31] Cicero himself seems to have borrowed money from Atticus for his journey from Rome to Cilicia in 51,[32] either because he could not draw his expenses until he reached his province or at least Asia Minor or possibly because he had used any advance expenses in *denarii* for some other purpose in Italy. This was perhaps what was bothering Atticus and Cicero in 59 about Quintus' money: they preferred to take Roman *denarii*, which could be used in Italy against a credit to Quintus in Asia with Atticus' associates, rather than have the bother of shipping the Asiatic *cistophori* back to the east. At the end of his governorship Cicero deposited the surplus of his expenses, equivalent to 2,200,000 *sestertii* (550,000 *denarii*), in Asiatic *cistophori* at Ephesus with the local office of the tax company, intending to draw on that credit with other representatives of the company at some other time and place.[33]

In short, there were in the late Republic facilities for transferring credit through bankers and tax companies, but it is not clear how far this was used systematically by Roman public authorities. Nor was there an elaborate credit system for private commerce such as the bills of exchange available in the Renaissance period.[34] Although much tribute money was kept in local circulation, the treasury still provided cash for at least part of the payments to magistrates sent to provinces, and it was up to the recipients to decide how they were to move this to their sphere of operations.

MILITARY RESOURCES

The Roman magistrate with *imperium* was above all a military commander, and a normal feature of his appointment was a vote about the troops he could use (this routine business actually formed part of the *lex de provinciis praetoriis* of 101–100 BC). Late Republican governors in Sicily, Sardinia or Africa, for example, normally used local non-Roman levies, except for a few officers. Major commands, on the other hand, involved the use of Roman legions, as well as a wider range of non-Roman auxiliary troops.[35] The magistrate, who was simply fighting a campaign and not governing a province, normally brought his army back with him. Thus Scipio Africanus brought back from Africa in 201 the army that had defeated Hannibal,

T. Flamininus withdrew from Greece in 194 that which had defeated Philip V of Macedon. Where, as in Spain from the second century BC onwards, there was a continual need for Roman troops, legions were kept in the province for long periods and supplemented by fresh recruits, which also allowed the demobilisation of men who had completed their term of military service.[36] After a time a whole legion or a whole army might be withdrawn.

In the late Republic many legions had become standing armies in provinces. When Pompey took over the Mithridatic command in 66 BC, he acquired some really old soldiers who were 'hard cases' – the remnants of the forces that L. Valerius Flaccus had led to Asia in 86. Caesar inherited four legions when he succeeded to the command of the Gallic provinces.[37] In Cilicia Cicero found himself leader of two meagre legions. However, commanders had considerable discretion to recruit on the spot, where necessary. Cicero supplemented his forces by recruiting Roman citizens living in the province, including *evocati*, those with military experience recalled to the standards. He also acquired the equivalent of 12,000 legionaries from king Deiotarus of Galatia and a useful force of 2,000 cavalry.[38] A standing army, however, would not automatically retain its senior officers and it is these and the rest of the governor's staff that we must now consider.

THE GOVERNOR AND HIS STAFF

A provincial governor's staff was essentially the entourage with which any magistrate or promagistrate would surround himself when he went abroad, and this in turn was only a cut-down version of the household and circle of *amici* of a Roman aristocrat, modified by a small dilution of public officials. The entourage as a whole was known as the *cohors*.[39] The only other regular magistrate with the governor was his quaestor (in Sicily exceptionally there were two, one at Syracuse, the other at Lilybaeum).[40] The quaestor was not merely a financial official, like those quaestors at the treasury at Rome, but a deputy to the governor in all respects.[41] Yet quaestors were young men at the beginning of their career as magistrates (at least 30 years old in the late Republic, they could be younger before Sulla and in the Principate their minimum age was 25).[42] So a governor might prefer as his deputy a senior man, such as he might find among his *legati*. These were usually men of senatorial rank, whom the governor selected as his chief assistants. Cicero took to Cilicia his own brother Quintus and C. Pomptinus, both ex-praetors and former provincial governors, and it was his brother whom he originally wanted to leave in charge of the province on his departure rather than his suspect quaestor, Mescinius Rufus, or the latter's untried successor, Coelius Caldus.[43]

Below the *legati* there were tribunes of the soldiers, prefects of the cavalry and at least one master of works (*praefectus fabrum*), who was a general aide-de-camp.[44] Caesar's *praefectus fabrum* Mamurra was notorious.[45] Except for the sixteen tribunes of the four first legions, who were elected by the assembly, all these posts were in the governor's gift and were often awarded to unmilitary men. Caesar was generous in granting posts to such men, but could not resist commenting ironically on their nervousness before his great battle with Ariovistus at Vesontio in 58 BC. Cicero obtained a post as tribune with Caesar for Trebatius Testa, a clever young lawyer, and then had fun in a subsequent letter about his trying to employ his knowledge of the civil interdicts about violence in the Gallic War.[46]

The *legati* undertook military duties either as subordinates to the governor or when detached on independent commands. In judicial matters they not only provided the governor with a *consilium*, a panel of advisers or jury,[47] but also sometimes handled cases themselves – for instance, M. Gratidius, Q. Cicero's legate in Asia, and Q. Volusius, sent by M. Cicero to Cyprus.[48] In due course under the Principate a legate came to be designated as the chief legal official in the province, the *legatus iuridicus*.[49]

Apart from those already mentioned, there were some men whom the governor simply took as friends or companions (*comites*), like Catullus' friends, Veranius and Fabullus, the companions of M. Pupius Piso.[50] Such men were not given any official post. In particular there were the *contubernales*, young men sent with the magistrate to learn what in due course would be their job, for example, Ti. Gracchus was sent with Scipio Aemilianus to Africa in the Third Punic War.[51]

The governor's personal staff included an *accensus*, of whom I shall say more below, a *scriba*, *lictores*, *viatores* (messengers), *praecones* (heralds) and *haruspices* to read omens, all of whom he would declare to the treasury, like the legates, tribunes and prefects, in order to draw expenses for them.[52] The quaestor had a special scribe, apart from the one assigned to the governor.[53] Scribes, heralds and *haruspices* would have been chosen from the panels (*decuriae*) of those registered as possessing the appropriate technical expertise, though the governor probably had a free hand in choosing whom he wanted from among them. The *accensus*, on the other hand, was usually a freedman or slave chosen by the magistrate himself, often from his own household, to run the governor's office and be his adviser. 'Your *accensus*', Cicero tells his brother, 'should have that status which our ancestors desired him to have. They used to confer the post, not as a favour, but as a task requiring service, not casually, but to their own freedmen.'[54] Governors would have used their own personal slaves and freedmen anyhow to help them in their administration; the *accensus* was originally one of these singled out for an official position of special importance. We know of a number of *accensi* in the late Republic. P. Tettius, who served C. Claudius Nero in 80 BC, may have been an exception in being freeborn. Verres had Timarchides; Q. Cicero had Statius, who in Cicero's view got above himself, especially when he was manumitted.[55] A. Gabinius employed an ex-painter, his own freedman Gabinius Antiochus, while Cicero himself chose Pausanias, a freedman of Lentulus Spinther, perhaps because of his experience, if he had been in the province previously with his patron. It is possible that *accensus* was the position held by Pompey's freedman, Demetrius of Gadara, famous for the wealth he acquired in Pompey's service. Caesar by contrast was exceptional in employing as a secretary a knight of Gallic origin, Cn. Pompeius Trogus, entrusting him with his seal-ring after the manner of Hellenistic kings.[56]

Furthermore, there were personal attendants like doctors and cooks. Verres is criticised by Cicero for making his doctor Artemidorus a member of a judicial panel (*consilium*) – a position he also conferred on a scribe, a herald and a *haruspex*.[57] However, Verres was not the only man to elevate personal servants. M. Antonius Artemidorus, the trainer and masseur (*aliptes*) of the triumvir Mark Antony, was sufficiently influential for his patron to cite him in his letter to the *koinon* of the cities of Asia as the promoter of the benefit Antony was conferring.[58]

The Principate was to bring important changes. Soldiers seconded from their units became an important part of a province's administration and a financial organisation developed, which became to some extent independent from the governor (see pp. 122–4). However, there had been little change in the personal staff of proconsuls two centuries after Cicero's death. An inscription from Samothrace shows P. Antius P.f. Orestes being initiated into the mysteries there in AD 165. With him are named four *amici*, three or four *lictores*, three *viatores*, some ten slaves of Antius himself, ten auxiliary soldiers and six other slaves.[59]

WARFARE

'I have in mind to set out straightway to my army, to devote the remaining summer months to military affairs, the winter months to jurisdiction.'[60] Such was Cicero's intention shortly before he entered Cilicia. These were the fundamental tasks for any governor, even if in most provinces their importance was not as nicely balanced as in Cilicia under Cicero. Most of Caesar's ten years in Gaul as proconsul was spent campaigning. Yet he regularly came back at some point in the winter to hold assizes in Cisalpine Gaul and Illyricum.[61] He presumably also spent some time in Narbo, Tolosa and other parts of southern Transalpine Gaul. At the other end of the spectrum governors in Asia or Sicily normally had only to deal with internal security. We know that governors of Sicily were expected to move about the province in the summer, when the harvests were being collected and large slave-gangs had been assembled.[62] However, Verres and Caninius Niger were also drawn into naval operations in Sicily against pirates,[63] while L. Flaccus, Q. Cicero's predecessor in Asia though governing in the aftermath of Pompey's success, also felt it necessary to assemble a squadron to deal with piracy.[64] In general, nevertheless, there would have been a considerable difference between a governor with Roman legions and their accompanying allied auxiliaries at his disposal and one with only a few allies.

The commander's desire for military glory and booty, supported by the military axiom that troops should be kept busy, if they are to be happy and well-disciplined, would have led governors into picking quarrels with border peoples or supposed subversives in the province itself. Cicero, after raising a considerable force to meet the threat of the Parthian army in Syria (above, p. 50), had to do something with it and so chose to attack the people of Pindenissus in the Mons Amanus, the watershed between Cilicia and Syria.[65] Even if they had been perpetual enemies of Rome, they do not seem to have worried previous governors. On the other hand, in the situation of 51 BC such operations could be justified as helping to scare the Parthians away, and it would have been detrimental to Cicero's authority if he had appeared to have raised a large army to no purpose.

In Macedonia, with its long and uncertain northern border, some active demonstration of military power may have been regarded as the best available form of frontier defence. It was probably partly with this in mind that the *lex de provinciis praetoriis* of 101–100 required governors of Macedonia to spend no less than sixty days in the newly acquired territory beyond the Hebrus, not merely to supervise tax-collection.[66] Spanish governors until the time of Augustus could always plead that part of their peninsula was unsubdued, but Appian remarked that, when Roman forces were under considerable strain elsewhere from the Germanic invasions, there was no fighting in Spain, because no fresh troops were assigned there.[67] The level of aggressive military activity under the Republic would obviously have been constrained by the availability of forces. Under the Principate it became more a matter of conscious imperial policy.

JURISDICTION AND LOCAL GOVERNMENT

Roman government would have been impossible without immense delegation of administration. The governor and his staff would have been too few, and they were neither trained to carry out, nor conditioned to believe that they should carry out, the comprehensive regulation of the life of the people subject to them. They were there to fight Rome's wars, collect Rome's taxes and exercise such supervision of the *socii* as was necessary for the security of Rome, Romans living in the provinces and the *socii* themselves.

Where local government already existed through a city or some other local commune (*civitas*), Rome made use of it; where it may not have existed already, as in certain areas of Spain, Rome encouraged its development. Most of our evidence for this process comes from the period of Julius Caesar's death onwards in the shape of the colonial and municipal charters and other documents about town and city administration. This is a topic to which we will return in Chapter 8. However, it is worth noticing that Rome took an interest in the way cities allied to her were managed from the earliest times. We may suspect that it began in Sicily after the First Punic War. Our first evidence, however, is of Flamininus' constitution-making in Thessaly in 195–4 BC.[68] Aemilius Paulus may not have touched city administration in Macedonia in 167 but he did impose new regional authorities.[69] Later, Fabius Maximus' letter to Dyme, now probably to be dated to 145, refers to the constitution given by Rome to the Achaeans (in 146), which the local rebels had tried to subvert.[70] In Sicily we find that Agrigentum's senate was regulated by the *leges antiquae* of Scipio (probably L. Scipio, pr. 193, honoured by the Italian residents at Halaesa): both the senate and the assembly are attested in an inscription from the Roman period.[71] As for Halaesa, C. Claudius Pulcher, pr. 95, helped the city to draw up regulations for its senate: senators had to be at least 30 years old, possess a minimum census and have not been involved in certain degrading professions (this sort of regulation reappears in later inscribed municipal charters).[72] In general censors were elected by the cities in Sicily to register property as a basis for their yearly local taxation. This too looks like an innovation imposed by Rome.[73]

A governor's relationship with cities centred on taxation and jurisdiction. Cicero's first action on entering his province was to spend twenty-five days in total in five different assize-centres. The following year he spent three months over one combined assize at Laodicea for the western *dioeceses* (the term meant originally an administrative district before it became connected with the church), followed by about a month at Tarsus in the east.[74] Reading Cicero, we tend to assume that this was always the provincial governor's lot. But how far back can we confidently trace this extensive jurisdiction and how did it arise?

From the time when Roman magistrates began to exercise direct authority over the civil life of peoples outside Italy subordinate to Rome, they must have been required to perform functions amounting to jurisdiction. This period began in 241 BC at the end of the First Punic War. Nevertheless, it is almost a century before we have good evidence of what this jurisdiction amounted to. Thus the early stages of development are a matter of conjecture, but it seems probable that this was a process of casuistry, where there were few, if any, ground rules existing at the beginning, and the growth of jurisdiction was, at least initially, a response to demand.

We have three fundamental data. The first is that a magistrate with the *imperium* that enabled him to command troops and require obedience from Romans and their allies in general – that is, a consul, praetor, proconsul or propraetor – also possessed standard powers of jurisdiction. These are conveniently itemised in a chapter of the law of 101–100 BC about the praetorian provinces which specifies that any deputy who takes over from a governor, when the latter abdicates or is deprived of his office, shall have all the judical competences of that magistrate in civil and criminal matters, not only in the province which he takes over, but anywhere else he is until he returns to the city of Rome. These powers comprise the appointment of judges and juries, the taking of securities and pledges, arrest, punishment and the application of other forms of physical force.[75]

The second datum is that local communities in the area subordinate to Rome would normally have their own systems of jurisdiction. In the Greek and Semitic east, in Sicily and Punic Africa this would be based on cities; in the west, too, there were some Greek and Punic cities, while the Celts and Celtiberians had urban centres, in which it seems likely that their arrangements for jurisdiction were centred (cf. the operations of the senate of Contrebia, p. 40). Obviously, there were some areas, especially those that were mountainous or remote from the sea and other communication routes, in which any rule of law was weak and intermittent before the arrival of Roman power. It is unlikely that this situation was changed much by the Roman presence.

The third datum is that, although the governor might delegate jurisdiction, though not (it appears from Cnidos IV and later imperial doctrine) capital punishment and his coercive powers, to a deputy (*legatus*) concurrently with his own activities, his scope for action was limited by his inability to be in a number of places at once: indeed he might find it difficult to visit more than a limited area of his province in the whole course of his administration. By the time Cicero became governor of Cilicia in 51 BC a system of assizes (*conventus*) had developed, one for each *dioecesis*. We tend to assume that such assizes had always been the governor's lot in any province, but it is more likely that they were the result of a process of evolution following an initial period of unsystematic touring by governors who were primarily concerned with the province's military and financial affairs. We can reasonably postulate two converging tendencies: on the one hand, the governor deliberately took cognizance of certain types of offence or legal dispute through his concern for security and the reliable extraction of Rome's tribute; on the other, there were pressures on him to intervene from friends, whether Roman or non-Roman, and indeed those who were being worsted in some local court might well decide to try their luck by appealing to the Roman authority.

We know of one province, where, in the late second century, some thirty years before the law about the praetorian provinces, a clear system of demarcation was created, perhaps for the first time – Sicily. There the consul of 132, P. Rupilius, advised by a commission of ten, enacted a decree, which the Sicilians called a law, so stable were the arrangements it introduced, which defined the respective judicial competences of Roman and Sicilian judges.[76] In the same period, the inscriptions from Claros show us that the notion of a Roman court, which contrasted with the local jurisdiction of cities, had become established in the new province of Asia. A few years after the law about the provinces, *c.* 95–4 BC, Q. Mucius Scaevola produced his famous edict for Asia which Cicero was to copy.[77] It is hard to gauge how fast Roman jurisdiction in the provinces had developed during the second century. As far as private law is concerned, it may to some extent have been affected by changes in that law at Rome by the praetors, which, whether this was a major purpose of the changes or not, made it more accessible to foreigners. These changes were well on their way by the middle of the second century BC, but chronological precision is elusive.[78]

What evidence we have suggests that the Romans began to take the problem of defining spheres of jurisdiction seriously in the later second century. That is the implication of the *lex Rupilia* in Sicily. The acquisition of the provinces of Macedonia and Asia, filled with Greek cities, would have stimulated similar decisions there, as Scaevola's edict shows. In Spain, too, the growth of towns and a more regular approach to taxation and administration from the governorship of the elder Ti. Gracchus (179 BC) onwards[79] seems to have led to a more systematic approach to justice, to the extent that Contrebia and its neighbouring communes in 87 BC could be expected to understand the procedures of Roman private law.[80]

We should not expect there to have been everywhere a clear once and for all division of competences between the governor and local communes. Even where on our evidence there was the sharpest division, as in Sicily, some boundaries may have remained blurred: it is not clear from Cicero's account that the governor's criminal jurisdiction was strictly limited.[81] For this reason and because of gaps in the evidence I shall discuss the matter province by province. However, a fundamental point should first be stressed about the governor's *modus operandi*. He employed the procedures and to a considerable extent the substantive law of Rome both in civil and criminal matters. In criminal cases, outside the realm of the standing courts (*quaestiones perpetuae*) established by law or plebiscite, which functioned at Rome, a magistrate with *imperium* would investigate a case with a panel of assessors (*consilium*), generally according to the categories of offences established in Roman law. He would consult his assessors over verdict and penalties but, unlike the president of a standing court at Rome, he was not necessarily bound to follow their opinion, though obviously under some moral pressure to do so.[82] In civil matters a magistrate might, instead of investigating the entire matter himself, use Roman civil procedure. After examining the pleas, he would decide whether an action should be allowed, how the issue was to be formulated and what the outcome in the form of penalty or restitution should be, if the case was proved. He incorporated these points in a *formula*. This was based on either Roman statute law or the concept of *bona fides* (good faith, akin to our concept of equity) or the magistrate's discretion to create a remedy for a certain unjust state of affairs. A single judge, who himself could use a panel of assessors, or a tribunal of judges (*recuperatores*) was then appointed to decide whether the facts alleged justified condemnation or acquittal according to the formula.

In Rome and Italy, when a magistrate wished to apply Roman statute law to a foreigner (*peregrinus*) in a civil case, he might do so by introducing a fiction of citizenship. Where a provincial magistrate was dealing with civil cases involving Romans he could have operated, and no doubt usually did, as if he were a magistrate at Rome. Where he dealt with civil cases involving only foreigners, he could have used principles in Roman law which were regarded as part of *ius gentium* (the law common to all nations) or he could have tried to adapt himself to local law, especially if the judge or jury who were to hear the case were themselves local. Cicero himself, and Scaevola before him, formulated their edicts in terms of Roman law, while permitting the Greeks to use Greek judges. Our other sources on the Republic, especially the *tabula Contrebiensis*, suggest that Roman governors not unnaturally tended to think in Roman terms.[83] However, it is a striking feature of the *tabula* that, although Flaccus had behaved like a Roman civil magistrate and had produced a decree embodying Roman *formulae*, the *ius* (system of rights), according to which the case was to be judged, was local. We should consider the possibility that in many other cases, which were to be heard by a local judge or judges, the Roman magistrate produced a *formula*, which allowed the indigenous law of the relevant community to be applied to the judgement, so reconciling local tradition and Roman authority.

Before coming to matters of detail we should also ask what the objects of the governor were in jurisdiction. Some magistrates in the provinces, like Cicero himself, were indeed concerned with justice and their own personal integrity, even if this was not exactly an altruistic zeal for abstract justice but closely connected with their interest in their own reputation.[84] Two further respectable purposes can be discerned, both related to the preservation of stability and order in the provinces, the prevention of excessive oppression by leading allies of those below them and the prevention of faction among the local governing classes, especially that which would bring the enemies of Rome to the top. The first aim can be seen behind Augustus' first Cyrene edict, which deals with conspiracies among juries in the province; the second behind his letter to Cnidos preventing Euboulos and Tryphera being victimised by their enemies.[85] Related to these purposes was the grant to individuals of the privilege of having their cases heard in a forum of their own choosing, perhaps at Rome itself.[86] However, some governors decided that it was more in their interest to co-operate with faction and oppression. This was the burden of Cicero's charges about Verres' behaviour in Sicily and of Pliny's accusation of Marius Priscus over 150 years later, and it seems to have been specifically designated as an offence by Caesar's *lex de repetundis*, if not earlier.[87]

JURISDICTION IN INDIVIDUAL PROVINCES

Sicily

From 132 BC onwards the governor's edict and judicial arrangements in Sicily were expected generally to conform to the decree of the consul P. Rupilius, which had been drawn up according to the advice of ten *legati*. The fact that the Sicilians referred to this decree as a *lex* emphasises the subsequent stability of the arrangements.[88] When a dispute arose between Sicilians of the same *civitas*, they used their local law.[89] When the case lay between Sicilians of different communities, the Roman praetor appointed judges he had chosen by lot (we find Verres dismissing five nominated judges in favour of three chosen by lot and his quaestor using *sortitio* at a *conventus*).[90] It is not clear whether Romans resident in the communities were eligible to be judges in such cases; in the cases described by Cicero they were probably Greeks, as he tended to mention Roman citizens by name. If a dispute arose between a private citizen and his own community, then the senate of another community was appointed to try this, after each party had been granted the option of rejecting one or more of the senates offered (presumably by the governor). When a Roman sued a Sicilian, there was one Sicilian *iudex*; when a Sicilian sued a Roman, one Roman *iudex*.

For the rest – that is, cases between Roman citizens, cases involving non-Sicilian *peregrini* and probably all criminal cases in which the governor chose to intervene – judges were appointed from the roster of Roman residents, the *conventus* (a term which also means the assize at which they would tend to foregather). These might sit in the *consilium* of the praetor himself or examine a case remitted to them as either individual *iudices* or a jury of *recuperatores*. For example, when Sopater of Halicyae was tried on a capital charge, Verres used a jury of Romans, including M. Petilius, a knight, just as Licinius Sacerdos had done previously in 75 BC.[91] Actions arising from the collection of tithes under the so-called *lex Hieronica* took place before three *recuperatores* from the *conventus* of Roman citizens, although at one point Cicero talks of the participation of a Sicilian magistrate (perhaps he first received the case).[92]

Certain items of Roman law are attested in the governor's edict. L. Metellus (pr. 70 BC) included in his the *formula Octaviana*, invented six years previously, which provided for the restoration of property seized by violence or threats. It was also possible in this period to bring an action for *iniuriae* (personal affront arising from assault on oneself or one's property) under the terms of a law of Sulla.[93] Although we cannot be sure that these procedures were used for non-Romans, parallels from Asia suggest that they might have been.

According to Cicero, Verres disregarded established principles completely. He gave cases within local communities to a Roman judge from his own entourage, and, when he should have selected jurors from the resident Romans, the *conventus*, he chose them instead from personal attendants in the *cohors* – his doctor, herald or *haruspex*.[94] Verres' defence to this charge would have been that he needed judges on whom he could rely. Cicero himself in an unguarded moment when writing to Atticus anticipates that the latter will call his Greek judges 'no-goods' and adds, 'What does it matter? They still think that they have got independence.'[95] Members of the jury trying Verres no doubt shared his opinion of foreign judges and may have reckoned that Verres' offence here was more neglect of public relations than perversion of justice.

Cilicia

It is tantalising that, although we have Cicero's letters as a source for his administration of Cilicia in the last years of the Republic, we know relatively little about how he performed jurisdiction there in individual cases. The most valuable information he provides concerns his edict. Where a long-term system had not been established by the decree of a commission, as in Sicily, the governor's edict, which announced his future judicial methods in the same way that the edicts of the *praetor urbanus* and *peregrinus* gave notice of procedures to be followed at Rome, was the fundamental source of law.

Cicero in fact largely followed the classic edict employed by Q. Mucius Scaevola in his governorship of Asia, which had apparently been declared a model for future governors by the senate.[96] In particular, Cicero took from that edict his general principle that Greeks should be allowed to settle disputes between themselves according to their own laws. This meant that such cases were in the end handed over to Greek judges, but it may be that Cicero himself formally received the cases first and reviewed the pleadings to check that they did not involve any Roman interest.[97] Cicero's edict had three sections, of which two were elaborately drafted, while the final item was a bare statement that his other decisions would be in accordance with those of the praetors at Rome (this made the edict much briefer than usual). The first detailed section was the *edictum provinciale* which dealt with the finances of cities, debts, interest, contracts and especially tax-collection. This was a field which a Roman governor had to supervise because not only the interests of the *res publica* but also those of many wealthy Romans were at stake. Cicero laid down the standard interest rate of 1 per cent a month,[98] and it was in this section that he included a cautious clause, inherited from Scaevola, which excepted from recognition contracts made in such a way that one was not in good faith obliged to stand by them. Bibulus' Syrian edict had dealt with this problem more brutally in a manner prejudicial to the *publicani* (so Atticus thought) – presumably by references to *metus* or *dolus*, threats or fraud, by the tax-collectors.[99]

The second section dealt with matters of purely private law relating to property, which could not be satisfactorily handled except by edict – the entry of heirs into inheritances, the seizure and sale of debtors' possessions by creditors. These were procedures whose legal justification at Rome depended on conformity with the praetor's edict.[100] We do not know whether Roman rules were applied to cases only involving Greeks in this field or the procedure was adapted to fit the pre-existing laws and customs of the communities in the province. Indeed did every provincial who wanted entry into property as an heir or creditor have to apply to Cicero? This seems highly improbable in practice. However, the prominence of this part of the edict suggests that every provincial who normally used due process of law in these circumstances (not, for example, wandering mountain shepherds) was expected to obtain Cicero's authority according to the procedure prescribed.

While Cicero was in Cilicia he held three assizes (termed *conventus*) – in the west in August 51, at Laodicea again from 13 February to 1 May 50 (for all *dioeceses* except Cilicia Tracheia and Pedias) and at Tarsus in May to June 50. He says nothing about any important hearings in civil or criminal matters, but clearly spent much time on tax cases. Even here his work seems to have been more that of a negotiator or arbitrator than of a magistrate or judge, and this is a warning that in public matters it is not easy to separate a governor's judicial and his administrative functions.[101]

Asia

The importance attached to Scaevola's edict of 95–4 BC, in which Greeks were allowed to sue one another according to their own laws, suggest that in the preceding thirty-five years since the creation of the province intervention by governors had been wide-ranging and unsystematic.

Two honorary decrees from the sanctuary of Claros in Colophonian territory, which have been recently published, show considerable uncertainties about the relationship between the jurisdiction of governors and the local jurisdiction of Colophon (in theory a free and autonomous city). In one inscription, the decree for Polemaios, we are told that an embassy to Rome was required to save a local citizen 'condemned in a Roman court' contrary, it is implied, to Colophon's own laws. In the other, the decree for Menippos, it is claimed that governors in general were transferring cases from local jurisdiction to their own courts. Moreover, a Colophonian was summoned to Rome on a capital charge – apparently for trial before the consuls – after either being acquitted or not brought to trial for the murder of a Roman citizen in Colophonian territory. Vigorous embassies of protest and the exploitation of patrons at Rome secured for Colophon the recognition that its autonomy separated it from provincial jurisdiction: the senate decreed that on Colophonian territory Romans, whether they were accusers or accused, must be judged under Colophonian law. We find a similar provision later in the *senatus consultum* of 80 BC about Romans on the island of Chios.[102]

Evidently, governors of Asia had been exercising jurisdiction in cases which might, or indeed should, have been decided by local courts. We cannot tell whether they followed principles about the categories of cases to be judged by them, such as had been introduced by Rupilius' decree in Sicily, or their selection of cases was as haphazard and arbitrary as I have suggested above. The case of the man believed responsible for the death of a Roman was a particularly awkward problem. No doubt, the governor would have been happy to handle this, if he had known about it in time and had been able to secure the presence of the accused. As it was, the senate encouraged the consuls to summon the suspected assassin to Rome – a procedure of which we know only one other example, but one which shows how the Romans claimed ultimate jurisdiction throughout their empire for themselves.[103] It is, further, clear that there was no general principle of non-interference with the jurisdiction of a free city before this *cause célèbre* at Colophon. The concession obtained by Colophon about the autonomy of its local jurisdiction was an important precedent, but the decree of the senate was specific to Colophon, as the later decree was specific to Chios. We cannot talk of the secure establishment of a general principle even then.

The agreement between Ephesus and Sardis in Scaevola's governor-ship, exchanging rights of litigation between the citizens of the two cities, shows that the traditional system of city-based Greek law was still in force among the free cities at least. Nevertheless, even after this date observance of this edict left considerable scope for the governor's jurisdiction and the use of Roman law. Not surprisingly, a capital case involving a Roman of high rank, that arising from the riot at Lampsacus in 80 BC against Verres, was heard by the governor, P. Claudius Nero, with a *consilium* including his tribunes of the soldiers, prefects and some local Roman businessmen (creditors of the Greeks, Cicero calls them here). Twenty years later Cicero's brother Quintus was applying, or threatening to apply, Roman capital, penalties to both Greeks and Romans, including the grotesque penalty for parricide of sewing the condemned man in a sack.[104]

Quintus is also found intervening in a legal dispute which had arisen from the legacy of one Roman citizen to another in the Greek city of Apollonis.[105] The case was apparently being handled under the local law of the city, since Q. Cicero was trying to give the city instructions. He ordered the agents of the heir, L. Flavius, not to take anything from the estate before a debt had been repaid to C. Fundanius, a friend of the Cicero family, and he ordered the city to ensure that Flavius' agents obeyed these instructions. Cicero does not comment on the fact that his brother had intervened in the jurisdiction of a free city and this is surely significant for attitudes at the time.

He does, however, point out that his brother's instructions were contrary to the principles of Roman law (they are unlikely to have been in accordance with Greek law either).[106]

Quintus' predecessor, L. Valerius Flaccus, was also involved in civil cases involving a Roman citizen and intervened at Apollonis, though at the request of the local authorities. Cicero contrasts the free city of Apollonis, where Appuleius Decianus sought help from a succession of Roman praetors, with Pergamum, Smyrna and Tralles, 'where there are many Roman citizens and jurisdiction is performed by our magistrate'.[107] The implication seems to be that, because these cities are not free, they fall within the Roman magistrate's competence and, because of the number of Roman citizens, he might choose them as judges. Thus, even if Greek judges were allowed in private cases involving Greeks in these cities, according to Scaevola's principles, it was the Roman praetor or his deputy who performed the introductory jurisdiction and one could expect some Roman judges at least in any case involving Romans.

Flaccus gave both tax cases and a case between Greeks over a debt contracted in Italy to Roman *recuperatores*.[108] Again, a claim that someone treated as a slave was in fact a free man (*causa liberalis*) was heard by three Roman knights, presumably also *recuperatores*, while the Greek Nicomedes is said to have been condemned *furti et pro socio* for theft and defrauding a partner. Were the cases heard by Roman judges decided according to Roman law, or is Cicero's use of Roman legal language deceptive, being simply the reproduction of Greek concepts in Roman legal language?[109] While we cannot rule out that a Roman term is simply the translation of a Greek one, it remains probable that a Roman magistrate expected Romans to judge casses according to the law with which they were familiar and thus all cases except those judged exclusively by Greeks were handled under Roman law. Finally, it seems probable that the supremacy of Roman magistrates entailed the introduction into the Greek world of the Roman practice of separating civil actions into two parts – that before the magistrate and that before the judge or jury. This seems to be one of the implications of Cicero's contrast of the subject cities with the free city of Apollonis.

Cyrene

We can deduce from Augustus' Cyrene edicts the judicial regime which operated in that province before they were issued – one which had presumably grown up after Cyrene's formal annexation in 75 BC. Panels of Roman judges had been drawn from the whole body of adult Romans in the province with a capital of at least 2,500 *denarii* (this would have qualified them for membership of the fourth class in the Roman *comitia centuriata*). In 7 BC these amounted to 215 men. Capital cases had been reserved for them exclusively, but Augustus modified this system by prescribing for suits involving Greeks (whether as prosecutors or defendants) mixed juries with a higher property qualification. In the fourth edict it is laid down that for non-capital cases between Greeks the governor should either investigate himself or provide a *consilium* of judges (more probably the equivalent of Roman *recuperatores* than the jury in a Roman *quaestio*, since these were not cases of major political importance). These judges were to be Greek, unless the plaintiff required Romans, but should not be from the same city as plaintiff or defendant.[110]

It seems that in this province under the Republic Greeks had tended to be judged by the resident Romans, often men who would have been of no great standing at Rome. Moreover, cases between citizens of the same city were not necessarily left to be settled within that city. If the Cyrenean cities all had similar constitutions as a result of their subjection to the Ptolemies in the Hellenistic period,[111] then the judging of cases by men from a different city to the plaintiff or defendant would not have subjected them to an alien system of law. However, the use of Roman judges suggests that cases were on the whole dealt with under Roman rather than Greek law. It may also have been more usual for governors to investigate minor cases themselves than in populous provinces like Asia and Cilicia.

THE JUDICIAL SOVEREIGNTY OF THE GOVERNOR

Jurisdiction in the provinces and the powers of coercion associated with it were reserved for the governor or, when he was unavailable, for the man to whom he had handed on his *imperium*. The Cnidos text of the law about praetorian provinces provides specifically for the mandating of jurisdiction and capacity to punish – together with the power to grant *iudices* and *recuperatores* and to perform formal acts like manumission – to one man, if a governor abdicated or was deposed. This may also imply that, when a governor delegated his jurisdiction for a period without himself ceasing to be governor, he was normally expected to transmit it to one man only at a time. We may also wonder if a governor would have passed on his powers in such a sensitive matter as capital jurisdiction, except when he left the province. However, if there was no one else available, a magistrate who happened to be travelling in the vicinity could act. The Cnidos text states that the man with mandated jurisdiction can exercise it until he returns to Rome. The same must apply to regular magistrates. We know, for example, that L. Lucullus on his way to the Mithridatic War in 74–3 BC heard a capital case at Chaeronea.[112]

At the same time the decision of the governor or the man to whom he had mandated his *imperium* was usually final. Reference was sometimes made to Rome, but this was not automatically available to the defendant as a form of appeal.[113] Cicero tells us of one occasion when an important provincial was summoned to Rome by letters of the consuls after a debate in the senate. The summons was provoked by a violent attack on the quaestor M. Aurelius Scaurus at Ephesus by this local aristocrat. The Claros decree for Menippos has now provided us with another example of this procedure. Cicero argues that the same course should have been followed with the men who had stirred up a riot against Verres at Lampsacus, when the latter had tried to rape Philodamus' daughter.[114] In his letter to Dyme Q. Fabius Maximus, probably the praetor of 145 BC, ordered a certain Timotheus, who had taken a prominent role in the sedition there but was thought less guilty than the ringleaders already executed, to be sent to the *praetor peregrinus* at Rome. We find a similar procedure used by P. Sextius Scaeva in the second Cyrene edict and it remained a feature of the Principate.[115] The cases in question, it should be noted, were criminal matters which affected the security of Rome and her allies.

In civil cases the practice was different. A recent careful study of the *litterae commendaticiae* sent by Cicero to Ser. Sulpicius Rufus, governor of Achaea in 46 BC, has shown that not only Cicero's letters but those of the consul M. Lepidus – referred to as *quasi commendaticiae* – must have been urging the jurist Sulpicius to oblige them in a way he might have felt to be legally improper. Sulpicius was being asked to send to Rome an inheritance suit between two Roman citizens – Cicero's former quaestor L. Mescinius Rufus and Oppia, the widow of Mescinius' brother or cousin M. Mindius – although the defendant Oppia, domiciled as she was in Achaea, was reluctant.[116] In fact the case was settled in the province. More relevant to justice for provincials is Cicero's request that the governor of Asia in 50 BC, Q. Minucius Thermus, should order the free cities of Alabanda and Mylasa to send *ecdici*, judicial delegates, to Rome in order to settle a debt with Cluvius of Puteoli.[117] Alabanda and Mylasa were only being expected to submit to a form of arbitration procedure with Cluvius. Nevertheless, the governor was not supposed to intervene in the free cities' jurisdiction over such matters after the *senatus consultum* of 60 BC and the *lex Iulia de repetundis*,[118] and there was also the general principle that the case should be heard in a court native to the defendant. So the request seems to have been improper. It is at all events clear that the governor could not be forced to send a civil suit to Rome, which otherwise he would have dealt with himself, nor could provincials be forced by a Roman plaintiff to have their case heard by judges in Italy.

An interesting case from Sicily illustrates the point that even a Roman citizen could not secure appeal from a provincial governor in a civil suit. A Roman knight, P. Scandilius, used the procedure of challenge by wager (*sponsione provocare*) to expose Verres' corrupt conduct in collecting the taxes of Sicily, that is, he promised to pay a wager if his allegation was not proved true.[119] Verres appointed *recuperatores* from his own retinue to hear the evidence; Scandilius rejected these jurors on grounds of bias and demanded that the case be referred to Rome since, he claimed, impartial jurors could not be found in Sicily; Verres refused. Thereupon Scandilius abandoned his suit, but Verres compelled him to pay his wager anyhow on the ground that the suit had not succeeded. This was really a Roman quarrel fought out in a province, where the defendant was also the source of law. However, if Verres was invulnerable, while he was still in post, against a challenge from a Roman knight, he was *a fortiori* invulnerable against provincials.

There is indeed positive evidence for reference to Rome in the laws relating to Cisalpine Gaul but this derives from the special political conditions of that area. By the close of the Social War in 89 BC all the free inhabitants of Cisalpine Gaul south of the Po had been theoretically made Roman citizens.[120] Furthermore, a great many of those living north of the Po were Romans or possessed Latin rights (which included the right to use Roman civil law). During the late Republic there was agitation that they too should be granted Roman citizenship – something finally granted by a law of Caesar's in 49 BC.[121] We possess a fragment of a law from Ateste and a much larger text from Veleia which refer to the removal of cases in the first instance from the jurisdiction of a local magistrate to that of the praetor in Rome. This occurred when the suit was above a certain monetary value or when condemnation entailed *infamia* for the defendant, provided that he did not wish the case to be heard by a local magistrate.[122] The second fuller text is of doubtful relevance to provincial administration, since it probably derives from the period after the province of Cisalpine Gaul was abolished in 42 BC.[123] The Ateste fragment may belong to the same period (it has been held to belong to the same law) or to the period when the province was still in existence, but in any case it only implies the possibility of referring suits to Rome after a certain *lex Roscia* (usually assumed to be the citizenship law of 49 BC).[124] Nevertheless, this may be explained by the close association of the province with the rest of Italy and the large number of Romans and Latins settled on the far side of the Po, who would have expected access to the same sort of jurisdiction that was available to the inhabitants of Italy.

In general, then, under the Republic neither Roman citizens in the provinces nor provincials had the right to demand the removal of a lawsuit from the provincial governor to a court in Rome. Moreover, appeal against the governor's judgement was *de facto* almost impossible even for Roman citizens. *Provocatio* against capital punishment was closely tied to its origins in the self-help of the Roman plebs and required the backing of tribunes to make it effective.[125] Sthenius of Thermae was protected by the senate by being excused from returning to stand trial in Sicily before Verres, and the tribunes refused to recognise his condemnation in absence by a Sicilian court as a justification for expelling him from Rome. However, neither the senate nor the tribunes could have protected him in Sicily.[126] Again, Cicero asserts that the court which tried Cn. Dolabella, former governor of Cilicia, overturned Dolabella's conviction of an ambassador from an allied community, but, even if it is true that the *quaestio de repetundis* had the right to abolish any prior legal judgement by the man on trial, not merely decisions in financial matters, its action was effective here only because Philodamus had been tried in his absence and could subsequently campaign against the condemnation.[127]

In capital cases the best source of protection for the Roman citizen or for the ally, who had been rewarded with *provocatio* in return for distinguished military service or for a successful prosecution *de repetundis*,[128] was the fear in the governor's mind that he would be later prosecuted himself for disregarding *provocatio*. Where an ordinary *socius* was concerned, even this threat was lacking. In noncapital cases *de iure* there was no basis for appeal (even at Rome this only occurred exceptionally through intervention by another magistrate with *imperium* or by tribunes). We do, however, find problems being referred to the senate, when a matter sufficiently affected the whole community to merit an embassy of protest. This was how Oropos' dispute with the *publicani* came to be referred to the senate in 73 BC, and in Cicero's consulship Apollonis protested there about its long-standing quarrel with Appuleius Decianus, in which Decianus had asked governors to intervene.[129] Furthermore, the governor might in effect promote an appeal against himself. In 59 BC Quintus Cicero, probably at the instance of Greeks in the province of Asia, referred to the senate a question regarding the customs-dues on goods being taken from one part of the province to another by sea (*portorium circumvectionis*) after holding a prior hearing himself with a *consilium*.[130] His brother insists in a letter that Quintus was not obliged to do so, but his references to the conflicting interests of the *publicani*, on the one hand, and the provincials, on the other, show us why Quintus wished to shift the burden of decision from his own shoulders.

5

TAXATION AND CORVEES

THE BEGINNINGS OF TAXATION

In the early days of their expansion the Romans were accustomed to demand not only military service but also financial contributions from their Italian allies. Although tribute was discontinued for Roman citizens in 167 BC, it continued to be required from non-Romans in Italy down to the Social War.[1] This money was chiefly, if not solely, conceived as providing payment for allied units in their joint operations with the Romans. As soon as Rome began to contract alliances outside Italy, it was in principle likely that she would see these as a possible source of financial, as well as military aid. The considerations which prompted the imposition of taxes and other burdens on these new allies at any particular time seem to have been largely practical – the need for money and the ease with which taxes could be collected. Conditions favouring taxation were the existence of a traditional system previously exploited by another power and the regular presence of Roman officials (though the latter was not a *sine qua non*, as the tribute imposed on Macedonia and Illyricum in 167 BC shows).[2] On the other hand, the Romans were more cautious in sensitive areas where they were anxious to maintain goodwill and where there was a diplomatic advantage in conceding immunity, for example, in peninsular Greece before 146 BC and in pro-Roman cities which had been formerly subject-allies of Carthage after 146.[3]

If we can trust Livy's account of a senate meeting early in the Second Punic War, it was complained then that the tribute of Sicily and Sardinia was being swallowed by the armies there.[4] This implies a previous policy that the provincials should not only pay for their own protection but provide a surplus profit for Rome. As a result of the First Punic War Rome had acquired in Sicily three categories of allies – first, Syracuse and her dependent cities; second, the cities, both

70

Punic and Greek, within the old Carthaginian province at the west end of the island; third, the remaining Greek and Sikel cities. Hiero II of Syracuse was enrolled as a friend and ally of Rome. He seems not to have paid any official tribute, but nevertheless made freely considerable contributions of grain and money in the Second Punic War.[5] Of the cities in Punic domain three were free from tribute in Cicero's day – Panormos, Halikyai and Segesta – and their status may have originated in the settlement at the end of the First Punic War (Segesta, significantly, claimed Trojan descent and kinship with Rome).[6] The rest of the cities in this area were probably treated by the Romans as they had been previously by Carthaginians – granted local independence but subjected to demands for financial aid as well as military support. It is likely that tribute was also imposed on the other Greek and Sikel cities outside Hiero's domain, apart from a few specifically exempted from taxation – Messana (which had a treaty), Halaesa and Centuripium. The latter two had surrendered to Rome early in the First Punic War and are attested as *immunes* by Cicero. A late Republican inscription shows that Centuripium claimed kinship with both Rome and the Latin town of Lanuvium.[7] Sicily was unusual in the late Republic in having two quaestors, one of whom was posted to Lilybaeum in Punic Sicily.[8] His position may have derived from the need to supervise taxation in the earliest years of the province before the incorporation of Hiero's kingdom.

After the defection and recapture of the island in the Second Punic War the cities that had revolted, including Syracuse, were given back their local autonomy, but the whole island was now subjected to Roman administration. In a speech ascribed by Livy to a Macedonian addressing the Aetolian council, Sicily is said to be subordinated to the *fasces* of the Roman praetor on his tribunal. The Romans allegedly intended that the province should supply Rome with food: with this in mind the consul of 210, M. Valerius Laevinus, had turned the Sicilians' minds back to agriculture.[9] Some land was confiscated – the outstandingly productive *ager Leontinus* and, probably, the *ager Recentoricus* – and rented out by the Roman censors.[10] However, the main revenue came from a system of taxation apparently used by Hiero II, called the *lex Hieronica*, which was based on a proportion of crops produced. This was extended to the whole of the island apart from the cities with treaties or immune from tribute. Neaetum and Tauromenium now joined Messana in the former class.[11]

About developments in Sardinia we know almost nothing. By 176 BC some states were paying *stipendium*, money-tribute, others

71

only contributing grain.[12] The likelihood is that the Romans adapted the system previously used by the Carthaginians. Meanwhile, in Spain, which was potentially richer but politically more volatile, taxation seems to have been developed in a more haphazard way. From 218 BC the Romans were committed to campaigning in Spain and extending Roman power south of the river Ebro. Initially the commanders there were cautious about financial demands, although we hear of fines imposed on peoples which seceded from Rome. Then the two Scipiones wrote home in 215 asking for money for pay, clothing and grain, saying that, if there was no money in the treasury, then they would begin a policy of extracting it from the Spaniards in some way.[13] By 206 we hear of *tributa* (*eisphorai*) imposed on cities for the benefit of the armies, including the provision of soldiers' pay. After the second revolt by Mandonius and Indibilis in 205 double *stipendium* was imposed for that year, a six-month supply of grain was required and also cloaks and togas for the army.[14] One may regard these last impositions as indemnities rather than taxation. From another point of view, in a situation where Rome was reluctant to offend friends by heavy demands, the opportunity of inflicting seemingly just financial penalties on defectors was too convenient to be missed.

It is a debated point among scholars whether there was a regular system for collecting direct taxes immediately after Spain had been turned into two provinces in 197.[15] During Cato's governorship as consul in 195 we hear of his probity in securing the supply of grain for the army by the Spaniards (he was later to attack P. Furius (pr. 174) for unjust calculation of the equivalent price in money for the grain demanded).[16] Conceivably, the grain or its value in money was in 195 the chief direct contribution that the allies had to make. In 180 it appears from the remarks made by a *legatus* and a *tribunus militum* of Q. Fulvius to the senate that enough grain and cash was being raised from Spain to make supplementation from Rome unnecessary: previously, it is implied, there tended to be a shortfall. The governor of 180–8, Tiberius Gracchus, father of the famous tribune, was remembered for fixing rates of tax, granting immunities and establishing treaties, which were greatly missed by the Spanish later, and it was perhaps then that the tax system began to be stabilised. The 600,000 *denarii* exacted by M. Marcellus from Celtiberia in 152–1 may have been the regular total assessment.[17]

In 171, at the time of a Spanish complaint about the corruption of governors, the senate passed a decree forbidding a magistrate calculating the price of grain arbitrarily or using *praefecti* (military officers) to collect the money: presumably, the money had to be paid by the communities direct to the governor or his quaestor. This decree also forbad a governor forcing the Spanish selling the right to collect a 5 per cent levy at the price he himself should determine. It is unjustifiable to identify this automatically with a tax on corn, whether raised in kind or cash.[18] It was a tax which the Spanish communities collected themselves through contractors and whose proceeds were then passed on, in whole or part, to Rome – perhaps a *portorium* (transit-due) rather than a tax on produce.

Meanwhile, the Romans had seized on another obvious major source of revenue – the silver-mines, whose profits were considerable. Strabo quotes Polybius to the effect that within a circuit of 20 stades (2.5 miles) round New Carthage there were 40,000 workers who brought in a total of 25,000 *denarii* a day. According to Diodorus, some individual silver prospectors had extracted a Euboic talent of silver (*c.* 6,000 *denarii*) in three days. He also describes the exploitation of the mines by Italians through slave-labour and the introduction of technology into the workings with elaborate tunnels drained by Archimedian screws.[19] Cato is said to have been the first to establish large taxes on the iron- and silver-mines. It has been argued by Richardson that the right to work them was originally leased to relatively small-scale operators, who perhaps made an initial down-payment and then paid a proportion of the produce. Only much later in Augustus' time did management pass into the hands of large *societates publicanorum*, which were granted the mines on long leases.[20]

We should probably connect with Roman taxation the appearance of 'Iberian *denarii*'. These are silver coins struck to a Roman standard (just under 4 grams) and bearing the *denarius* sign (X) but with local types – a young man's head on the obverse and a horseman with lance on the reverse. They are found chiefly in northern Spain, especially the region of Osca on the Ebro, and are now believed to have been in circulation from *c.* 150 BC down to the time of Sertorius.[21] Whether these were originally minted on Roman authority, out of bullion received in tribute, or on the initiative of the Spaniards themselves, they would have provided a convenient medium not only for tribute-payment by the Spaniards but also for the purchase of goods and services by the Romans.

Even if we know comparatively little of the details of taxation in Spain, the history of the two provinces there illustrates the Romans' growing concern with the public exploitation of the resources of her overseas dominions. A similar trend can be detected elsewhere. The settlement of Macedonia in 167 BC after the defeat of Perseus was a compromise. Although the country was not subjected to a Roman governor but divided into four autonomous regions, it was nevertheless required to pay to Rome half the tribute, that is the property tax, formerly paid to the kings. Moreover, royal land was taken over as Roman *ager publicus*.[22] This had the effect of exporting funds which had previously been spent in the country on the Macedonian army and administration. Gold- and silver-mines were for the moment closed, while iron- and copper-mines were allowed to remain open at half the former rent. Later in 158 the gold- and silver-mines were reopened, possibly on similar terms.[23] The Roman governing class seems to have been both a little embarrassed at the wealth now available to it and reluctant to provoke revolt by inflicting heavy burdens, but, in the same way that a momentum of conquest had been generated, so too there was a momentum in the pursuit of the financial rewards that had been available to the previous dominant powers in the areas conquered. When it came to the settlement of Carthage's old territory in 146, there seems to have been no doubt that the land was at Rome's disposition and there to be enjoyed by Romans and allies at the discretion of the senate and people. The ten-man commission set up by the *lex Livia* allocated land within the province to the free cities and the *stipendiarii*, while apparently keeping the rest as public land to be leased out by censorial contact: it was the latter which was in part sold off in the Gracchan period or used for allocation to colonists by C. Gracchus himself.[24]

DIRECT TAXATION IN THE LATE REPUBLIC

Cicero distinguished between two basic forms of direct taxation imposed on the provinces in his time.[25] First was the *vectigal certum* or *stipendiarium*, for example, the taxes in Spain or Africa. *Stipendium*, as we have just seen, came to be demanded regularly from Spanish peoples as maintenance for the army until it became consolidated into an annual tax, while in Africa it was imposed immediately on the conquered in 146 BC. Cicero calls the tax 'a reward for victory and a penalty for having made war', which was indeed its origin, but before his day it had developed into something more permanent. His second category was the *censoria locatio*, as established by C. Gracchus for Asia. This is the only example Cicero gives of direct taxation of a province contracted out by the censors in Rome. Late Republican inscriptions, on the other hand, reveal the *censoria locatio* of Delos and perhaps Euboea, though the nature of this taxation is unclear.[26] The censors in any case leased out the land retained in the public domain, for example the territory in Sicily[27] and that in Africa mentioned earlier (p. 74).

Thanks to Cicero, we know most about the Sicilian system, which was, unfortunately for us, unique, though in various elements analogous to what occurred elsewhere. It was embodied in the *lex Hieronica*, a code which must have derived from that employed by Hellenistic Syracuse in its own and allied territories, but was extended by the Romans to the rest of Sicily some time after the Second Punic War. The principle was a tithe (*decumae*) on produce – not only on grain, but on wine, oil and other fruits (*fruges minutae*). The right to collect these was normally sold to contractors in Sicily by the quaestors there, but in 75 BC the contracts for all but the grain tithes were sold at Rome by the consuls (there were no censors at that time).[28] The rate for grain seems to have been a standard one used, for example, by Hellenistic rulers in Asia[29] and by the Romans themselves in Italy, but that on fruits was more generous to the producer that the fifth demanded in Italy.[30]

Farmers were required to make a *professio* (declaration) of the land under seed.[31] Such declarations were probably regularly used as a basis for tax-collection in other provinces, as they were in Ptolemaic Egypt.[32] From calculations made in the light of these declarations and the known past yields of different districts, the relevant tax contractors (*decumani*) (who seem to have been mainly residents of Sicily) made bids before the provincial governor in Syracuse for the tithes of the various city-territories, and the highest secured the contract. The bids were made in kind – in *medimnoi* of grain, for example – although on one occasion Cicero talks in terms of a monetary equivalent, and this valuation would have been necessary if guarantors or security were given, as they must have been, for the sum of revenue to be delivered.[33] The collectors of the tithe then met the farmer when his grain was on the threshing-floor and agreed in a *pactio* the tax to be collected. One passage suggests that there was a regular payment to the tax-collector of an additional 6 per cent of the produce (not 6 per cent the tax assessment), although other evidence suggests that 10 per cent of the assessment, i.e. 1 per cent of the original sum declared, would have been a more normal administrative charge by a Roman tax-collector.[34]

The grain then had to be conveyed to a port (*ad aquam*) perhaps by the farmers, perhaps by the *decumani*. The fact that there is no sign that Verres tried to profit from any obligation on the farmer is perhaps an argument for this duty belonging to the collectors. On the other hand, where extra grain was bought by Roman officials on instructions from Rome, the fees sought for inspection, money-changing and the services of scribes suggest that the grain had to be delivered to an official place of reception by the farmer.[35] The revenue grain was then presumably shipped to Italy. There is little evidence and much obscurity here. Did the tax-collectors' duties cease at the Sicilian port, when they handed over the grain to the Roman quaestor or his representative? Or were they also bound to convey the grain to Italy? We hear of *mancipes* (contractors) charged with moving the tithe grain, and Cicero later claims that Clodius put all public and private grain and the *mancipes* in the hands of his agent Sex. Cloelius. Moreover, one family of grain-transporters, C. Avianius Flaccus of Puteoli and his sons Gaius and Marcus, are known to us from Cicero's letters.[36] There are two main possibilities: either the original contract with the tax-collectors stipulated delivery to a port in Italy on pain of forfeiting the monetary equivalent of the bid for the tithes, or a secondary contract was made by Roman officials with operators of ships, either in return for a fee or perhaps on condition that the grain should be left in their hands for a price less than its market-value, but providing in any case that the full value of the grain should be paid to the treasury if delivery did not take place.[37] In this way the Roman authorities could best ensure that the grain reached the Italian market, as was politically desirable, without having to undertake the risk of transporting it themselves. Grain was in fact occasionally sold by Roman magistrates in the middle Republic and regularly (apart from a decade between 82 and 73 BC) in the late Republic after C. Gracchus' grain law of 123, but there is no evidence that the grain was in the hands of public officials on its journey from its port of origin to the warehouses in which it was stored in Puteoli, Ostia or Rome.

Our knowledge of the Sicilian system has its blind spots but it is in strong contrast with our ignorance of the direct taxation of the province of Asia through *censoria locatio*, that is, the letting of contracts in Rome introduced by the controversial law of C. Gracchus in 123 BC. It appears from remarks attributed to M. Antonius by Appian that, as in Sicily, direct taxation was basically levied on farming and derived from a percentage of the produce. Cicero at one point talks about *decumae* at Ephesus and this seems to have been formerly the tariff under the Pergamene kings.[38] L. Lucullus is said to have put a 25 per cent tax on crops in Asia but this was an emergency measure to deal with arrears which had probably arisen through failure to pay Sulla's indemnity. We still hear of tithes in Asia in the dossier on *portoria* from Ephesus published in Nero's reign (see below).[39] However, at some point some tithes were replaced by a tax on the quantity and quality of land possessed. An imperial inscription shows land liable to tax at the rate of 12 *drachmai/denarii* an *uncia* (the latter seems to mean one-twelfth of a *iugerum*, which is itself one-quarter of a hectare). The system of collection from the producers in this province changed when Julius Caesar removed this from the contractors and put it in the hands of local communities.[40]

It is a fair inference from silence that, when Caesar was dictator, no other eastern province had a tax system like that of the province of Asia, where *publicani* bid at Rome for the right to collect tax from producers. Collection by communities was the most common medium of direct taxation, in operation, for example, in Cilicia during Cicero's governorship. It was probably regarded by the Romans as a favour to the locals if they, rather than the Roman *societates publicanorum*, were allowed to collect the tribute. Nevertheless, Cicero talks of *pactiones* between the cities and the *publicani*, which had entailed high interest on arrears as early as the governorship of Servilius Isauricus in the early 70s BC. It is most improbable that this refers to the collection of Roman *portoria* (see below), since the dossier from Ephesus implies that the collection of these, not only in the former Pergamene kingdom (now Asia) but also in neighbouring provinces, was directly in the hands of the Roman company. It is far more likely that the *publicani* had contracts for collecting the total sums of direct taxation owed by the cities. Such contracts were for a *lustrum* (five years). They may have been let in Rome or by the governor or his quaestor in the province (an early imperial inscription suggests that the latter may have been true in the province of Africa; it may also be significant that Cicero only mentions the letter-carriers coming from Rome for the company that had leased the *portoria*).[41] The communities themselves had to farm out the collection of taxes in order to raise the necessary sums. Cicero found the cities of his province in trouble on his arrival. They had already sold in advance the 'ὠναί', the franchises to collect taxes – described as *venditio tributorum* in Latin – and, he implies, had spent the money thus raised. Hence the expenditure on embassies, which Appius Claudius, the outgoing governor, was requiring them to make, had led them to impose poll-taxes ('ἐπικεφάλαια'). Although at one point Cicero refers to this imposition as the tribute of Appius, it is clear from Cicero's contemporary letter to Claudius himself that at this point a poll-tax, like the tax on doors which is linked by Cicero with it, was not a direct imposition of the governor with or without authority from Rome, but a local measure to raise money in an emergency.[42] We may compare the fragmentary letter about Mylasa after the devastation caused by Labienus' invasion in 40–39 BC: 'For the city has no money nor public revenues to rely on, unless in face of the collapse of the taxes it should wish to make levies on the firewood (?) of each individual and to inflict a poll-tax.'[43] It is true that Caesar accused Metellus Scipio of greedily raising money in 48 BC by a poll-tax on slaves and free men and taxes on doors and columns.[44] However, even if Scipio had taken the initiative here, the cities would have had to act as his agents and in any case this was a time of civil war when money had to be raised somehow and any pretence of legality or normality was a discount.

In general, then, outside Asia and Sicily the cities were given a global sum to collect and pass on to the governor or the tax-collectors: it was up to them how they raised it. The local taxation of Greek cities was immensely complex. A second-century BC decree from Cos tells us of levies on bread, grain, ship-borne wine, wine from the vineyards, whores, firewood, rents, four-footed animals, carts, fleeces, vine-pruners, female slaves, tunny-fishing, incense-selling, pickled fish and purple dyes. In the same period the Dionysiac artists at Teos were freed from taxes on beasts of burden, pigs and sheep, on wool-working and on the profits of their slaves selling firewood and doing other jobs.[45] However, the majority of revenues like these are likely to have been earmarked for maintaining the civic life of the community and, in order to obtain the sums required by Rome, either a levy on the chief form of production, agriculture, or a capital levy was necessary. In my view, the inscription from Messene praising the secretary Aristokles for tax-collection in a crisis (it has been dated variously to the early first century BC, the triumviral period and AD 35–44) does not describe a Roman 1 per cent (eight obol) tax on property, but rather one used by Messene in order to raise money to discharge a block sum required by the Romans.[46]

Roman citizens were liable to such taxes on property they owned within the city's territory. (Cicero assumes that the property of Appuleius Decianus is liable for tribute to Apollonis and we find Caelius pleading with Cicero that his friend M. Feridius should not have to pay tax on lands he has leased from a city.)[47] Nor were Roman citizens excluded from becoming the local tax contractors. The *fructus Trallianorum* that Falcidius had bought must have been some form of local revenues worth apparently at least 2 million sesterces.[48] It was of course easy, though in the long run unwise, for a city to pledge the proceeds of future taxes to those who lent it money, and the money-lenders would often have been the same people as the contractors.[49]

Where cities or other communities were responsible for providing Rome with tribute there was more flexibility than under the regime of the great *societates publicanorum* in Asia and something of a buffer between those who paid tax and the ultimate recipients. Moreover, there was less likelihood of disputes between the tax companies and cities over who had the right to exploit a particular source of tax, such as that concerning Priene and certain salt-pans in the 90s BC. Yet in any financial crisis, whether the community borrowed against future revenues or actually sold the right to collect taxes in advance or combined the two options, it came under similar pressures from the *publicani* to those which regularly obtained in Asia. Cicero gleefully pointed out that, when the cities of Asia were themselves responsible for collecting the indemnity imposed by Sulla in 84, they could not manage this (as opposed to the regular taxation) without a *publicanus*.[50] That was true, but it was a fact of civic life and reflected no particular credit on the Roman *publicani*.

Poll-taxes were only an emergency measure under Roman admi-nistration in Cilicia and Asia, but they were imposed on the *stipendiarii* in Africa in 146 BC (conceivably this was the way Carthage had extracted taxes from subject communities earlier). They had also been a traditional form of tax in Palestine and almost certainly elsewhere in the Seleucid realms (together with a crown-tax, salt-tax and tax on grain).[51] Under the Principate they were also used for the Jews, Syrians and Cilicians, though the last two peoples only paid 1 per cent of their assessed valuations.[52] We have no details of the tribute imposed on Syria and Judaea in the late Republic by Pompey.[53] Badian has argued that Pompey is likely to have extended the *censoria locatio* at Rome to the new Asiatic provinces of Bithynia and Syria, but we hear nothing of this system being abolished in these provinces by Caesar, as it was in Asia.[54] More probably, taxation in these provinces took the traditional Seleucid forms, except that now Roman magistrates were the ultimate recipients. While governor in 57–4 BC, Gabinius came into conflict with the *publicani*.[55] Amid Cicero's rhetoric it is possible to discern that he removed collection of some taxes from the *societates publicanorum* and used local dynasts or cities as his agents. It is difficult to tell whether the contracts which Gabinius transferred from their former collectors were for direct taxes or indirect taxes. In favour of the second hypothesis there is the parallel a decade later of Caesar's granting to Hyrcanus the right to collect the transit-dues at Joppa in return for 20,175 *modii* of corn. Under Caesar's settlement, at any rate, the direct taxes of the Jews were to be paid over to the quaestor at Sidon without *publicani* as intermediaries.[56]

OTHER REVENUES

Land-leases

Stipendium or *tributum*, as it later came to be called, was only one form of revenue which accrued to the Romans. There were other forms of rent or taxation in every province, which were normally exploited through Roman contractors and their companies – the *societates publicanorum*. The exploitation of mines, as we find it in Spain, has already been discussed (p. 73). We have also already encountered the public lands subject to *censoria locatio* in Sicily (p. 75). Such lands were to be found in most provinces, as indeed they were in Italy. If cultivated, they were subject to a rent in the form of a percentage of the produce (10 per cent on grain and other crops, 20 per cent on fruits), if grazed, to a fee (*scriptura*) probably depending on the head of cattle kept there, as in Egypt – though our texts are not so specific.[57] The *lex agraria* of 111 BC, which says little about the payers of direct tax (*stipendiarii*), is more informative about leasing of the land remaining public in Africa for *vectigal, decumae* or *scriptura*. This was done either by the censors or, if necessary, by a consul.[58] We shall have more to say about this procedure below.

An important general question arises about the land rented out by the censors in the provinces on similar terms to those applying to public land in Italy: was it also subject to tax as part of the province? In Sicily, for example, the *ager Leontinus* was Roman public land with, according to Cicero, only one Leontine actually working it in his day.[59] Those who worked it must have leased it from the censors like any other public land. Among them were the citizens of the free city of Centuripium, who farmed everywhere in Sicily.[60] Yet we also hear of tithe-gatherers (*decumani*) operating there, which would be only reasonable, since, *qua* resident agricultural producers in the province, the farmers were liable to tax, while *qua* lessees of the *populus*

Romanus, they were liable for rent.[61] This distinction helps to explain the provision in the *lex agraria* of 111 BC about land sold in Africa, (which is likely to have applied elsewhere), whereby such land was to become *ager privatus vectigalisque*.[62] It was once held by scholars that this *vectigal* was a token rent like that applied to *ager quaestorius* in Italy.[63] However, the point of that was to denote that the land was still public, whereas this land in Africa was specifically private. Hence it has been rightly argued recently that the *vectigal* was substantial and reflected a policy of retaining part of the revenue after sale.[64] The law itself provides an inference that this *vectigal* was considerable. An elaborate procedure for collecting money is detailed in lines 70–2 of the law which is most naturally interpreted as a means of collecting tax on this land. There is a reference to the start of a new tax period and to the buying by contractors of the right to collect the money. (By contrast, if a purchaser failed to produce the purchase price of land sold by the treasury, this was followed by seizure of securities or sale for cash to another man.)[65] Such sales should not be regarded as confined to Africa. The clause mentioning *ager privatus vectigalisque* in the central part of the law may well be separate from the African section. Furthermore, it is certain that sales of land and buildings were to take place in Greece in 111 BC – one possible location is Euboea, from which the Romans collected taxes in 78 BC, but which was not one of the territories on the sale-list of P. Servilius Rullus in his agrarian bill of 63 BC.[66]

Rullus, it is true, was accused by Cicero of planning to dispose of many *vectigalia* of the Roman people by a massive sale of Roman public land. Yet his behaviour would have been more politic and plausible if the land he was selling was to become *ager privatus vectigalisque* like the African lands. Rome would thus forego future rent in return for a lump sum but retain the right to tax. We cannot trust Cicero to be completely honest in this sort of situation and it is more likely, in my view, that the long list of provincial lands retailed in Cicero's second speech *de Lege Agraria* had previously produced both rent and tax, even if both had not been exacted at the highest possible rate.[67] Rullus was also planning to impose a *pergrande vectigal* on the land remaining public.[68] This is best explained as a large rent increase, since in Sicily, for example, it would have been difficult to tamper with the system of *decumae* and Rullus' exemption of the *ager Recentoricus*, farmed by locals, is more likely to have been a remission of rent than of the basic tax paid by provincials.

There remains, however, a question about the land formerly

belonging to the Pergamene kings in the province of Asia annexed by the Romans in 133–2 BC. In the speeches on the Rullan bill Cicero only mentions the Attalid lands in the Thracian Chersonese (over the Hellespont from Pergamum) as being now up for sale,[69] but this may be a reflection of the fact that other ex-Pergamene public land had either already been sold or was too burdened with debt to be satisfactorily privatised. Rostovtzeff believed that the whole of the province of Asia, whether previously royal land ('χώρα βασιλική') or belonging to the cities, was subjected by the Roman settlement to *decumae* contracted out to the *publicani*, on the ground that Rome, like the Hellenistic kings, taxed on the principle of being the ultimate owner of the territory.[70] Frank reasonably objected that only certain provincial lands were treated by the *populus Romanus* as its own under the Republic, in the same way as *ager publicus* in Italy. However, he then went on to argue that the old royal lands of the Attalid kings were not subjected to rental as *ager publicus*: they were merely subjected to tax from 123 BC; only the personal estates of the kings were treated as Roman public property.[71] Frank may have been right to exclude from the Roman public sector lands granted by the kings to temples or mountain villages,[72] but the crown lands given to friends of the kings as quasi-feudal holdings seem as likely to have been annexed to the property of the Roman people as the kings' personal estates. As such, it would have been appropriate if they had been liable to both rent and taxes and, if sold, continued to be liable to tax.

Might this double exaction have been an excessive burden on the producers? In practice the censors could only lease out public land, also subject to tithes, at rents which the lessees were prepared at the time to pay. Thus there was a safety mechanism, if the land was viewed merely from the economic standpoint. However, where lands worked by a community became Roman public land, then sentiment and convenience might have led the locals to pay rents which they could not afford for their traditional holdings. The *ager Recentoricus* was clearly farmed by locals and was treated by the Romans as an exception to the rule that one should extract the maximum return from *ager publicus* probably for this very reason.[73] By contrast, the Leontines apparently could not afford to farm their own land. Where Roman public land in the provinces was being rented by wealthy provincials or Romans, there was no fiscal objection to extracting the maximum market rent. This in conjunction with the 10 per cent tax also payable still compares favourably with the 33.3 per cent on grain and 50 per cent on fruits demanded by the Seleucids from Palestine.[74]

Taxes on grazing

We only hear of *scriptura* in passing in the Verrines in spite of the fact that pasturage figures importantly in the stories of the two Sicilian slave-revolts at the end of the first century BC.[75] It appears that Verres could not turn it into a source of profit. L. Carpinatius was the local representative of the tax company which had bought the right to collect both the *scriptura* and *portoria*.[76] As for Asia, the satirist Lucilius declared about 130 BC that he did not want to change his life for that of a *scripturarius* and *publicanus* there.[77] In Africa, as we have seen, it was one way of exploiting the land which remained in public hands after the sales and allocations prescribed by the agrarian law. If a man only chose to raise stock, he would have escaped the double burden that fell on the agriculturist who leased public land. However, he probably was only allowed to use the more marginal terrain for which agriculturists would have paid little rent.[78] Moreover, he may have had to pay tolls on the movement of his herds from one pasture to another.[79] There was a logic in any case in entrusting the contract for *scriptura* and *portoria* to the same company, as in Sicily, Asia (where we know that P. Terentius Hispo was *pro magistro* of the company contracting for these two taxes) or in Cilicia during Cicero's governorship,[80] since the best opportunity of imposing a tax commensurate with the size of a herd would have been when it was comparatively compact, while on the move.

Transit-dues

The Latin word *portorium*, which is a literal translation of the Greek equivalent 'λιμέναιον', covered more than customs duties. As Cagnat pointed out, under this heading the Romans subsumed duties imposed at the frontiers of the empire or provinces (*douanes*), duties at the gates of towns (*octrois*) and tolls at bridges or points on roads (*péages*).[81] In the *lex Antonia* about Termessus, the community is granted the right to fix its own regulations for *portoriis terrestribus maritumeisque* (duties on land and sea).[82] Such dues had been exacted in areas under Roman jurisdiction in Italy since at least the third century BC. In 199 we find the censors contracting out *portoria venalicium* at Capua and Puteoli. *Portoria venalicium* should probably be understood as tolls on goods for sale, i.e., not on personal possessions, which were exempted from duty according to the late Republican jurist Alfenus Varus, citing the regulations governing the customs duties of Sicily (he could also have cited the Asiatic customs law).[83] The dues instituted by Rome and the other Italian communities would have become consolidated under Roman administration after the Social War and the unification of Italy. They were abolished by a bill of Metellus Nepos, when praetor in 60 BC, but reinstituted by Julius Caesar for foreign goods, probably at ports alone, since it would often have been difficult to prove a foreign origin of goods once they were on the roads of Italy.[84]

Portoria also figure early in Rome's relations with the Greek world. In 189 BC the senate recognised the right of the Ambraciots to exact their own *portoria*, provided that they did not apply these to Romans and Latins.[85] Then in 170 the senate restored to Thisbai in Boeotia the right to her own *'limenes'* and later this was one of the privileges conceded to Stratonicea by Sulla.[86] The grant made to Termessus, probably in 68 BC, was similar to that made to the Ambraciots: this time not all Romans and Latins were excluded from transit-dues, but only the *publicani* who had a contract with the Romans and these merely on the proceeds of their tax-collecting.[87] Thus in the Greek world local collection of transit-dues by the free cities continued alongside Roman collection in their provinces. The regulation of 17 BC in the Ephesus dossier shows the Romans carefully forbidding the installation of customs posts on the territory of free cities and ordering them to be placed instead on the border between the city's land and the rest of the province.[88] We know that many of the cities lost their right to exact local taxation under the Principate. However, some remained – for example, at Veii in Italy, Stratonicea and Aezani.[89] Some detailed tariffs of duties survive: there is a major customs law from Palmyra and two fragments of *leges portus* from Zarai and Lambaesis, which seem to be local. The same may be true of the tariff recorded by Marcian and preserved in the Digest.[90] In the Celtic world there was a tradition of customs-dues and tolls before the arrival of the Romans: they are attested on cross-Channel trade, in Aeduan territory and on passes over the Alps.[91]

From the literature of the late Republic we can glean some scattered information about the Roman collection of *portoria*. There are the agents (*pro magistro*) of the relevant tax companies – L. Carpinatius in Sicily, L. Canuleius at Syracuse, P. Vettius Chilo, the *magister scripturae et sex publicorum* there, P. Terentius Hispo in

Bithynia and their counterparts in Cilicia.[92] There are references to customs posts (*custodiae*), and in Cicero's *Pro Fonteio* we find that Cicero's client was accused of conniving at the introduction of new posts on the wine-route up-country from Narbo, which had not been provided for in the *lex censoria*.[93] The local collectors appointed by the *societates* seem to have been slaves. At Tergeste a certain Agato was *portitor sociorum*; at Aquileia a similar post was held by Epagatus. Nevertheless under the *lex censoria* these slaves had a right to search.[94] In Sicily there was a standard 5 per cent duty, but in Gaul we hear of variable amounts per amphora on the wine trade. (I have already mentioned the vexed question of liability to a multiple duty in Asia through the *portorium circumvectionis* – a question remitted by Quintus Cicero to the senate.)[95] We get an idea of the range of goods liable to duty from the tariffs surviving from the Principate – slaves, hides, beasts for sale, garments, cloth, perfume, wine, oil, fruit, nuts, pitch and pine-cones.[96]

The best evidence, however, for *portoria* is now provided by a dossier inscribed at Ephesus in the reign of Nero deriving from the commissioners for public taxes of AD 62 (their appointment and the publication resulted from the senate's resolution in AD 58 to publish the regulations affecting each public tax company.) This contains a series of regulations laid down for contracts stretching back to those of 75 and 72 BC (the earliest contains references to the situation under the Attalid kings). These affect the standard rate (2.5 per cent), the types of goods liable (not, for example, money, books or other documents), the duty of carriers to declare, the penalties for failure to declare, the towns where customs posts are to be sited and their exact location, the treatment of free cities and other forms of exemption and, most important, the procedures for letting contracts and the liabilities of the chief contractor (*manceps*).[97] The dossier gives, on the one hand, the impression of a fundamental continuity, whose origin lies in the rule of the Pergamene kings, and, on the other, of manifold exemptions from tax, which were no doubt chiefly granted in response to special appeals and pressures from those affected. Although the collection of direct taxes had been removed from the *publicani* by Julius Caesar, in AD 62 these were still as active in indirect taxation as they ever had been. Though there had been some modifications in the procedure for contracting, the principles of this and the mechanics of collection were much what they had been in 123 BC or earlier.

THE TAX COMPANIES (*SOCIETATES PUBLICANORUM*)

The importance of the Roman tax-collectors should be already evident. Who were they and how did they operate? A *publicanus* was a man who dealt with *publica*, Roman public contracts. These might be for building, transport, supply or revenue collection, but tax contracts were so important that *publica* became shorthand for these alone – for example, the *sex publica* of Sicily or the *quattuor publica* of Africa.[98] The earliest description of their operations is given by Polybius, when describing the position of the plebs in the Roman constitution:

> For, inasmuch as many public works are contracted out by the censors throughout Italy for the construction and repair of public property, so many that one could not easily count them, and on the other hand many rivers, ports, fruit plantations, mines, estates, in short everything that has fallen under Roman power, it happens that all these activities I have mentioned are handled by the plebs and almost everyone, so to speak, is devoted to buying and performing the contracts arising out of these: for some buy the concessions from the censors themselves, while others give personal guarantees for those who have bought the concessions and others give their property as security in these matters to the treasury.[99]

By the time Polybius died in the late second century BC the contractors' activities had spread to either end of the Mediterranean.

The censors or, when they were not in office, other magistrates, usually the consuls, auctioned the concessions at Rome in public.[100] Bids were made by the lifting of hands and the successful bidder was known as *manceps* – probably because he was the purchaser rather than because he used his hands.[101] He was expected, as Polybius describes, to provide *praedes*, personal guarantors, and *praedia*, property which was mortgaged to the *aerarium* as security for the contract (there was some precedent for this double security in Ptolemaic Egypt). However, he might in certain circumstances be his own guarantor.[102] The titles of the properties to be mortgaged were put under a seal at the treasury (*praedia subsignare*). The liability of guarantors descended to their heirs.[104] Whether a man who contracted to collect revenues for the Roman people was required to make a cash deposit is unclear. The elaborate procedure for obtaining security suggests that, even if there was a cash deposit, it was comparatively unimportant. Moreover, the contract regulations (*leges*) from the Augustan period in the Ephesus dossier make no mention of any such down-payment.[105]

A *manceps* was permitted to have partners (*socii*): hence the growth of *societates*, men who regularly worked together in undertaking contracts and were sufficiently organised to appoint directors (*magistri*) and local representatives (*pro magistro*). These partners might also be guarantors, if they wished, but this was not a necessary consequence of the contract.[106] We also find *adfines* to a contract and those who are said to hold shares (*partes*) in the large *societates* (the latter included senators like Caesar and Vatinius). Here interpretation must be highly conjectural: it is uncertain whether these shares were bought or might be simply granted by members of the *societas*, perhaps to guarantors as a reward for their services. According to a scholiast to Cicero, *adfines* had some right to a share in the proceeds of any dissolved partnership, but only up to a fixed sum: they would not, like partners, have been able to demand the dissolution of the *societas* themselves.[107]

The successful bidder was bound by the contract regulation (*lex*) laid down by the censors or whoever had let the concession. This, as our literary and epigraphic sources, especially the new Ephesus dossier, show, fixed the tax payable, immunities and penalties for failure to declare what was liable to rax or rent; further the measures allowed to tax-collectors in order to enforce their demands and perhaps the percentages which a collector might legitimately add as reward for himself (we hear of 10 per cent and 6 per cent, perhaps both of the sum collected); finally the procedures which the *manceps* himself must follow in undertaking the contract.[108]

The contracts in Asia, Cilicia and no doubt other provinces were normally for a *lustrum*, the five-year period associated with the Roman census in the Repubic.[109] Questions, however, arise over this. How exact were the time-limits? When precisely was the money for the contract demanded from the *manceps* and his *socii*? At what point were the securities seized, if this proved necessary? According to Macrobius, March was the month in which tax contracts were let; moreover, in the years when an intercalary month in February (an extra month intended to harmonise a basically lunar calendar with the solar year) was corruptly inserted or omitted, this was often to gratify the *publicani*. The Ides of March was the date from which the contract for exploiting the whetstone mines in Crete ran in the time of Julius

Caesar or Augustus.[110] In the *lex agraria* of 111 BC the coming Ides of March are first mentioned as a date by which controversies over possession of land in Italy should be brought before a magistrate. Later in this law taxes on *ager privatus vectigalisque* are owed from the first Ides of March which follows the first fixing of taxes after the passage of the law. This suggests that the Ides of March was treated as the beginning of a new financial period (this may have been a survival from the time before 153 BC when March was also the beginning of the consular year) and the tax arrangements applying during that period were fixed in the preceding months. It seems that a new tax contract was imminent in 111 BC, whose operation would probably begin in 110 (the Ides of March 111 must have been past when the agrarian law was enacted).[111] Cicero recalls an occasion when the herald Granius was accosted by the consul of 111 BC, P. Scipio Nasica, when the latter was going home after proclaiming a *iustitium* (cessation of public business): why, asked the consul, did he look gloomy? Was it because the bidding for the taxes had been adjourned? No, replied Granius, because the hearing of embassies had been adjourned (see p. 8).[112]

Censorship did not occur at precisely five-year intervals. For example, in the period preceding the agrarian law there were censors elected in 154, 147, 141, 136, 131, 125, 120 and 115 BC; following the law in 109 and 108, 102, 97 and 92. In the absence of censors the consuls could operate, as happened, for example, in 75 BC.[113] It may be that on some occasions there was a delay before a new tax period came into operation and the contract for this period was retrospective, but this would have produced an awkward hiatus in the areas where the taxes were collected (one can hardly imagine a customs post for instance simply closing down) and the inevitable tax arrears would have created additional problems. It is more likely that the Romans kept rigidly to the five-year *lustra* for tax purposes, even if the terminal dates did not coincide precisely with the presence of censors in office. For example, in 50 BC a *lustrum* of tax-collection had come to an end before the new censors were elected (see below). Thus, although short-term delays before the beginning of a new tax period might occur through political and private pressures, a delay of a year or more would not have been permitted. In fact if we assume that the tax periods before the Social War lasted strictly five years and that one terminal date fell in the year 15 March 111–15 March 110, censors were available in 141, 136, 131, perhaps in 120 and 115 but not in subsequent years. In the late Republic it seems that a strict succession of five-year tax period was maintained. The consuls let contracts in 75; there were censors in 70, 65 and 61–60; in 55 Pompey was settling accounts with the *publicani* in April, at a time when the tribunes were obstructing the censorship; and in May 50 Cicero talked of communities paying the collectors even the residue of the previous *lustrum* as well as their contributions for the current year.[114]

As I have argued earlier, the corollary of the complex system of guarantors and pledges was the lack of any significant deposit by the contractor. The regulation of 17 BC in the Ephesus dossier envisages yearly payments but this may have been an innovation. It is in my view likely that under the Republic the *publicani* only became liable for the sums they owed at the end of the *lustrum*. If the term could be marginally delayed by intercalation, that, as Macrobius suggests, would have helped a tax company which was having difficulty in collecting the necessary ready cash at the last moment.[115] If it failed to do so, its *praedes* became immediately liable and its *praedia* were exposed to seizure. Against this background we can, I believe, better understand the famous episode of 61–59 BC when the tax-gatherers demanded a reduction in what they owed on a tax contract. In November 61 the company which had contracted for the Asiatic taxes requested that the contract should be cancelled because they had bid too highly. They were backed by Crassus and Cicero himself, but opposed by Metellus Celer, consul elect for 60, and by Cato. The latter maintained his obstruction into the following January and later (Cicero tells us in May that Cato had prevailed). The following year, perhaps in March, Caesar relieved them of a third of the price of their contract.[116] Cn. Plancius, the father of the ex-aedile whom Cicero defended, was a leading figure in the major *societates*. According to the scholiast on Cicero's speech, the reason for the complaint in 61 was the losses the company had suffered through enemy invasion. We also learn that the *publicani* were supported in the senate by 'Caesar', who cannot be the later dictator (since he was currently away in Spain) but must be the consul of 64 and the censor of 61–60.[117]

It is normally assumed that what was at stake was the new contract let by the censors of 61–60. This is highly unlikely if L. Caesar was supporting the *publicani*, since the censors could probably have cancelled their own contract themselves and much of the point of the debate would have been to put pressure on the censors then in office. A greater difficulty is that, if the issue was an alteration to the new contract let by the current censors, there should have been objections from rival unsuccessful bidders who might have originally obtained the contract, if it had been let for less. Yet we hear nothing of any division among the *publicani* either in the early stages of the dispute or in 59, when any remission would have seemed more unjust to defeated competitors. Further, it is hard to see how a company could have a case at all for claiming that a bid was too high, when the actual auction was only a few months old and the period of the contract (which on the calculations above should have started on 15 March 60) had not yet commenced. The damage done to the Asiatic provinces by Mithridates' advance in the 70s and subsequent piracy was well-known in 66, when Cicero delivered *De imperio Cn. Pompeii*. The tax-collectors may have had illusions about a quick recovery in the wake of Pompey's appointment to the Mithridatic command, but, five years later, there was no excuse for miscalculation. Indeed, their sponsor Crassus had visited Asia himself in 62.[118] It is surely more plausible that the issue in 61 was the contract due to end in March 60, probably let by the censors of 65, the excessive optimism of which became apparent as the term of the contract came nearer. If the money owing was not paid soon after March 60, their guarantors would be called on to make up the deficit and their real securities would be seized. The fortunes of a number of eminent men, among them senators, would have been affected. From the senate's point of view there was no longer any question of a second auction to replace the contracting company with a rival firm. The probable result of Cato's obstruction was that by May 60 the partners in the *societas* or their guarantors had had to put their hands in their own pockets. Caesar's measure of 59 would then have been retrospective. Ironically this misfortune may have made the company all the more ready to take on the new contract, so that its agents could be on the spot to collect any arrears and they might in general have the chance to recoup their losses.[119]

In theory, the procedure for letting taxes insured the treasury against serious loss and imposed strict conditions on the tax-collectors in the field. In practice it was hard to supervise and enforce the *leges censoriae*, even later during the Principate. The Roman people had to wait a long time for their money, and the senate might be reluctant to be firm with organisations in which not only the fortunes of the *publicani* themselves but those of other wealthy 'names' were involved.

One final problem should be noticed, even if there is no easy solution. Roman company law was primitive by our standards. Originally, any partnership was legally dissolved at the death of a single one of its members or at his decision to end the association. The *societates publicanorum* were large and possessed considerable staffs: indeed the Asiatic company is now revealed to have taken over the posts used by the Attalid kings.[120] With contracts of such importance continuity of operation was vital. Hence it has been held that they formed an exception to the Roman law of partnership in being allowed a corporate personality.[121] Certainly, in the second century AD the jurist Gaius, when discussing the associations (*collegia* and *societates*) permitted in a province, says: 'Few people are allowed bodies [*corpora*] of this kind, for example the partners in public taxes or in gold, silver or salt-workings: such men are allowed by law to have a community with common property and a public representative.' However, the significance of this should not be exaggerated. The Romans, especially in the Principate, did not recognise a free right of association, regarding any such grouping as a potential threat to public security. This is principally why an exception had to be made for the companies which exploited taxes and mines.[122]

It was of course convenient that the companies were allowed a local agent who could act regularly for the company, but this did not give the company more of a corporate personality overall. At Rome or in the provinces contracts were let to a single man, the *manceps*, with or without partners, whose financial backing came from specified guarantors and pledged properties. Any other financial associates of the contractor were not legally involved. A problem might occur if he died. The Flavian municipal law assigns liability to the heirs of the contractor as well as to the partners and guarantors. The imperial regulations preserved in the Ephesus dossier show that, although it was possible for the contractor to change his legal representative or leading guarantor during the five-year period, he remained personally responsible for the contract throughout: if he died, therefore, his guarantors, partners and heirs would bear financial liability.[123] There is no question of a contract being made with a company. As for the staff of a company in a province, it is significant that the attested collectors were slaves and their superiors masters (*magistri*) or men commissioned to act as masters (*pro magistro*). The higher officials of the company were responsible for the actions of the staff according to the general principle that masters were responsible for the actions of their slaves, if undertaken with their consent.

OTHER DEMANDS AND REQUISITIONS

Originally, we are told, Roman commanders in Italy were expected to provide themselves and their army with transport, tents and military equipment, not to demand supplies and hospitality from allies. If commanders did stay in the houses of local people, it was through private links of hospitality. Then in 173 BC the consul Postumius complained (unjustly) that he had been inadequately entertained and supplied by the Latin city of Praeneste, some 20 miles from Rome.[124] We may think that Livy's story is too pat and that Postumius is likely to have had some precedent for his demands. It seems more probable that by the second century BC the Romans had come to make requisitions from their allies which before had been contrary to tradition. These swiftly gained momentum. In a speech of 124 or 123 BC C. Gracchus related a horrific tale about a Roman consul who had been arrogant and abusive in demands for baths for his wife.[125] Much later, when Horace journeyed with Octavian's envoys on the road to Tarentum in 37 BC, they spent one night at what was probably a public resting-place. The bijou dwelling (*villula*) next to the Campanian bridge, that is the *aedes publicae* there, gave them a roof, while the *parochi*, those neighbouring the road, provided firewood and salt. (*Paroche* is a Greek term for the compulsory provision of entertainment for travellers, associated with *kataluma*, lodging.)[126] The building of an *aedes publicae* on the road from Capua to Rhegium is commemorated in an inscription of 132 BC , while the agrarian law of 111 shows that in this period certain public lands and buildings were allocated to *viasiei vicanei*, villagers by the roads.[127] These men were probably required to be *parochi*, providing supplies and services for travellers, as well as perhaps helping to maintain the roads.

In the Greek world, which Rome came to dominate, we learn most about the practice of billeting and compulsory entertainment from the measures which granted cities immunity from it. This was, as we have seen earlier (pp. 36-8), a major item in the declarations of freedom made by Hellenistic rulers and was incorporated, following a decree of the senate, in Flamininus' declaration at the Isthmus of 196 BC. Such immunities continued to be granted in the late Republic, but to be granted as special privileges. Octavian's edict about the status of veterans, for example, declares that they should not have to entertain magistrates, legates, procurators or tax contractors against their will.[128] Moreover, apart form granting immunities, the Romans also tried to check corruption and excess in demanding supplies and entertainment. A *lex Porcia*, probably of 101–100 BC, mentioned in the Cnidos text of the law about praetorian provinces as regulating a governor's departure from his province, also limited the hospitality and provisions that he could legitimately demand. This is attested in the *lex Antonia*, which conferred freedom on Termessus and, interestingly, did not exempt the city entirely from billeting and other requisitions, but merely provided that these should be within the limits laid down by the *lex Porcia*. (For comparison, we find a treaty-ally, Epidauros, a few years earlier liable to billeting as well as the provision of troops.)[129] Further strict limits were laid down by Caesar's *lex Iulia de repetundis* (see p. 105).

It appears from these measures that when the Romans expanded overseas, their expectation of receiving and their allies' expectation of being required to give soon combined to produce a heavy burden. There were exceptions. Cato prided himself on not receiving free wine or money in lieu during his provincial commands in the 190s. When Cicero was on the move in Cilicia, he contented himself with a roof and beds, and these not always. Nor did he ask for hay, firewood and the other traditional requirements legitimised by Caesar's law. The cities beyond the Taurus and in Cyprus had expected that he would require billets for his troops and expect large sums of money in return for exemption (the Cypriots had provided in the past 200 Attic talents, that is, nearly 5 million sesterces). Cicero did not make such demands himself and, meanwhile, his entourage, with one exception, did not ask for free hospitality.[130] Another governor who avoided offending against Caesar's law was C. Memmius in Bithynia, to judge from the protests from the poet Catullus who was on his staff.[131]

Roman exploitation of the local corn-supply is already visible in the early history of the Spanish provinces. Cato claimed to have used the grain regularly supplied by the Spaniards actually to feed his army and not for sale to traders. Spanish bitterness over the money required in place of grain came to a head in 171 when complaints were lodged against recent governors.[132] Verres had no Roman troops when he was in Sicily, but he was permitted to demand *frumentum in cellam*, grain for his own storeroom, or, if a city had no grain to spare, 4 sesterces in place of a *modius* of wheat, 2 sesterces in place of a *modius* of barley. In fact he demanded 12 sesterces per measure of wheat and 4 per measure of barley.[133] Over 250 years after Cato's consulship Tacitus praised Agricola's restraint in not forcing his British allies to pay excessive prices in place of grain so demanded or to transport grain unnecessary distances.[134] Other demands, which the

Romans recognised in principle as proper, but which easily gave rise to exploitation, concerned gold for crowns to celebrate the magistrate's victories (*aurum coronarium*) and money to pay for statues.[135]

Allies of Rome were of course liable to furnish military aid. This was explicit in the traditional formulae of Roman treaties (see pp. 16–17). However, soldiers were also recruited from cities without treaties.[136] Tauromenium in Sicily was exceptional as a treaty ally in not being required to provide ships, when as a coastal city it could reasonably have been expected to so. Free cities, like Halaesa in Sicily, were also liable to ship contributions.[137] Even if a city did not provide manned ships of its own, it might be ordered to build them. In 61–60 L. Flaccus demanded both ships and rowers from the cities of Asia, but seems to have accepted financial contributions in their place. Equally, even if contingents for armies were not demanded, war material might be. Scipio apparently exacted arms, siege-engines and transport from Asia in 49 bc.[138]

There is little evidence for demands for transport under the Republic, which contrasts with the wealth of documentation now available about the Principate, but some extrapolation from the later period backwards in time is reasonable. According to Livy, up to 173 bc demands had been restricted to the provision of single animals for ambassadors dispatched in haste. In the late Republic we know from Cicero's criticism of L. Piso for his indiscriminate issue of *diplomata*, that the use of these certificates entitling the bearer *inter alia* to requisition transport as a public appointee had already begun.[139] *Angareia*, the term originally used to describe the Persian public post,[140] had been applied to the system of requisitioning transport under the Seleucids, which probably followed Persian precedent in many respects, and such requisitioning is also to be found in Hellenistic Egypt.[141] An elaborately regulated system of *angareia* under Roman administration is now attested by the edict of Sextus Sotidius Strabo, governor of Galatia *c.* AD 15, which was found at Sagallassus. This edict was composed on the basis of instructions by the emperors Augustus and Tiberius. According to it, transport could be requisitioned by officials and senators or *equites* on military service at standard rates, calculated by the *schoenos* (the distance covered in a certain time, perhaps an hour) and varying also with the means of transport – cart, mule or donkey.[142] There has also survived a series of directives from emperors or other magistrates concerning either immunities from *angareia* or the repression of violence, corruption and excessive demands. These range from Germanicus' edict of AD 19, arising from his visit to Egypt, to a dispute in Phrygia adjudicated in 213 and 237.[143] As Sotidius stressed, the problem was not that there were no regulations, but that these were disregarded.

THE ROMAN ATTITUDE TO TAXATION

At the beginning of their expansion through the Mediterranean the Romans were cautious, indeed tentative in some areas, when it came to extracting resources from their subjects and allies, but in the long run they were ready to take what was there to be taken, especially when they could employ traditional forms of taxation and compulsory services. The demand for money increased with the regular mainten- ance of legions abroad and at home with public expenditure on welfare, that is, land allotment and subsidised grain.[144] Romans clearly learnt techniques from their predecessors, the Hellenistic rulers. We cannot imagine them using the form of taxation applied in Sicily without the example of Hiero's system before them. Similarly, in the east the range of taxation was infuenced by Pergamene, Macedonian and Syrian precedents.

The normal level of taxation does not seem to have been especially oppressive. Tithes on cereals compare favourably with the tax of a third attested in the Seleucid realm. It is also striking that when Lucullus wished to arrange for the arrears of Sulla's indemnity to be paid off by the province of Asia in 70 BC, he chose to consolidate the tax at 25 per cent.[145] Obviously, the incidence of direct taxation was felt more severely, when it came on top of a considerable rent, and this, as we have seen, probably applied to those who used Roman public land as well as those renting from private landlords. The lessees of Roman public land probably tended to be wealthy landlords who were not working with the narrow surpluses of the peasant. Where tenants were renting from private landlords in an area subject to tithes on crops, the tax-collectors, whether local or Roman, would probably have sought to ensure that their demands were met first. What happened then in a bad year would have depended on the generosity of the landlord and, above all, on whether there was a ready supply of alternative tenants. If the latter were scarce, he might be forced to make concessions on his rent.[146]

The tax-farming system was traditional in the Greek world and is also attested among the Celts.[147] It had the merit from the point of view of the administration of letting the contractors, rather than the *populus Romanus*, carry the risk of an unpredicted drop in yield, although on the debit side it appears that there was a considerable time-lag before the proceeds actually reached the Roman treasury or the provincial *fiscus*. When Rome operated through local authorities in collecting direct taxes, it was the Roman magistrate who had to apply pressure on the cities, if necessary forcing them to borrow from *publicani* or other *negotiatores* in order to raise the cash. Moreover, the local people may not have benefited owing to corruption or the size of the percentages permitted to magistrates and collectors who raised revenues within the city's territory. In crises a great deal of money could be squeezed from prosperous areas, as the civil wars showed. Sulla's heavy indemnity on Asia in 84 BC (which perhaps took into account the seizure of land formerly owned by Romans during the Mithridatic invasion as well as lost taxes) did prove too much, but only in the aftermath of one major war and the depression created by a new one. Over a period the Romans preferred to settle for rates of taxation, which time had ingrained, if not hallowed, and could be collected without provoking major unrest. Nevertheless, it did not take much to make these oppressive, whether the difficulty was caused by poor harvests or the illegal supplements of the tax-collectors. On such occasions both peasants and landlords in the provinces had reason to complain.

6

RESTRICTIONS ON MAGISTRATES AND THE PUNISHMENT OF DELINQUENTS

Our investigation of the organisation of the Roman empire and the history of a number of the provinces has already shown how much discretion Roman magistrates had *de facto* under the Republic. From the constitutional point of view, it was as a governor or military commander abroad that a magistrate was most easily able to exercise that unfettered power which, theorists have argued, was the essence of *imperium*.[1] What restraints were brought to bear on this power?

In dealing with Roman citizens the magistrate was expected to obey Roman laws, in particular the *provocatio* laws which sought to guarantee the immunity of citizens from summary execution or flogging. However, in a crisis, as a military commander he could claim that it was in the interests of the state to disregard them.[2] The notorious execution of T. Turpilius Silanus by Q. Metellus (Numidicus) in 108 BC for cowardice and desertion could not have been excused on the ground that he was not a Roman citizen (Sallust's phrase, *'nam is civis ex Latio erat'* must mean that he was a Roman citizen of Latin extraction), but politically he carried less weight and he seemed a convenient person to be made into an example.[3] The magistrate was in theory supposed to respect the terms of a treaty or, more generally, the status of those recognised as friends and allies of the Roman people. He might also receive formal instructions from the senate or people (for modifications to this under the Principate see pp. 112–18) as to how he was to act. For example, the law about the praetorian provinces of 101–100 BC instructs the governors of Asia and Macedonia to do specific things – visit certain areas, protect certain areas, write letters to friendly kings and cities (cf. pp. 23, 44). Furthermore, by the last century of the Republic a magistrate was constrained by legislation, which forbad certain kinds of conduct and threatened offenders with prosecution.

97

The most familiar of these are the laws *de pecuniis repetundis*. Though the phrase itself means 'concerning the recovery of money', the laws became more complex than their name implies and performed a broader function. The origins of legislation of this kind can in fact be detected before 149 BC, the year in which the first permanent *quaestio* (tribunal) *de repetundis* was established by the tribune L. Calpurnius Piso. We have also a little evidence for the formulation of rules about a governor's behaviour. In 171 BC the senate forbad governors in Spain to buy the twentieth of the grain crop regularly demanded as supplies at prices fixed by themselves, or to use their own *praefecti* to collect taxes from towns. Restrictions may also have been placed by this time on the purchase of land or slaves by Roman officials abroad.[4]

As to the punishment of delinquent magistrates, the Romans initially tried to adapt existing legal machinery and to create new procedures without conspicuous success. The oldest form of prosecution was before an assembly. This was mainly employed against magistrates whose offence lay more against the *populus Romanus* than the *socii* – leading Roman troops to disaster, for example, or embezzling funds owned to the treasury. However, in 170 BC tribunes prosecuted two praetors before an assembly for their conduct in Chalkis during the Third Macedonian War. This led to a find of 1 million asses (that is, 400,000 sesterces) and the release from slavery of some Greeks wrongly deprived of their freedom. Similar measures were taken against the consul of 171, P. Licinius Crassus, and may have been repeated in 156–4.[5]

Sometimes a special tribunal was set up. The first example of this is the most unusual, arising out of the conduct of Q. Pleminius, who, as garrison commander of Locri after its capture in 205, allowed his soldiers excessive freedom to rape and pillage. A commission was sent out to investigate this, including a praetor, two tribunes and an aedile of the plebs, and they condemned Pleminius and thirty-two others to a capital penalty. The condemned men were sent to Rome, where they were kept alive for a time by the intervention of tribunes, but they were eventually executed after failing in an attempt to break out of custody. This form of investigation on the spot was not, to our knowledge, repeated. However, we do hear of tribunals at Rome set up, or unsuccessfully proposed, in the assembly of the plebs – concerning L. Scipio Asiaticus, M. Popilius Laenas and Ser. Sulpicius Galba.[6]

The most interesting initiative, however, was the procedure set in motion in 171 BC by the senate, after Spanish envoys complained that their people had been robbed. The senate voted for a special form of private process, whereby the Spaniards could seek back their money (*pecunias repetere*) with the aid of distinguished Romans as their *patroni*. It would have been theoretically possible at this time for a foreigner to go to the *praetor peregrinus*, the magistrate who dealt with private actions involving foreigners, and ask for an action for theft against a Roman citizen by praetorian formula, but in practice he would be reluctant to proceed against a consular or praetorian senator without the support of powerful patrons. On this occasion, after five senatorial *recuperatores* (judges dealing with recovery) had been appointed for each defendant, M. Titinius (pr. 178 BC) was acquitted at the third hearing, while P. Furius Philus (pr. 174) and M. Matienus (pr. 173) retired into exile after one adjournment, thus leaving their prosecutors with nothing but the value of their bail (*vadimonium*). Furthermore, it was alleged that the *patroni*, who included Cato the Censor, Aemilius Paulus, Scipio Nasica and Sulpicius Gallus, had prevented their clients summoning as witnesses leading members of the nobility.[7] Thus, even when the provincials had powerful patrons, these may have been unwilling to back them to the hilt for fear of spoiling their own relations with the accused (the later provisions about appointing *patroni* in C. Gracchus' *lex de repetundis* were designed to avoid the selection of anyone connected with the accused).[8] We also find in this period that ex-magistrates might be challenged by a wager to defend their conduct in their provinces, but this procedure, if not just a legal curiosity, was a form of infighting among the wealthy and powerful, which in itself could bring no remedy to the injured ally.[9]

Generally, there were obvious defects in the arrangements for prosecuting officials for their conduct abroad. First, there was no permanent machinery which was easily available to the allies; second, there was little attempt to view the problem from the allies' side and to consider their welfare as important as the reputation of Rome. Rome's measures seem to have been essentially directed to preserving the *maiestas populi Romani* and its own interests.

Permanent machinery for the recovery of property was introduced in 149 BC by the *lex Calpurnia de repetundis*, but it is not clear how far it advanced the allies' cause. The kernel of the procedure used by the *lex Calpurnia* and its obscure successor the *lex Iunia* was an ancient legal ritual, the *legis actio sacramento*, which could only be performed by citizens. It has been recently argued that these laws were not intended for the benefit of non-Romans at all but only for Roman citizens who had suffered improperly from the actions of a magistrate in office or to enforce the claims of the Roman people itself. This seems to be a possible but improbable explanation of the laws and I prefer to believe that in some way they were intended to help the allies too, as has been traditionally held. If allies had exploited these laws, the co-operation of Roman *patroni* would have been essential, and this is confirmed by the evidence we have of actual prosecutions – the only prosecutors known to us are Scipio Aemilianus, P. Cornelius Lentulus and C. Rutilius Rufus. It seems as though the complaints of the allies were deliberately channelled through a single prosecution and this was carried out by an eminent Roman.[10]

We now come to what is recognised to be the most important evidence for the development of the *quaestio de repetundis*, the law on one face of the fragments of the bronze tablet which once belonged to Cardinal Bembo (hence usually called by classicists the *tabula Bembina*, although, as it is now recognised, the fragments were earlier in the library of the Dukes of Urbino).[11] This is not the place to deal with the technical arguments concerning this piece of evidence. Essentially, I believe that Mommsen was right to identify this text as a law of C. Gracchus, even if not all his arguments remain valid. The alternative view, that it is the *lex Servilia* of Servilius Glaucia, recently revived by H.B. Mattingly, has been comprehensively refuted by Sherwin-White. Some points relevant to this argument will emerge in the following analysis of the content of the law.[12]

The law dealt with wrongs to Latins, other allies, friends and subjects of the Roman people. It may also have covered Roman citizens. Cicero's later claim that the law was set up for the benefit of allies alone is formulated in a very strained way and suggests that Romans did not necessarily use the ordinary processes of civil law. Epigraphically, there is room for the insertion of the term *civis Romanus* in the first line.[13] The law provided for the recovery of compensation for the loss of property, but for no other redress, when this property had been improperly taken by Roman magistrates or senators or senators' sons through coercion, threats, negotiation or deceit.[14] The penalty was restitution of twice the value of what had been taken. There is no evidence in this law either for a capital penalty or for the automatic infliction of *infamia*, that is, loss of senatorial privileges.[15]

Prosecution could be initiated by both Romans and allies, either acting for themselves or as representatives of a king, community or fellow citizen. The plaintiff denounced the offender to the praetor by *nominis delatio*. He could be subsequently given a *patronus* to act for him in court, if he wished (he was allowed to reject those who were unsatisfactory), but even an ally was permitted to handle the case himself.[16] The non-Roman who was successful in leading a prosecution was offered as a reward Roman citizenship and freedom from military service: if he did not want this, he might be granted *provocatio*, freedom from military service and from public duties in his own community, provided that he did not come from the ranks of their magistrates. There were also rewards for Roman citizens who prosecuted successfully.[17] The prosecutor was afforded some special assistance by the court. He could subpoena (the Roman phrase is *testimonium denuntiare*) up to forty-eight witnesses from Italy and probably search for evidence and stolen property there. There is no evidence, however, for investigation (*inquisitio*) being permitted abroad, as it was under later legislation. Plaintiffs from the provinces would have been expected to bring their witnesses and documents with them.[18]

A new form of trial was devised. This was not on the model of private law procedure with the praetor granting a *formula* according to which the judge or judges were later to evaluate the evidence, nor was it a *quaestio*, as this had been previously understood, an investigative tribunal conducted by a magistrate with a small group of advisers. A large jury was appointed to hear the case and to be autonomous in finding a verdict, while the praetor presided over the enquiry and enforced the provisions of the law. There were two parts to the action: the first to determine guilt or innocence; the second, where the verdict was 'guilty', to establish the exact amount of the damages to be paid to each injured party. At the same time as this second part of the trial measures were taken to obtain guarantors from the defendant for the likely sums at stake or, if these were not provided, to seize and sell his property.[19]

The composition and method of appointment of the jury was also new. A panel of 450 men was set up every year, which excluded senators and their close relatives and those who had held minor magistracies. The positive requirements are hard to establish, but both a financial qualification and some reference to membership of the equestrian order are likely. However, it should be noted that the jury would exclude the upper echelons of the equestrian order who were closely connected with senators. For each trial an elaborate process of selection and rejection took place, in which both prosecution and defence participated and which was intended to remove relatives and other associates of the two parties from the trial jury of fifty men.[20]

This statute, the product of immense legal and political ingenuity, introduced a new era of public law. For *quaestiones* with large juries and regulated by a rigid founding statute became the dominant form of public criminal trial in the late Republic.[21] The allies had a far more open avenue to prosecution than before. However, limitation to the redress they could obtain was inherent in the penalties prescribed. The law could remedy loss which could be converted into money, but it was not easy to punish a brutal and corrupt governor. In particular, little could be done against a man who took bribes, since the original givers of bribes would have had to bring a prosecution and they were unlikely to receive a friendly hearing from the court: it would not have seemed right that they should have their money returned to them.

The struggle over the composition of the juries which followed the Gracchan law is significant here in so far as it shows the danger this new law posed to ex-governors and other Romans back from the provinces. However, detailed investigation belongs to works on Roman domestic politics, to which I must refer the reader.[22] There are other important developments which generally receive less attention. In the last decade of the second century there were two *leges de repetundis* in quick succession – one passed by the consul of 106, Q. Servilius Caepio, in the optimate interest, the other by C. Servilius Glaucia, tribune in either 104 or 101, as a *popularis* countermeasure in the interests of the *equites*. Caepio's law introduced mixed juries of senators and *equites*. It is also likely that it introduced the procedure known as *divinatio*, whereby the prosecutor in court was selected beforehand by a jury from among those who demanded the right to prosecute. In practice this meant that in Cicero's day Roman accusers were selected and were not necessarily those whom the injured parties would have preferred as their representatives or *patroni*. We have evidence of *divinatio* occurring in 100 BC or a little earlier in the cases of T. Albucius and C. Servilius, also perhaps in that of Valerius Flaccus (if he is the consul of 100).[23] All these episodes may have taken place after the introduction of Glaucia's law, but this becomes unlikely if Glaucia's law is dated as late as 101. In any case *divinatio* is more plausibly to be viewed as an invention of the leading aristocrats known to be behind Caepio, who would have been eager to limit the allies' right to prosecute.[24] This was not rescinded by Glaucia for reasons which will become apparent.

Two significant innovations are specifically assigned by ancient sources to Glaucia's law: first, *comperendinatio*, the compulsory division of every trial into a first and second action; second, the extension of the pursuit of the money improperly taken to the man 'quo ea pecunia pervenerit', that is, to a receiver of the stolen money, when this was the only way to compensate a successful plaintiff.[25] However, this is not all. Another possible change is that the breach of specific rules laid down for magistrates was made an offence under the *repetundae* laws. We have seen that the *lex Porcia*, probably of 101–100 BC, which is mentioned in the text from Cnidos, regulated departures by the governor from his province and the demands he might make from allies.[26] We may conjecture other possible elements in the *lex Porcia* – a restatement of the rights of Roman citizens to appeal and the restrictions on the purchase of slaves and land abroad by Roman officials; the introduction of the regulations about the collection of money for temples and statues to governors and the ban on moneylending by them, which were in operation later under the *lex Cornelia* at the time when Verres was tried.[27] We know that a clause limiting a governor's exactions from allies had its place in Caesar's *lex Iulia de repetundis* of 59 BC.[28] This, then, had been taken over from the *lex Porcia* by the current *lex de repetundis* at some point. Was Caesar the first to enact this and Sulla the first to regulate temples and statues? Or might all these clauses go back to Glaucia's law? At all events, it would have been appropriate if the trend to incorporate specific rules in the *repetundae* law began about the time when the *lex Porcia* first laid down general terms under which a governor should operate.

There is also a good case for believing that Glaucia adapted the procedure of the court so that the receipt of bribes became actionable under it, as it was under Sulla's *lex Cornelia* and later laws. In 91 BC the tribune M. Livius Drusus proposed to prosecute equestrian jurors for bribe-taking. This failed, but it suggests that senatorial jurors were already liable and the court which later dealt with bribe-taking by senatorial jurors was the *quaestio de repetundis*.[29] If the *quaestio* already dealt with bribe-taking by jurors in the 90s BC, why not that by officials also? Cassius Dio states that the notorious prosecution of P. Rutilius Rufus *de repetundis* was for receiving bribes (the only source which gives the ground for the accusation). This point has been generally neglected by scholars, but in fact makes sense of what is otherwise puzzling. Rutilius had been hated by the tax-collectors but popular with the allies. It must have been alleged that the allies had bribed him to defend their interests against the tax-collectors. Indeed Rutilius may have been guilty as charged according to the provisions of the law, however good an administrator he was in other respects. We should not let ourselves be confused on this point by the later protests of orators and historians.[30]

Thus Glaucia's *lex Servilia* seems to have extended the remit of the *quaestio* to offences which lay more against the Roman people and its rules for the administration of the empire than against individuals subject to a magistrate abroad. Such crimes could not be dealt with merely by allowing a victim to sue for and recover what he himself had lost, but required a prosecution in the name of the Roman people and a penalty to be paid to it. This change in the substance of the law fitted excellently with the change in the type of prosecutor introduced by *divinatio*. If the latter had in fact been introduced by Caepio as a reactionary measure, we can see why the radical Glaucia retained the system whereby prosecutions were still channelled through Roman *patroni*. In this situation it is appropriate that we now find evidence of *inquisitio* – investigation by the prosecutor himself in the province where the offence was committed.[31] Without this it would have been difficult for someone based in Italy to acquire sufficient knowledge of the griefs of the provincials and the behaviour of the Roman magistrates.

We must assume that, when the charge brought under the *lex de repetundis* was not theft from the plaintiffs, the penalty was paid to the state. Originally it was probably a fine,[32] but after Sulla there is some evidence for the introduction of a capital penalty. Cicero twice refers in *pro Cluentio* to a *lis capitis* being admissible in a *repetundae* case. On the first occasion it is possible that the capital charge might result from the accumulation of massive financial penalties so that they exceeded the fortune of the condemned man, but in the second passage the charge is clearly viewed as capital from the start.[33] We know from the Fifth Cyrene Edict that capital charges were possible under the current *lex de repetundis*, the *lex Iulia* of Julius Caesar, and capital penalties continued to be exacted under the Principate.[34] Cicero talks in *pro Cluentio* of *repetundae* being valued at the level of *maiestas* (treason) and it is not difficult to see what the charges might be – major breaches of rules, like leaving a province without permission and fighting an unauthorised war against allies, or receiving bribes in return for condemnations, especially those on capital charges (this last was an offence at Rome under the *lex Cornelia de sicariis et veneficis* following an earlier specific law devised by C. Gracchus).[35]

The character of the *lex de repetundis* in Cicero's day was already very different to what it had been after C. Gracchus' legislation. The complication of the law, the multiplication of charges and penalties seem originally to have been the policy of *populares*, but it suited Sulla not to change laws which were conducive to the control of provincial magistrates. The legislation was brought to a climax by Caesar's *lex Iulia* of 59 BC. This law is said to have been very severely and sharply drafted. It was certainly immensely long. Chapter 101 dealt with the *litis aestumatio*, which comes in line 59 of the bronze copy of C. Gracchus' law and is there about twenty chapters from the end of the text.[36] This law, we know, incorporated a number of provisions regulating a governor's conduct, some clearly deriving from previous laws, others apparently new. The clause of the *lex Porcia* forbidding a magistrate leaving a province without permission unless *rei publicae causa*, also incorporated in the *lex Cornelia de maiestate*, reappeared. The restrictions in the *lex Iulia* on the requisition of grain and the raising of fleets or ship money, as well as the requirement that magistrates should respect privileges granted to individuals or communities, seems also to go back in outline to the *lex Porcia*, to judge from the allusion to this law in the *lex Antonia* about the people of Termessus of 68 BC.[37] New, perhaps, were the restrictions on the grant of *diplomata*, certificates entitling the holder to demand hospitality and transport from the allies. Furthermore, a magistrate was not to demand help and hospitality from the provincials beyond basic requirements like shelter, beds, firewood, fodder and salt, nor to receive gifts (the last provision, which went beyond the receipt of bribes, had a precedent, according to the Digest, in a previous plebiscite), nor was he to demand *aurum coronarium* (gold for crowns) unless decreed a triumph.[38] At the end of their tours of duty every governor and provincial quaestor were required to deposit copies of their accounts in two cities of the province and deliver a further copy to the treasury in Rome.[39] There may also have been a veto on a governor organising laudatory decrees from provincial cities on his own behalf.[40]

As to the major crimes against subjects dealt with under the law, apart from extortion of money, the law dealt extensively with the receipt of bribes, to judge from the stringent clauses known to us from the Digest, which can plausibly be assigned to the original bill.[41]

Under the Principate we find brutality (*saevitia*) by magistrates prosecuted under the *repetundae* law and these men could incur the capital penalties mentioned as being available under the *lex Iulia* in the Fifth Cyrene Edict.[42] Brutality against Roman citizens, which infringed *provocatio*, and that which involved the receipt of bribes were certainly covered here, but I doubt whether we can safely attribute to Caesar's law a ban on all unmerited violence against allies.[43]

It is helpful to look ahead to the new *repetundae* procedure introduced by Augustus through the *senatus consultum Calvisianum* of 4 BC reported in the Fifth Cyrene Edict. The emperor found it desirable to create, as an alternative to the full procedure of the *quaestio*, a simple abbreviated process before a small panel of *recuperatores*, which was available to allies who applied to the senate, provided that they had no intention of making a capital charge on the same facts (see note 34 above). The penalty was simple restitution of the value of what had been stolen. Ironically, there seems to have been a return to the methods of 171 BC. What was the attraction of this? The provincials were being offered a swift and inexpensive form of prosecution in which the guilty defendant might be more co-operative because his whole life and dignity was not at stake.

The fact that Augustus introduced such a measure at this time is a judgement on the development of the *repetundae* court up to this point. It had begun as a means of securing for those robbed by officials repayment of what they had improperly lost, thus satisfying their complaints and rehabilitating Rome's reputation abroad. These aims were paramount in the laws down to and including that passed by C. Gracchus. However, from about 100 BC onwards, when the court was reformed to be also a general instrument for controlling magistrates, the legislators gradually lost sight of the interests of the subjects themselves. Crimes multiplied, penalties were intensified, but the attempt of a man to secure recompense for himself might get lost in an action on a vast scale, which was at the same time a political trial of strength, usually between a young prosecutor and an important senator backed by imposing *patroni*. If the defendant retired into exile, especially if this occurred before condemnation and the official seizure of his property (as in the case of Verres), it would have been difficult to obtain adequate compensation. Cicero claimed at the end of the first Verrine that Verres had stolen 40 million sesterces from the Sicilians. This apparently contradicts Plutarch's statement that Cicero's *aestimatio* was 750,000 *denarii*, i.e., 3 million sesterces.

However, we can reconcile the two passages if we assume that Plutarch's figure represents the actual amount collected and shared out – an inadequate return for the plaintiffs from Cicero's energy and eloquence.[44] In 4 BC Augustus gave the victims the chance to get their money back and be grateful for that.

Part II

7

THE IMPACT OF THE
MONARCHY ON THE EMPIRE

> Nor did the provinces reject that state of affairs, since they
> regarded with suspicion the sovereignty [*imperium*] of the
> senate and people on account of the feuds of dynasts and the
> greed of magistrates. The protection they had received from the
> laws was feeble, since these were subverted by violence, intrigue
> and ultimately money.
>
> (Tacitus, Annals 1.2)

Tacitus' comment on the reception of Augustus' monarchy by the
peoples of the empire shows that he had no doubt that it had changed
their lives as much as the lives of the Romans themselves – in this
case for the better. However, the nature of the changes needs
definition, and this definition may help us to judge how far they were
deliberate reforms by Augustus, or the natural consequences, foreseen
or unforeseen, of monarchy.

In the provinces monarchic rule had a prehistory. During the last
century of the Republic magistrates and promagistrates had been
granted overarching commands, embracing more than one province,
or had themselves usurped vast fields of discretion. In 84 BC Sulla
reorganised Asia into forty-four districts and imposed a package of
taxation, including an enormous indemnity, on the cities without
consulting the senate and people at home.[1] No senatorial commission
was involved in Pompey's settlement of the Asiatic provinces after
the Mithridatic War in the 60s BC (it is conceivable that this was
justified by a specific clause in the *lex Manilia* which had conferred
this command on him).[2] In any case he created two new provinces,
Bithynia-Pontus and Syria, and allocated some half a dozen major
kingdoms, not to mention the minor principalities and temple-states.
In consequence he had to face a long investigation of his *acta* in the
senate, which was only finally resolved by a law passed by Caesar or

Vatinius about March 59 BC.[3] Caesar was apparently granted the right to found colonies during his Gallic command under the *lex Vatinia*. He was suspected of exploiting this to grant in effect Roman citizenship to those living north of the Po in Cisalpine Gaul (Gallia Transpadana) – a measure which he had planned long before.[4] Beyond the Alps he concluded settlements with Gallic and British peoples and imposed tribute on them apparently without any senatorial commission or specific authorisation from the senate (references to ten *legati* are more likely to signify commanders for his ten legions than a commission to supervise a peace settlement).[5] Gabinius left his Syrian province in 55 to instal Ptolemaios Neos Dionysos ('Ptolemy the Fluteplayer') on his throne in Alexandria: in spite of the fact that this created an uproar in senatorial circles at the time and he was charged with treason (*maiestas populi Romani minuta*) on his return to Rome, he was able to produce a defence that this was in the interests of the state and was in fact acquitted on this charge.[6] Senatorial prerogative might thus be usurped on a grand scale by confident proconsuls. On the other hand, there had been a trend to restrict the conduct of governors by legislation (see Chapter 6) – one to which, ironically, Sulla and Caesar made major contributions.

At Rome, however, the theoretical primacy of the senate in supervising imperial administration was respected down to Caesar's death, notwithstanding the fact that the policies of powerful individuals, including Caesar himself as dictator, tended to be determinative. Sulla settled Asia, as we have seen, and granted privileges to Cos and Oropos on his own authority, but once back in Rome as dictator he operated through *senatus consulta*.[7] Caesar granted the Jewish ethnarchy and high priesthood to Hyrcanus and dynast status to Antipater on the spot (the grants were relayed to Rome to be recorded). He followed this up by a number of decrees regulating Hyrcanus' behaviour.[8] However, in Rome he employed the machinery of the senate and people, as in the treaty with Mytilene. It must be conceded that the constitutional rectitude was more apparent than real, if we believe Cicero's account of the forging of *senatus consulta* relating to allied kings.[9]

Perhaps the turning-point in the administration of the empire from Rome was the senate's decision, two days after Caesar's murder, that his *acta* were to be treated as law. This allowed M. Antonius the discretion simply to validate by publication alleged decisions of the dead dictator, which would have been embodied in either law or *senatus consultum*, had he not been murdered. 'But look how

Antonius, after a huge bribe, has posted a law, passed by the dictator in an assembly, which makes Sicilians Roman citizens. Not a word of this when the man was alive.[10] A recently published document provides an interesting example of a decision, apparently taken by Caesar shortly before his death, which was never actually translated into a *senatus consultum* but simply transmitted by M. Antonius to the interested parties after the Ides of March. This concerned the asylum of the temple of Artemis at Sardis. Caesar granted this privilege in respose to a Sardian embassy on 4 March 44 BC, and it was displayed at Sardis as a *decretum* without any reference to the Roman senate or people. (This right of asylum was among those rights whose validity came to be investigated under the reign of Tiberius.)[11]

The conflict after Caesar's murder displayed the impotence of the senate over events in the province even more sharply than its impotence at home. The commanders on the spot took the decisions, however dubious – whether this was Brutus deciding to besiege Xanthus or Lepidus offering sanctuary to the fugitive Antonius.[12] The founding of the triumvirate on 27 November 43 BC by the *lex Titia* seems to have legalised in advance any instructions given by Antonius, Octavian and Lepidus to Romans and allies subordinate to them. It may have been intended that these dictatorial powers should only be used by each in his assigned area of influence. So, not unreasonably, Antonius could lay down regulations for the Jews and confirm the privileges of the union of victors in artistic and athletic contests in Asia, as he would have done if he had been the proconsul of the particular province.[13] More interesting is the decree of Octavian and Antonius providing privileges and relief for the city of Aphrodisias. It anticipated the *senatus consultum* of 39 BC, which gave the city autonomy, immunity from taxation and asylum status for its temple, and was made on their own authority. This first decree was confirmed by the *s.c.* of 39, but Octavian also sent letters to a certain Stephanus and to the city of Ephesus about Aphrodisias' plight, which are clearly instructions, in spite of the fact that Aphrodisias was within Antonius' sphere of authority, and there is no suggestion of the backing of a *senatus consultum*.[14] Before the end of the triumviral period we find Octavian making edicts on his own authority about the general privileges of demobilised veterans and the particular rewards of his admiral, Seleucus of Rhosos. There are also letters of instruction to Mylasa and to the proconsul of Asia.[15] Amidst the turmoil of the civil wars a unified authority over the empire was emerging. Even if there had been no Actian War at the end of the triumvirate, it is unlikely that provincial governors could have recovered the independence they enjoyed under the old Republic.

In fact the three became one: 'when he had sloughed off Lepidus and killed Antonius, Caesar was the only leader left to the Julian party'.[16] The regime that followed confirmed and developed the methods of the triumviral period in two ways. First, and perhaps foremost, were the changes in practice, reflecting the power-relations now in being, which have been the theme of much of the recent work of Fergus Millar.[17] Provincials, not without encouragement from the emperor's own self-presentation in sculpture, coinage, epigraphy and cult, saw Caesar Augustus' authority as paramount in everything and strove to enlist his support over matters which were of great importance to them but often of little account in the administration of the empire as a whole. Strabo's story of the fisherman from Gyaros travelling to meet Augustus in 29 BC in order to seek a relief from tribute is symptomatic. A few years later Chaeremon of Tralles travelled to Cantabrian territory in Spain to find Augustus, so that he might seek help for the rebuilding of his city.[18]

The attitude of Rome's subjects was reinforced by the readiness of proconsuls, who from 27 to 23 BC were in theory independent of Augustus, to accept his authority. An inscription from Cyme attests the response of the proconsul of Asia, Vinicius, to a problem concerning the occupation of a site sacred to Dionysus as a private house by a non-member of the band of worshippers.[19] The proconsul quotes a letter or edict of Augustus and Agrippa as consuls (either in 28 or 27 BC) forbidding the sale of public or sacred property – which would not have been sufficiently authoritative under the Republic without a *senatus consultum*, since the consuls at Rome could not give orders to a proconsul[20] – and then refers to the wish of the worshippers to restore the sacred property to the god *'iussu Caesaris Augusti'* ('on Caesar Augustus' order'). It has been supposed that this indicates some further instruction from the emperor which has been ellipsed, but it would have been remarkable that his further authority had not been recorded on the stone and it is most plausible that the phrase *'iussu Caesaris Augusti'* was used by the proconsul or the representative of the worshippers to describe the joint letter or edict of the consuls. This voluntary subordination is also attested by the coinage issued by proconsuls of the period with Augustus' head on the obverse.[21]

Nevertheless, in spite of the fundamental importance of the perceptions of Rome's subjects and Roman proconsuls in establishing

Augustus' authority over the empire, it was not long before this authority was formalised. In 27 BC Augustus, who had by now laid aside his triumviral powers and officially brought the period of national emergency to an end, was assigned a large package of provinces – the Gauls, the Spains, Syria with Cilicia Pedias, Cyprus and Egypt – for which he, the consular governor, appointed in his absence *legati pro praetore* as deputies (with the exception of Egypt, where a prefect had probably already been put in post).[22] The emperor was thus in charge of the most important military provinces. In time he relinquished the most pacific parts of Spain and Gaul, Baetica and Narbonensis, and Cyprus to ex-praetors appointed by the senate, but took over himself the Balkan provinces of Illyricum, Macedonia and, at the end of his reign, Achaea. He also was to take personal control of the provinces created on the Rhine and Danube – the Germanies, Raetia, Noricum, Pannonia and Moesia – as well as Galatia in Asia Minor (annexed in 25 BC).[23] In the years following 27 BC his unformalised authority in other areas remained strong, if we draw the natural conclusion from the case of M. Primus, who, when accused of having fought an improper cross-border war in Macedonia, apparently claimed that Augustus and Marcellus had encouraged him (see Chapter 3, pp. 23–4 for the interests of the state, *rei publicae causa*, justifying breaches of the laws limiting the movements and campaigns of governors: it is interesting that Augustus defended his appearance as an unsolicited witness at the trial on this ground).[24]

However, when in 23 BC it appeared that Augustus was not going to die in the near future of natural causes and that the majority of Romans expected him to stay in his dominant position, new constitutional devices were invented. One, *maius imperium proconsulare*, apart from perpetuating his *imperium* without the need to hold the consulship, specifically permitted him to intervene in provinces of which he was not the appointed governor. This meant that any instruction given to proconsuls by Augustus, whether in person, by edict or by letter, had the backing of his *imperium* and disobedience was treason. A similar wide-ranging power, equal to that of the governors but not superior to them (*aequum*, not *maius*), was to be conferred in 13 BC on Augustus' political partner M. Agrippa.[25] It is not clear how soon and how much Augustus exploited this power. Perhaps the earliest datable evidence is provided by his edict of 12 BC about the Jews. The subsequent edicts sent to Cyrene (in 7–6 and 4 BC), are excellent illustrations of *maius imperium*. The first is diplomatic in its instructions ('I think governors of Crete and Cyrene

115

will be acting correctly and appropriately, if'), but this follows the phrase, 'until the senate deliberates about this or I myself find a better solution', where it is clear that the governors are acting as much under Augustus' authority as that of the senate and people. In the second edict he informs the provincials that they should not criticise their governor, P. Sextius Scaeva, over a certain matter and, in the fifth edict, when it is a question of transmitting to the province a *senatus consultum de repetundis* (see p. 106), he dispatches it under his own prescript in order to show the province the care he is taking of it.[26]

Evidently by the time of the edicts *maius imperium* was neither latent nor a last resort, but was paraded to attract the attention of Rome's allies and subjects. The emperor might write a letter to a governor or produce an edict which was addressed directly to the population of the area it concerned. Furthermore, cities might write letters to him, as Greek cities had done in the past to the Hellenistic kings: these might be channelled through a provincial governor or brought directly to him by an embassy. At a lower level *libelli* (petitions) might be submitted (the mechanics of this are obscure) by villages and individuals, to which the emperor replied by a *subscriptio*, a note at the bottom of a petition, which was then publicly posted.[27] And there were other means by which the working of *maius imperium* was formalised. The historian Cassius Dio claimed that the system of written instructions (*mandata*) for governors, not only Augustus' deputies in his own provinces but proconsuls in public provinces, originated under Augustus. Though long doubted, this has now become a certainty through two pieces of epigraphic evidence relating to *mandata* at the beginning of Tiberius' reign, in one case those given to Sextus Sotidus Strabo, the imperial legate of Galatia, in the other those given to Germanicus Caesar, who as proconsul and himself possessing *maius imperium* in the east is said to have been operating '*ex mandatis Ti. Caesaris Au[gusti*'.[28]

Another innovation was the provision for appeal. Of course, even without the development of formal appeal procedure, it is likely that individuals and communities would have essayed to get their cases put before the emperor. An example of what became in effect an appeal is provided by Augustus' letter to the Cnidians (they came under the authority of the proconsular governor of the province of Asia).[29] Euboulos and his wife Tryphera had been besieged in their house at Cnidos by Philinos and another Euboulos. When they tried to resist by getting a slave to empty a pail of slops, the pail had dropped and killed one of the besiegers: hence Euboulos and his wife had been treated as murderers by the local authorities and fled to Rome, pursued by a Cnidian embassy. Augustus examined the case himself, after getting the proconsul of Asia to take evidence (under torture) from the slaves involved, and judged Euboulos, who had died in the meantime, and Tryphera not guilty.

However, the possibility of appeal was enshrined in legislation. The *lex Iulia de vi publica* of 18 BC rendered liable to a capital charge any governor or other offical who punished or tortured a man in defiance of *provocatio (adversus provocationem)* or, in the later formulation of the jurist Paulus, 'in the past appealing to the people, now to the emperor' ('*antea ad populum, nunc imperatorem appellantem*').[30] Under the Republic *provocatio* had been the right to appeal to the Roman plebs as a whole or to their spokesmen, the tribunes, against capital punishment or some other use of physical force by a magistrate. It was the cornerstone of the personal liberties of the Roman plebs. In 30 BC, after the news of Octavian's victory at Alexandria, the Romans, according to Dio, voted Octavian 'the powers of tribune for life, such that he could give *auxilium* to people inside the *pomerium* and outside within the first mile from Rome (something not permitted to any of the tribunes), he could judge on appeal and he could cast the vote of Athena in all trials'.[31] It is not the place here to discuss whether Dio has unhistorically retrojected these powers from 23 BC or the implications of the 'vote of Athena' (it does appear that Augustus in fact both judged appeals and exercised a sort of royal prerogative of mercy). It is sufficient to note that an extended version of the protective powers of Republican tribunes was voted to Octavian or Augustus, which he could exercise without the restraint of the tribunes themselves, but that in principle it was confined to Roman citizens and effectively to the current extent of the city of Rome. The *lex Iulia de vi publica* implies that the right of appeal was valid throughout the empire, and subsequent practice suggests that it was not confined to Roman citizens.[32]

It may be that the *lex Iulia* acknowledged a *de facto* development, whereby men had appealed to Augustus, as if his tribunician power was valid for non-Romans and throughout the empire. Alternatively, when a reinforced tribunician power was assigned him in 23 BC, his powers to receive appeals were legally extended. Paul's appeal to Caesar in Claudius' reign is the first occasion when we find a formal appeal described in our sources.[33] But the practice must have been becoming common both in criminal and civil cases, since we learn from a letter of Corbulo, when he was proconsul of Asia under Nero, that by then it was necessary for every appeal to be channelled through the governor, and later, under Titus, we hear of a penalty for unjust appeal.[34] A recently discovered inscription contains Marcus Aurelius' responses to a sheaf of appeals from Athens, while the writings of the Severan jurists and later law-codes reveal how a great deal of case-law built up over appeals of all kinds.[35]

Imperial edicts, decrees and constitutions are given the same authority as laws, plebiscites and decrees of the senate in the Flavian municipal law and this is the doctrine of later lawyers.[36] Even if this was not declared in Augustus' reign, it was implicit in the operations of his administration. Moreover, the combination of his constitutional powers and perceived authority created a general impression of dominance. Strabo talks of him becoming 'lord of peace and war' by virtue of his people awarding him supreme power over the empire, and notes his supervision of allied kings and princelings – something which seems to have arisen more *de facto* than through any specific grant.[37] This does not mean that the senate lost all supervision over imperial administration. A number of matters were regulated by *senatus consultum*, for example, the treaty with Mytilene in 25 BC and the new *repetundae* procedure in 4 BC, although frequently, as with the *SC de repetundis*, this resulted from an imperial initiative. Under Tiberius we find matters of interest, though not of great importance, left to the senate's deliberations. Even though Achaea was now an imperial province, the rival claims of Sparta and Messenia to the temple of Artemis Limnatis were discussed there, as were the claims of many Asian shrines to the right of asylum – the latter proved so exhausting that it was eventually remitted to the consuls, who presumably investigated it with a committee (*consilium*), such as had been used to hear the case of Oropos against the *publicani* in 73 BC.[38] At the same time the emperor's responsibility for all the provinces with legions but one and his power to intervene elsewhere led to strategic decisions about the imperial administration devolving on him, as Strabo described.

It is prudent to admit that we simply do not know how far Augustus consulted the senate about strategic decisions relating to the management of the empire, in particular over the choice between territorial expansion and the maintenance of the status quo with its implications for recourses in money and manpower. However, if we can trust Tacitus' account of the debate in the senate on 17 September AD 14, after the dead Augustus had been devoted divine honours, the implication of this is that by the end of his reign Augustus had been keeping such strategic decisions to himself, his family and the political 'friends' who advised him. In face of the senate's pleadings that he should openly assume the burden of administration undertaken by Augustus, Tiberius demurred and eventually ordered a document to be read (called by Suetonius the *breviarium imperii*) which listed military units and fleets, provinces and allied kingdoms, direct and indirect revenues and, finally, regular and occasional expenditure. It had been written out by Augustus in his own hand.[39] Although Augustus seems to have given the senate financial accounts from time to time, the point of Tiberius' behaviour was that the contents of the document were not common knowledge in the senate, nor was the subjoined advice that the empire should be kept within its present bounds.[40]

The existence of this document is evidence of a dramatic change in the management of the empire since the Republic and indeed the beginning of Augustus' own reign. The emperor's control of the majority of the army and navy – the main cause of public expenditure – and his knowledge of the revenues collected allowed him to strike a balance, albeit very rough, between military operations and their cost. He was able to form a better estimate of the resources of the empire thanks to provincial censuses, attested for the first time in his reign.[41] Moreover, the entrenched supremacy of himself and his family made it possible to take a long-term view about imperial strategy. How soon Augustus in fact began to do so is problematic. Many of his military operations – the early expeditions into Ethiopia and Arabia, for example, and the original deep advances into Germany – resemble the old-style expansion for expansion's sake – that characterised the last century of the Republic. One may point to the strategic advantages of a Rhine–Danube or Elbe–Danube northern frontier, compared with one south and west of the Alps, and these certainly did exist; what is not clear is how far Augustus perceived these before his armies arrived there.[42] The will o' the wisp of limitless empire perhaps never evaporated while the Romans retained their military strength. Nevertheless, what in the person of Pompey or Julius Caesar might have been simply ascribed to greed, machismo, romantic imperialism or rivalry with the ghost of Alexander the Great, is likely in Augustus' person to have included a strong element of calculation: it is significant that Strabo tells us that an invasion of Britain was rejected on the basis of a cost–benefit analysis.[43] By the end of Augustus' reign such calculation had gained the upper hand and it continued to do so in Tiberius' Principate. Tiberius, one of Augustus' most successful subordinates as a field-commander, knew his own and his army's limitations:

> He had been sent into Germany nine times by the divine Augustus and had achieved more by policy than by force. It was thus that he had achieved the surrender of the Sugambri; thus the Suebi and Maroboduus had been tied down by peace-treaties.[44]

We should not, however, proceed too confidently on this basis to talk of a grand strategy of the Roman empire. The bureaucracy character-istic of modern war ministries did not exist to elaborate policy, intelligence from beyond the frontiers was poor and communication, in spite of the *cursus publicus*, was comparatively slow.[45] Hence, at the extremities of the empire military operations were frequently hasty responses to a sudden threat and the governors on the spot had to improvise. Yet it was possible to have a long-term policy or attitude, which could be incorporated into instructions to governors, and this would be confirmed over the years by conservatism. Moreover, decisions might be taken about military recruitment and the raising of revenues which of necessity would set limits to territorial aims.

What was left for the senate? We have already seen how Tiberius left comparatively trivial matters of provincial organisation to the senators' deliberations (see p. 118). By contrast, when it came to the Gallic revolt of AD 21, he did not brief them about the crisis officially until it was over.[46] Under Augustus some significant decisions were formulated in *senatus consulta*, such as the *SC Calvisianum* of 4 BC (see pp. 106, 116); in Claudius' reign there was the decree granting members of the Aedui the right of membership of the Roman senate, while Nero presided over an important, if largely fruitless, discussion of the operations of the *publicani*.[47] One development which affected imperial administration, as well as politics at Rome, was the use of the senate, sitting as a body, to conduct trials. We know of no law or indeed preliminary *senatus consultum* which established this as a senatorial function in principle. However, before he died, Augustus established the practice of bringing a case involving the *maiestas* of the whole senatorial order before the senate – the libels of Cassius Severus – and he also submitted to that body a particularly atrocious case of provincial misgovernment – that of Volesus Messalla, which would normally have been a matter for the *quaestio de repetundis* or, in so far as it involved official brutality in defiance of appeal, the *quaestio de vi publica* (see p. 117).[48] Under Tiberius this led to a great number of cases involving senators and *equites* being referred to the senate, including those arising from provincial misgovernment, cases which would have been previously dealt with in a *quaestio* or by the simplified recovery process before a senatorial subcommittee, established by the *SC Calvisianum*.

Trial before the senate might aggravate the charges brought (through the addition of the count of treason against the emperor) or the penalties, even if no extra charge was added.[49] It is not, however, evident that this led to more convictions than would have occurred anyhow in a *quaestio*. The senate's treatment of provincial misgovernment seems to have varied with the attitudes of the current emperor. Tiberius encouraged severity, but after him there is little sign of zeal to eliminate misgovernment until Domitian. Under Trajan it appears from Pliny's letters that even those manifestly guilty were handled with kid-gloves.[50] Left to itself, the senate tended to forgive its own members the sins they committed abroad – the problem that originally led C. Gracchus to create a new *quaestio* with a non-senatorial jury. The change of location for trials is unlikely to have promoted efficiency and rectitude abroad, while, in so far as senatorial procedure was not well-adapted to that body's functioning as a court, this might create injustice and encourage senators to treat such trials as something fundamentally repugnant which should be avoided in the interests of the solidarity of their order.

So much for developments at the centre, but what was the face of administration in the provinces? What changes actually occurred there? Dio Cassius in his summary of the nature of the Augustan regime draws his readers' attention to many of them.[51] Governors were still appointed from the senatorial class, except for the prefect of Egypt, who was a knight granted *imperium* and jurisdiction as if he were of praetorian rank in the senate.[52] The so-called public provinces, which were not the emperor's,[53] had governors of proconsular rank selected by lot, whether they were in fact ex-consuls or ex-praetors, who were normally expected to serve a single year. Only those governors were allowed to wear military uniform or carry a sword, who had the right to execute Roman soldiers – that is, presumably, those who commanded legions (it should be noticed that Dio accepts that governors in general had the right to inflict capital punishment.[54]) Theoretically, there was a gap of at least five years between holding an office at Rome and a provincial governorship, as under Pompey's law of 52 BC.[55] The emperor's subordinates in his provinces were called *legati pro praetore*: each had five *fasces* and the right to wear a sword and to execute Roman soldiers. This last seems to have been a new measure devised by Augustus, since under the Republic magistrates and promagistrates had not been able to mandate their capital jurisdiction unless they demitted office (see p. 55). Such *legati* were appointed by Augustus at will without any legal restrictions. Quaestors continued to be appointed to the public provinces and governors also had *legati* to assist them who had no power of capital punishment.[56]

Equites were employed in the provinces as tribunes of the soldiers and as commanders of auxiliary units (following a precedent of Julius Caesar's). Procurators, usually of equestrian rank but sometimes even freedmen, were sent out to all provinces to deal with public revenues and expenditure, but proconsuls were still to some extent in charge of collecting revenues from their own provinces.[57] All these officials received *mandata*, as we have seen, and also *salaria*, as opposed to the grants for expenses characteristic of the Republic (see pp. 48-9). Their *mandata* included a veto on raising troops or money, beyond what was laid down in these instructions, unless they received permission from senate or emperor. This was of course a continuation of Republican practice, except that the emperor was now an authority as well as the senate. In fact, Dio argues, although in theory public money was separated from his private money, all was spent in the light of the emperor's policies.[58]

The nature of Augustus' command in his own provinces led to something of an administrative hierarchy, with the *legatus Augusti pro praetore* governing the province and commanding all military units, while subordinate to him were *legati* commanding legions and other *legati* concerned with jurisdiction (although the post of *iuridicus* is only once attested outside Egypt before the Flavian period).[59] Procurators must have undertaken supervision of both public finances and Augustus' own in the emperor's provinces from the beginning; how quickly they came to dominate finance in the public provinces is another matter. Tiberius was angry when a procurator of his in Asia behaved as if he had public authority and used soldiers to collect money.[60]

Julius Caesar had abolished the system whereby there was an auction among companies at Rome for the right to collect the direct taxes of Asia at source from the taxpayers (see p. 77). The method of tax-collection that replaced this is uncertain. An inscription of the early Principate shows the quaestor in the proconsular province of Africa involved with the contractors for the tribute in that province:[61] perhaps the right to collect from communities was auctioned in the province, as probably occurred outside Asia and Sicily under the Republic (see pp. 77–9). It has been argued on the basis of the elder Pliny's account of Sicily that the system of letting out the taxes on produce there for direct collection by *decumani* was abolished by Augustus.[62] The institution of provincial censuses would have provided a helpful foundation for taxes on land or other capital, rather than produce. However, taxes by percentage on production had not been generally abolished, as the new Ephesus dossier reminds us.[63]

This inscription as a whole emphasises the continuity in the procedures for collecting indirect taxes. The contracts for collecting the *portoria* of Asia were still auctioned, apparently at Rome. Rates of tax, rules about customs-houses, exemptions for free cities, for those on public service and for personal possessions were maintained.[64] However, we find additions to the *lex* governing the *portorium* contract, for example, by the consuls of 17 BC, whereby payment was due in instalments on the Ides of October (15th) each year and security in the form of *praedes* (guarantors) and *praedia* (pledged property) had to be provided by the Ides of January (13th) followed the contract. In 12 BC the colony of Alexandria Troas was exempted and the contractor (*manceps*) was allowed to change his leading guarantor within three days of making the contract. Then in 7 BC Tiberius and L. Piso ordered the contractor to give up to fivefold security – a provision maintained in the contract of AD 5.[65] To sum up these and a number of other new provisions, we find minor alterations in the system of collection on the spot and some more significant alterations in the modes of making the contract. In any case the document makes clear that the *societates publicanorum* were still of great importance in Roman tax-collection.[66]

The Principate in the long run was to bring increased control of local government, partly through the creation of local constitutions on a Roman pattern – a topic which will be treated in the following chapter – partly through direct intervention by Roman magistrates. Intervention had occurred under the Republic even in free cities (see pp. 36–40) to solve specific problems. Usually this was a matter of a Roman magistrate promoting Roman interests, including his own and those of his friends. However, we find Cicero seeking to eliminate corruption among the local magnates in the cities of Cilicia.[67] Under the Principate we find a new official, the *curator rei publicae* (*logistes*), whose existence is attested for the Flavian period, if not earlier, sent to solve financial problems in cities. In fact an earlier example of an official similar to these *curatores* may be found under Tiberius – an ex-praetor M. Ateius, who was sent in AD 17 to assist cities damaged by earthquake in Asia.[68] As for the governors' dispensation of justice, the circuit of *conventus* performed by him in the course of jurisdiction became standardised (there had been in the late Republic a system of jurisdictional divisions (*dioeceses*) in Asia and Cilicia, but Cicero had not observed the latter rigidly – see pp. 60-2). Under the Principate cities came to compete for the status of assize-centre because of the financial advantages brought to the city from the crowds who gathered there.[69]

The collaboration of cities in a *koinon* or *concilium provinciae* was also encouraged. Under the Republic this is attested in the Greek provinces of Asia, Sicily and Achaea, while Caesar used to summon *concilia* of Gallic chiefs (see pp. 40-1). In Augustus' reign a new *concilium* associated with the imperial cult was established for the three Gallic provinces that formed 'long-haired Gaul' (as opposed to romanised Narbonensis), which met by the confluence of the Rhône and Saône at Lyons (Lugdunum).[70] Subsequently, *concilia* are either attested or implied in Africa, Spain, Narbonensis, Britain, Macedonia and other provinces of the Greek east.[71] Apart from their promotion of unity through the imperial cult, these assemblies developed a political function through their dispatch of embassies, especially when it was a question of registering a protest about a provincial governor. Claudius Timarchus from Crete, on trial in AD 62 for oppressing his fellow provincials, claimed in the senate that it depended on him whether a formal decree of thanks was made by the *concilium* on behalf of proconsuls who had completed their tour there. In the *repetundae* cases handled by the younger Pliny it is probable that the *concilium* of the province was involved in the prosecution.[72] In AD 238 a certain T. Sennius Sollemnis had a statue dedicted to him by the *concilium* of the Three Gauls in his home community of the Viducasses. Among the testimonies to his virtues engraved on the base was a letter commending him for his services in preventing the prosecution of the governor Claudius Paulinus.[73]

However, in spite of these developments and the change in administrative hierarchy in the emperor's provinces, civil administration still strongly resembled that under the Republic. A far more striking change was the position of the army in the provinces. In the late Republic legions were stationed in particular provinces for long periods (see pp. 49-50), but we have no evidence for permanent camps being constructed here and the theoretical period of service which individual soldiers were required to complete was comparatively low (Polybius' manuscripts give six years as the compulsory military service required from infantry and there is no evidence which directly controverts this).[74] Moreover, it is misleading to say that Marius' reforms created a 'professional' army. There is a great deal of evidence for conscription in the late Republic: although some men were volunteers – in particular time-served soldiers who had re-enlisted and would be most likely to achieve by promotion higher pay and higher status – it is likely that the majority of the rank and file were conscript amateurs, who did not see the army as their life and career.[75] Augustus and Tiberius seem to have tried to avoid conscription, although we find it still in emergencies, such as the Pannonian revolt in AD 6 and the German crisis three years later, and when there were difficulties in recruitment.[76] Augustus also made the army professional in another sense by requiring long service – a minimum of sixteen years from legionary infantry – and apparently forbidding Roman soldiers to marry.[77] Furthermore, after the subjugation of the Danube lands and the campaigns in Germany, a pattern of legionary distribution developed which remained undisturbed for long periods. Recruits tended to join units serving in the part of the empire in which their own homes were.[78] The proportion of Italian-born soldiers serving in the legions (the praetorian guard was an exception) dwindled to less than 50 per cent by the Flavian period. They developed a strong attachment to the regions in which they served, wherever they were recruited, and tended to settle there, once demobilised.[79]

Thus, where legions were based in the provinces, life inevitably came strongly under their influence. The legates of the emperor frequently visited their permanent camps. The manpower of the legions was deployed in construction and the industries associated with it as well as in military operations. The administrative staff needed in the administration of a unit or a garrison came to be employed for civilian purposes as well.[80] However, the military presence was not confined to the legionary bases. Throughout the empire, at points considered opportune to check internal or external threats, auxiliary units or detachments were deployed. There were even detached soldiers placed in post in otherwise civilian areas (*stationarii*) to be representatives of Roman authority and, no doubt, sources of intelligence.[81] Nor should we forget those whose job it was to be a kind of security service, the *speculatores* and *frumentarii*.[82] Where there was no organised local administration, the local military unit would become the source of civil authority and, even where local government did exist, the army might well be drawn into police matters and public works.[83] In the public provinces the situation would have been different. By Gaius' reign no proconsul commanded a legion. It is true that these governors had auxiliary troops at their disposal and, where appropriate, ships. Moreover, soldiers would use the strategic roads through public provinces to reach their posts elsewhere. Nevertheless, overall the military would have a lower profile.

'The empire was screened by the Ocean or distant rivers; the legions, provinces and fleets, all things were interconnected; there was law among the citizens and discipline among the allies.' So, according to Tacitus, said Augustan supporters at his death.[84] It did seem as if the consolidation of Roman conquest had at last been achieved. In what follows an attempt will be made to investigate some aspects of this consolidation. How real was it? In so far as it was real, how was it maintained? How far was it acceptable to the allies and what advantages accrued to them? In short, was the Roman empire politically coherent or was it simply an assemblage produced by conquest?

APPENDIX: A NOTE ON EGYPT

The kingdom of Egypt under the Ptolemies was administered politically and economically in a different way to the other Hellenistic realms. This system was modified under Roman rule so that it came to resemble more that of the other Roman provinces without, however, any really close approximation. Thus most generalisations about the Roman provinces need the caveat that they must not be thought to apply automatically to Egypt.

Under the Ptolemies, apart from the Greek cities of Alexandria, Naucratis and Ptolemais, the land was subdivided into *nomoi*, ruled by *nomarchoi* and *stratêgoi* (the latter with both military and political functions). These *nomoi* were frequently themselves subdivided into *topoi* and within these the basic administrative unit was the *kômê* or village. Some communities, largely for religious reasons, were given special importance among the *kômai* as *mêtropoleis*, but were not cities in any political sense of the word.[1]

After Octavian had conquered Egypt, it became the property of the Roman people, but it was managed in a peculiar way because of its enormous strategic and economic importance.[2] The governor was a *praefectus* from the equestrian order, who was given powers of civil jurisdiction and military authority, as if he were a proconsul – at first subject to Octavian, when he was still in effect triumvir, then subject to him as Augustus and proconsul, since Egypt was one of his allocated provinces. Senators, other than the emperor, were normally banned from the province.[3] The prefect was expected to hold assizes (*dialogismoi* = *conventus*) in Alexandria, Pelusium and Memphis on the model of other provincial governors,[4] though the procedure used to bring a suit was peculiar to Egypt (see pp. 156–7). As assistants, the equivalent of senior *legati*, he had a *iuridicus* (= *dikaidotês*) and for finance an *idiologus*, whose rule-book for judicial decisions we have preserved in papyri – both drawn from the equestrian order.[5] There was also a *dioikêtês* from among the imperial procurators. Originally there were three major subdivisions of the province – the Thebaid, the Seven *Nomoi* with the Arsinoite and Lower Egypt (the Delta). Each of these had *epistratêgoi* – an office which came to be held exclusively by Romans from the equestrian order. Underneath them were the *nomoi*, each with its *stratêgos*, who was now a purely civil official and an Egyptian. These *stratêgoi* were assisted by nomarchs concerned with the collection of taxes and 'royal secretaries' (*basilikoi grammateis*). The corresponding official in each village was the village secretary (*kōmogrammateus*). In the period down to AD 202 the *mêtropolis* remained what it had been in the Ptolemaic period – a superior kind of village with no independence or special political function – though the Romans did introduce there new officials concerned with administration, such as the gymnasiarch.[6]

Parallel with this there was a reorganisation of the land. In Ptolemaic Egypt all land was the king's and a source of rent (in produce), but from some land he forebore to exact this: hence there was a fundamental division between 'royal land' and 'land on release' (*gê en aphesei*). The Romans subdivided the land, now completely the property of the Roman people, into a number of categories which were frequently new.[7] Royal land, public land and 'land producing income' (*gê prosodou* – perhaps land seized against a public debt) was rented out for farming either according to voluntary contracts or imposed conditions (*epimerismoi*). The concept of 'sacred land' was changed, so that its exploitation was akin to that of the various types of public land. The *gê ousiakê* was imperial domain either held by the emperor himself or allocated to members of his family or other high-ranking Romans or Alexandrians.[8] There were also categories of 'private land' (*gê idiotikê, gê idioktêtos*), held by Egyptians themselves, including the old land of Ptolemaic military settlers. Thus the Romans could create a class of independent property-owners who could take on *leitourgiai* – unpaid service or financial contributions to their communities. Although administratively, more was changed in Egypt than in any other province, this did not in fact detract from its exotic character, whether viewed politically, juristically or socially.

1 The Byrsa hill at Carthage, as laid bare by recent excavations. The city was razed in 146 BC and under Augustus *Colonia Iulia Carthago* was built on the site. Here can be seen the substructures of a basilica forming part of the forum complex which was planted on top of the hill. Underneath are a Punic street and the remains of Punic houses

2 Corinth too was destroyed by the Romans in 146 BC, although some structures, like the archaic temple of Apollo, were left standing. The city was refounded by Julius Caesar with its civic centre to the south of the temple (a) The shops to the south of the agora with the temple of Apollo in the background

2 (b) Acrocorinth showing the Roman agora in the foreground

3(a) Trajan's column became the most spectacular monument to Roman conquest, when it was enveloped, probably after his death, with relief sculpture commemorating the campaigns of 101–2 and 105–6 AD which added Dacia to the Roman empire

3(b) The close-up of the top of the column shows the mopping-up
operations after the fall of Sarmizegetusa, including the suicide of Decebalus
(bottom right) and (at the top) the Dacians leaving their homeland with their
cattle

4 Military might and triumphalism dominated not only the architecture and sculpture of Rome but also that of the provinces
(a) The elegant triumphal arch of the first century BC from the town of Glanum (St Rémy-en-Provence)

4 (b) A fragment of relief from Hadrumetum (Sousse) which juxtaposes a second-century AD emperor in his triumphal car and a captive

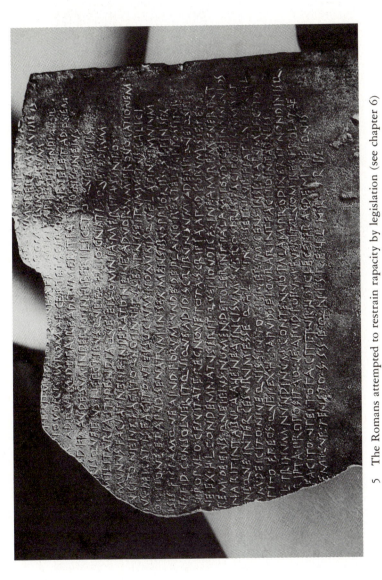

5 The Romans attempted to restrain rapacity by legislation (see chapter 6)

(a) This bronze fragment from Tarentum (Taranto) contains the final lines of a law against extortion (*lex de repetundis*) of
c. 100 BC

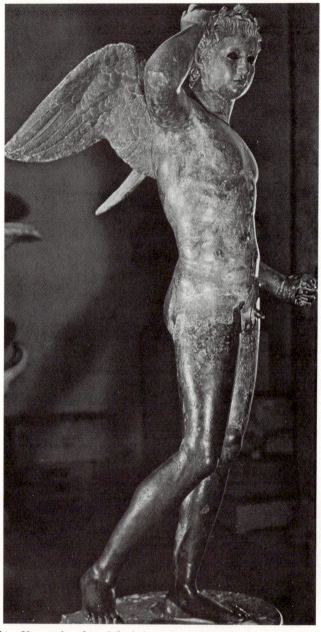

5 (b) Yet works of art left their native land by fair means or foul. This exquisite Hellenistic statue, a 'Winged *Agon*', was found with other items of Greek sculpture and two Athenian inscriptions in a late-Republican shipwreck off Mahdia on the coast of Tunisia

6   Under the peace of Augustus and his successors Roman influence was embodied in religion, architecture and public amenities. In a Roman town a major focus was the Capitol, the temple to Jupiter, Juno and Minerva. Examples are:

(a)   The 'Maison Carrée' at Nemausus (Nimes)

6 (b) The Capitol at Thuburbo Maius

6 (c) The triple temples in the forum at Sufetula (Sbeitla)

6 (d) Among the other monuments in the town of Nemausus is the 'Porta Augusta', the east gate dedicated to Augustus in 16–15 BC.

6 (e) The 'Pont du Gard' carried an aqueduct supplying Nemausus from the hills to the north over the river Gard

MAGERI

CRISPINVS

HILARINVS

BVLLARIVS

TALICOVANDOTALF
EXCAPLOQVARSIO
RVAMMVNSEDES
DERETVAMV
IVVSEDES
STADIES
AAGERIVSDO
NXIHOCSITHABI
RETHOCESTPOSSE
HOCISTIA·NOXEST
AMANIVRETVO
FACCISMAISSOS

7   Another amenity which strengthened links between the élite and the ordinary citizen was the shows given by local magistrates, to a considerable extent at their own expense. The mosaic, found at Smirat in Tunisia, now in the Sousse museum, was the centre-piece of a dining-room and commemorated a beast-fight promoted by its owner. The Latin text visible on the left is an account of the acclamations by the crowd. Such shows earned the wealthy local aristocrat the prestige and popularity appropriate to his status

8

CITIES, MUNICIPALITIES AND LOCAL GOVERNMENT

It is already clear that the *imperium Romanum* was founded on the *polis*. Cities provided Rome with a convenient channel for her commands and her demands for resources through taxation. The Romans themselves had neither the manpower nor the funds to staff the lower levels of provincial administration. The comparatively limited duties of the governor, described in Chapter 3, only made sense when they were the superstructure on a strong foundation of local autonomy, whether the communities in question had the privilege of freedom or not. Moreover, because of the ancient belief in the cultural superiority of urban life, the creation or maintenance of cities conferred prestige on the leaders of an empire individually and collectively.

Of course, this situation was nothing new in the ancient world. The empires of classical Greece, those of Sparta and Athens, subordinated other cities without necessarily subjecting them to direct rule by the imperial power. This principle was inherited by the Macedonian monarchs: Alexander the Great, although for the most part he simply took over the old organisation of the Persian empire in Asia, created new cities and his successors, especially the Seleucids, added more, either reinforcing old communities or creating them *de novo* from their demobilised soldiers.[1] The Phoenicians, too, had a civilisation based on cities and, when Carthage created itself an empire in the west, cities were, wherever possible, its constituent elements, whether on the coasts of Africa, in Sicily or in parts of Spain.[2]

Rome's relations with the Mediterranean world were in this respect a macrocosm of her relations with the rest of Italy. There she had both exploited pre-existing urban organisation and deliberately created new urban centres. In particular, after the unification of Italy, areas which before had been organised in *pagi* (districts) or *vici* (villages) became incorporated in the territory of new or former *municipia* – among the Vestini, Paeligni and Celto-Ligurian peoples.[3] In the Hellenised provinces she based her arrangements on their cities from the time she first organized Sicily onwards. In provinces, such as Spain, where there was an existing network of village communes, she used these as a basis, until the majority of them became *municipia* under the Principate after a process which should not be ascribed uniquely to the influence of Roman authority: we should add the influence of individual Roman settlers and the desire of the Spaniards themselves to imitate the urban life of the Roman and Hellenic worlds.[4] In Gallia Narbonensis the Celtic *oppida* were replaced by Roman towns near their sites, while in the Three Gauls to the north the old fortified strongholds were gradually abandoned and the tribes both received new *civitas* capitals and developed minor local centres as an urban substructure.[5]

By the end of the Julio-Claudian era the following hierarchy of communities had emerged. First in Roman eyes, as always, were *coloniae* – towns created or remade as settlements of Roman citizens, usually ex-soldiers. Such communities in the provinces had the prestigious status of Roman islands in a more or less foreign sea: their constitutions and laws were entirely Roman and they were freed from direct taxation as towns in Italy were. Second came *municipia*. In the provinces these were either of Roman or Latin status. Those with Roman status, whose citizens were Roman citizens, had similar privileges to colonies, differing from them largely in not being deliberately created foundations. Those with Latin status were pre-existing communities, whose constitutions were generally made to conform to a Roman pattern and where Roman law held sway. Ex-magistrates in these communities received the privilege of Roman citizenship. Latin *municipia* were a feature of the west. In the Greek east, apart from colonies with their Roman status, the most privileged communities were the cities which had been specifically declared 'free' (see Chapter 3, pp. 36–40). The majority of Greek cities did not have this status, but none the less remained communities with their own constitutions and local government. Corresponding to these in the west – including Africa from Tripoli westwards – were the *civitates peregrinae*, communities neither Roman nor Latin, which had institutions of their own and might be promoted to the status of *municipium* or exceptionally to that of *colonia*.[6]

However, this is not the whole story. The city might have been the most visible element of the *imperium*, but there were also political units of lower status which were of particular importance in the wilder and less populated parts of the empire. In the Greek east the *kômê* (village) had a long history and frequently survived the tendency to concentrate population in cities. Indeed, some Greek writers thought that certain cities, which lacked proper amenities, should be reclassified as *kômai.*[7] In the west we find a variety of small nuclei of habitation. Some of these were more urban in character than others, and would have been centres for the agricultural population or have grown up for a specific purpose – a staging post in communication or the exploitation of some resource or amenity, such as a mine or hot springs. We also find *fora* and *conciliabula*, which were not so much settlements as meeting-places for commerce, justice and festivals, performing the function of certain shrines in the non-urbanised parts of classical Greece.[8] The pattern of settlement varied from province to province. In the West Africa Vetus and Nova were remarkable for the number of towns that grew up, often only a short distance from one another. In southern Spain urbanisation was also widespread. In northern Gaul, on the other hand, the distances between the towns which were capitals for the tribes were so great that they left a great deal of room for the development of secondary settlements.[9] In Achaea the *polis* tradition remained strong, but to the north, in Macedonia, Thrace and the other Balkan lands villages came into their own. For example, an inscription tells us of the founding of an *emporion* or *forum* at Pizus in Thrace with its own council, based on a population drawn from neighbouring villages.[10] In the east the Hellenistic legacy of cities remained and more were added to it. Yet there was also a vigorous tradition of *kômai*, especially in remote areas, including those attached to a temple.[11] The preponderance of villages in Egypt has already been mentioned (see pp. 126–7).

There was one form of community living on its own territory with some claim to be regarded as a separate political organisation, which was a peculiar product of the Roman Principate. This was the *saltus* – the imperial estate, ultimately controlled by the emperor's procurators but leased as a business to a *conductor* (lessee). Such estates might exist throughout the empire, but the most important documented examples are from Africa and Asia Minor. The tenants subordinated to the lessee were subject to rent in the form of produce and compulsory labour. The inscriptions suggest harsh regimes and in one text the tenants appear to have been treated by the lessee and procurator with a violence which according to Roman standards was improper for free men.[12] It was a point of legal controversy, how far the inhabitants of such estates were free from civil obligations in local communities;[12] we do not know what rights they possessed there, for example, whether they could use the community's judicial system (they could not of course be removed from the jurisdiction of the governor).

Although it was Roman policy to encourage, rather than crush, these various forms of local government, both the central administration and Roman provincial magistrates had a considerable impact on them. One aspect of this is intervention from above in specific local problems – something for which we have already seen considerable evidence under the Republic (see pp. 36–40, 63–4) and which was even more common under the Principate because of the tendency to refer cases to the governor or the emperor. Plutarch complained about certain men that they were like those could not wash or eat without consulting a doctor, in that they brought in the ruling power on every occasion and forced it to become more despotic than it wished.[14] The constitutional basis for imperial action has been discussed in the preceding chapter (pp. 115–18). The evidence for the reference of disputes and problems to Roman authority is voluminous and we shall have occasion to return to it. A type of intervention, which is of equal importance and may be considered a reflection of Roman desire to strengthen local government, is the granting to communities of constitutions designed at Rome.

LOCAL CONSTITUTIONS IN THE WEST

Rome had a record of imposing or bestowing constitutional reforms from the early second century BC onwards. Flamininus encouraged oligarchic constitutions in Greece; so later did Mummius (see pp. 8–10, 37). We know of three occasions where Roman governors of Sicily had drawn up regulations for a local senate – at Agrigentum, Heraclea and Halaesa.[15] It appears from the younger Pliny's letters that the composition of the senates in the Bithynian cities was determined by the code laid down by Pompey when he established the province.[16] Regulation of the governing class was an important element in any constitution, but we should have a very imperfect idea about what receiving a local constitution from the Romans entailed, if we merely had to rely on these snippets of literary evidence. Fortunately, there survive, preserved on bronze, parts – in one case a very large part – of the Roman laws applied to colonies or *municipia*. Two features of this evidence should be recognised immediately. First, these are in a sense extreme cases, where we would expect a maximum of Roman regulation, since the communities involved were either comprised entirely of Roman citizens or had an upper stratum of Roman citizens. Second, some of the documents concern Italy, not the provinces. However, since there are clear links between the Italian documents and those from the provinces, it is best to treat them as series in which the development of constitution-making for Rome's subjects can be traced.

The first example arguably does not belong to the series at all, but will be treated briefly here to emphasise the contrast with the laws that follow. This is the constitution from Bantia in Lucania, whose obverse held the text of a Roman judicial law. The constitution is in the Oscan language, but it is influenced by Latin texts in that it is written from left to right and has elements of Latin vocabulary. What survives concerns the use of the assembly, especially for public trials, the holding of the censorship, the powers of magistrates to enforce the law and the hierarchy in which magistracies should be held. The provisions seem on the whole consistent with Roman practice (not all features of this code are definitely attested at Rome and there is a discrepancy, probably more apparent than real, between the number of assembly-meetings required for a trial at Bantia and at Rome). One attractive possibility is that it is related to that of the neighbouring Latin colony of Venusia. In the light of the law on the obverse, the Bantian constitution should belong to the 90s or 80s BC – the period in which Rome's war with her Italian allies occurred. Whether it represents willing adoption or enforced acceptance of Roman practice is hard to tell: the use of the Oscan language is an indication of the former.[17]

A document which is different in character from the others and illustrates an early stage in constitution-making is the so-called '*lex Iulia municipalis*' on the Table of Heraclea – a bronze tablet, whose obverse contained a record of land-division in Greek.[18] It must date from before 43 BC (when the month Quinctilis became Iulius – line 98) and after Sulla's proscriptions (line 122) and the invention of the *actio de dolo malo* by C. Aquilius Gallus (line 111).[19] It is a collection of regulations, some of which were designed for application in the city of Rome, others specific to communities of Roman citizens outside Rome. It has been plausibly argued that it results from the spontaneous action of the city of Heraclea itself (or perhaps, in view of the find-spot in a regional sanctuary, of more than one local community): in the knowledge that they now had to conform to Roman law, they collected Roman legal texts which they thought relevant.[20] If so, this is a stage of adaptation which logically precedes that of receiving a ready-made constitution devised by a Roman authority. Yet the latter process is referred to in the final section of the text on the bronze. Here we find a chapter from a Roman statute concerning men who have been selected to give constitutions to municipalities by previous Roman statutes – one which permits them to make corrections to these constitutions within a year from the date of this present statute.[21] In particular, it is interesting that Heraclea had collected a number of regulations regarding traffic and the upkeep of roads at Rome, whereas what seems to be the earliest Latin municipal law-code we possess, the *lex municipii Tarentini*, deals with this sort of problem in a brief chapter enabling magistrates to build roads, ditches and sewers – provisions which are repeated in a slightly expanded form in the *lex coloniae Genetivae Ursonensis* from the triumviral period and are adapted in the Spanish municipal law from the Flavian period.[22] Clearly, the Table of Heraclea is contemporary with the installation of constitutions by Roman commissioners in formerly non-Roman towns in Italy (though perhaps not yet in its neighbour Tarentum) but is itself evidence of something different – an attempt to pursue an alternative, self-directed procedure.

The Table of Heraclea has an interesting chapter on the taking of the census (the rules are somewhat different from those at Bantia and include the transmission of the results to Rome), but the most important section, which is directly relevant to communities outside Rome, concerns the qualification laid down for local office and membership of the *decuriones* (the local senate)[23] – matters which, as we have seen, Roman magistrates had regulated in certain provincial cities. The *decuriones* are a body with limited membership and election to a magistracy is a necessary, but not a sufficient, condition for membership of the *decuriones*. There is no mention of a property qualification for either holding a magistracy or being a member of the senate, but candidates for office must be at least 30 years old, have performed a term of military service (three full years in the cavalry or six full years in the infantry) and must not be in business as a herald, funeral attendant or undertaker (such disqualification may be best explained not by the sordid nature of the jobs, but by the fact that such men received salaries or entered into contracts with local author-ities).[24] In relation to membership of the senate a great many other disqualifications are also listed – conviction on a criminal charge in Rome or in an Italian town or in a civil suit which involved *infamia*;

bankruptcy in various forms; dismissal with ignominy from the army; receiving money for the head of a proscribed man; prostitution, pimping, employment as a gladiator, a gladiator's trainer or an actor.

As we have seen earlier, the final chapter of the Table of Heraclea concerns the process of giving law in a *municipium*: it permits the man, who was commissioned by a statute passed at Rome to give such a constitution, to make additions and corrections to it within a year of the chapter becoming law. This demonstrates how the Table of Heraclea itself is not a granted constitution. The earliest surviving text of this kind in Latin is the municipal law from Tarentum (we have only one column of text and the initial letters of the next column),[25] in which we find provisions which recur in similar form in later municipal laws. We have already noticed the permission granted to local magistrates to build roads, ditches and sewers.[26] A ban on the demolition or unroofing of houses without their being replaced by a building of equal quality similarly reappears in later local constitutions, though in this text exemptions may be granted by the local senate. Interestingly, the regulation employed in these new constitutions was not applied generally in towns up and down Italy. For an inscription found at Herculaneum contains two *senatus consulta* from Claudius' and Nero's reigns dealing with this very topic. This implies that the destruction of houses for profit had been flourishing unchecked at Rome and elsewhere and probably that there had been no local law about it at Herculaneum.[27] The other regulations in the surviving column concern magistrates – penalties for fraud, requirements that they should give financial guarantees before entering office and that they should have a residence in the town. The law apparently went on to deal with citizenship of the *municipium*, perhaps including that of freedmen.[28]

None of the documents so far mentioned refer to the use of Roman private (civil) law in local communities. Nevertheless, it is likely that the relationship between local and Roman jurisdiction was a necessary part of every constitution given to a community by Roman commissioners. The earliest evidence for this is in two inscribed texts relating to Cisalpine Gaul, which are in fact part of the laws passed in Roman assemblies, not of local constitutions. The fragment from Ateste is of a law passed in the same year as, but later than, a *lex Roscia* of 11 March. Otherwise it is hard to pinpoint it: on one argument it may be as late as the incorporation of the region in Italy in 42 BC; on another it may belong to the immediate post-Sullan period – its omission of the *actio de dolo* from the catalogue of actions, in which condemnation brought infamy (*actiones famosae*), may mean that it was passed before C. Aquilius Gallus invented this action.[29]

Two provisions survive: first that *actiones famosae* could be brought locally, if the damages sought were worth 10,000 sesterces or less and both parties agreed to this; second, that any jurisdiction handled by a local magistrate through treaty, plebiscite, *senatus consultum* or *institutum* before the *lex Roscia*, should not be subject to recall to Rome (*Romae revocatio*) by a private citizen, in such a way that the local magistrate would be deprived of the jurisdiction he had before the *lex Roscia*. It is clear from this that Roman law was being used in this town before the *lex Roscia*, as afterwards, and further that jurisdiction was shared between local magistrates and a higher authority. It is not certain that 'recall to Rome' existed before the *lex Roscia*, but it does seem implicit that this procedure was currently being made available for certain cases elsewhere in the law (otherwise there would have been no reason to mention it here) – presumably these cases included *actiones famosae* worth more than 10,000 sesterces, where at least one party was not satisfied with local jurisdiction. Cases, which were not judged locally before the *lex Roscia*, had been heard either by the praetor at Rome or, just as plausibly, by the provincial governor. As for the situation after the law on the Ateste fragment, what the text forbids is *revocatio* by a private citizen: this implies that *revocatio* was still possible for a magistrate, whether local or a Roman provincial governor.[30]

Thus, at the time of the law Roman legal procedure was in operation at Ateste as was part, if not all, of Roman private law. Local jurisdiction was compulsory in some types of case, unless a local magistrate chose to send them up to a higher authority or a higher authority himself intervened. Other cases might be heard locally, if the parties agreed, but otherwise were referred to a higher authority and sometimes this meant referral to Rome.

We have a much larger section of a *lex Rubria* concerning jurisdiction in Cisalpine Gaul, found at Veleia near Piacenza.[31] The law was passed in a period when the jurisdiction in that province had become closely related to that at Rome. The thrust of this text is to enable and encourage a magistrate on the spot in a community in the province to carry out aspects of civil jurisdiction according to Roman law, which were available to the praetors at Rome but up to that time had not been available locally. These included the extraction of a guarantee or financial security from a defendant against the likelihood of future damage; the grant of permission to a creditor to seize a confessed or evasive debtor in some actions for a defined sum of money (*pecunia certa credita*); the exercise of pressure against confessed delinquents in other cases by ordering the seizure of their persons or property.[32]

As in the Ateste text, it is implied that there are two levels of jurisdiction: in actions over fixed sums of money and certain other actions the limit of local jurisdiction is 15,000 sesterces. However, there is also a class of case where the local magistrate is empowered to act, irrespective of the sum involved.[33] Although it is not specified what the alternative jurisdiction is, except at one point where a reference to Rome under surety is mentioned,[34] it seems that in general it is the jurisdiction of the praetors at Rome that is the alternative. The two documents are arguably peculiar, in that they deal with communities possessing either Roman citizenship or Latin rights in a province which was being absorbed into Italy and by the time of the *lex Rubria* was almost certainly already part of it. However, they illustrate the extent to which in the last century BC Roman law was exported beyond the old frontier of Italy.

There are a number of inscriptions referring to Italian municipal laws from the late Republic or early Principate which give us a hint of the quantity of Roman constitutions imported into cities which were not originally Roman.[35] However, no fragment is big enough to make a significant contribution to our understanding of their nature. The remaining texts are on a much grander scale and come from Spain. The first is the law granted to the colony at Urso (*colonia Iulia Genetiva*) shortly after Julius Caesar's murder according to his directions.[36] The text itself derives from the first century AD and contains at least one indication of revision (ch. 127). Some fifty chapters of this law are more or less intact and there are others on recently discovered fragments whose content can be approximately reconstructed. This amounts to about a third of the original constitution. What survives may be summarised as follows (the categories inevitably involve some overlap):

A Instructions about magistrates: (i) their attendants (chs. 62–3); (ii) their financial operations (80–2); (iii) residence qualifications (91); (iv) powers on military service (102); (v) requirement of obedience to local senate (129).

B Religion: festivals, priesthoods and religious expenditure (64–72).

C   Funerals (73–4).
D   Public games (125–8).
E   Town-planning: roads, paths and ditches (75–9).
F   Public works and water-supplies (98–100, 104).
G   Measures against corruption in public contracts and elections (81–2, 93, 132, 134).
H   Judicial procedure in public cases – including trials before *recuperatores* and *quaestiones* (94–6, 102, 123–4).
I   Embassies by colony (91).
J   Co-option of patrons and grants of *hospitium publicum* (97, 130–1).
K   Membership of local senate (105, 123–4).
L   Wives of *coloni* to have rights and duties under the law (133).
M   Ban on illegal assemblies (106).
N   Private law procedure (61 and 108–22 from the new fragments).

The scatter of chapter numbers in certain major categories suggests a document somewhat unsystematically organised. This impression may be an unfair consequence of the choice of categories here: frequently one can see an association of ideas, which leads the legal draughtsman from one topic to the next, for example, from religion in ch. 72 to funerals and their sites in chs 73–4, and from funerary monuments and cremation-sites to other aspects of the physical fabric of the city in chs 75–9. Nevertheless, a number of chapters seem to have no context, for instance, that concerning the powers of the local magistrate at the head of the militia (103), nor is the separation of the section on games from that on other religious topics easily justifiable. The confused order of chapters does not make it easier to reconstruct what has been omitted. However, there must have been a section defining membership of the *colonia* and the different statuses of the members – i.e., *coloni* and *incolae* (colonists and resident aliens), Romans and non-Romans – to which ch. 133 about the rights of wives of *coloni* is a supplement. There must also have been rules about the local senate and elections to it, mentioned in ch. 67, about the election of magistrates, to which chs 101 and 123–4 are pendants, and about the selection of jurors and judicial procedure in public and private cases (what survives in ch. 95 is a special provision for a certain type of public case). Apart from the section on certain aspects of private law, inadequately preserved in the remains of chs 108–29, there may have been another important section on this topic ending in ch. 66. Both procedure and substantive law needed to be specified, if only by reference to the law dispensed by the praetor at Rome. Moreover, the relation of local jurisdiction, especially the *quaestio* mentioned in ch. 102, to that of the governor will have been clarified.

This constitution seems, where possible, to have been assembled out of pre-existing elements already used in Italy. The chapter forbidding demolition of buildings is a modification of that in the law from Tarentum; the formulation of the permission to magistrates to construct roads, ditches and sewers is, apart from minor adaptations, the same as that in the Tarentine law; the chapters concerning the residence qualifications of magistrates and their rendering of accounts are a recast version of the provisions at Tarentum.[37] Other chapters are prefigured in the Table of Heraclea: the ban on the candidature for magistracies of men ineligible for the local senate and that on the usurping of senators' seats at the public games.[38] Furthermore, the regulations about roads, paths and boundary-ditches (ch. 104) are identical with those in ch. 54 of a text which almost certainly belongs to the *lex Iulia agraria* of 59 BC, as one of the sources which cite it claims. Finally, it is evident that the provisions about magistrates' attendants derive from Italian precedents, in the light of their reference to exemption from military service except when there was and Italian or Gallic uprising.[39]

What other general conclusions can be drawn from the Urso text? First, the regulations are at times very detailed and specific – the salaries of magistrates' *apparitores* (chs 62–3); the money to be spent on games (ch. 71); the days of service to be required for public corvées (ch. 98); judicial procedures (chs 95, 102); the quorums required in the local senate for particular votes (chs 69, 75, 92, 97, 99, 130–1). In all of these matters, especially the last, the elimination of corruption must have been a major concern of the legislator and this appears most blatantly in chs 69, 72, 80–2, 93, 132. Magistrates have certain basic duties of performing jurisdiction, letting contracts, maintaining the public property, urban fabric and territory of the colony. However, unlike magistrates in Rome under the Republic, they were required by law to obey decisions of the local senate, and the implication of the quorum regulations is that their initiative would have been rather limited, if they could not compel attendance at meetings by fines. It seems likely that the local constitution at most permitted such fines in the case of failure to attend certain specified meetings, and one may infer from the phraseology of ch. 69, regarding the letting of contracts for religious ceremonies, that a duumvir might have to wait almost two months before he could get the necessary quorum. The extent to which the local senators (*decuriones*) were to form a permanent corporation to control the public aspects of life in the colony is apparent even from the partially preserved text, but it is also evident that they were not expected to do too much: a minimum amount of clean government was what was now required.

We finally come to grants of constitutions to communities in the provinces, which were in origin non-Roman. Surviving documents of this kind derive entirely from Spain, for the most part from the province of Baetica. This in itself is not surprising. Bronze inscriptions have been preserved comparatively well in Spain and Baetica was the most urbanised and romanised part of it. However, nothing of this kind has survived from the oldest and most romanised provinces Gaul and Africa – Narbonensis and Proconsularis. The recent discovery of a very large section of a Roman municipal law from the Flavian period at Irni, a neighbour of the colony at Urso, has made a critical difference to our understanding. This text overlaps two previously known sections of municipal law from Malaca and Salpensa, in such a way that the Malaca text can be used in part to supplement that from Irni. The result is two-thirds of a local constitution, known to have been engraved with only minor variations in all three towns.[40] Nor is this all: there are a number of other fragments of municipal laws, three of which at least, from Basilippo, Ostippo and perhaps Italica, seem to contain texts identical with those in the constitutions of Irni and Malaca.[41]

We seem to have evidence of a Flavian municipal law exported to the non-Roman communities of Spain. These had been generally given by Vespasian Latin rights, that is, a form of half-citizenship which could be converted into full citizenship by the tenure of a local magistracy.[42] Adoption of this constitution was not an immediate complement to the grant of Latin rights. The text from Irni has as a postscript a letter of Domitian sent on 10 April AD 91 (some fifteen years later than Vespasian's grant), which seems to have been engraved at the same time. Some allowance was made for differences between Irni and Malaca: the sum of money at stake in a public lawsuit which marked the boundary between two different kinds of public judicial procedure was fixed at 500 sesterces for Irni, but 1,000 for Malaca – an indication of the respective wealth and importance of the two communities.[43] Nevertheless, it is hard to believe that any community in Spain given Latin rights could in the long term avoid having a constitution of this kind (Domitian's subscript to the text shows that there was no alternative to obeying its regulations about marriage),[44] and, once a model had been provided which had the emperor's approval, the magistrate or commissioner entrusted with providing the town with a constitution would probably follow it. It is perhaps strictly inaccurate to talk of the imposition of a constitution, but in fact Irni had little choice or room for manœuvre.

Before the discovery of the text from Irni scholars had assumed that a municipal constitution was much less rigid and more determined by the discretion of the local community than that of a colony, on the basis of the advice Hadrian is said to have given to the *municipium* of Italica.[45] The conformity to Roman rules required from a colony may indeed have been more rigorous in administrative detail than that required from a *municipium* (though we should allow for Hadrian being a little disingenuous in his rejection of a request for colonial status). However, it is clear that, as a *municipium*, Italica had been forced to adopt a constitution approved by Rome and, further, was largely required to conform to Roman private law. Chapter 93 of the Flavian law at Irni laid down that in cases where there was no specific prescription as to the law the *municipes* were to use in suing one another, they were to conform to the civil law employed by Roman citizens.

The Flavian municipal constitution, as it can be reconstructed from the tablets found at Irni and Malaca, was a much better organised text than the constitution of the colony at Urso. The latter may well have been put together with haste and urgency in the confusion after Caesar's murder, while the former incorporates a further century of experience, in which standard formulae could be elaborated. The definitions of the local citizen-body, rules about resident aliens, rules about marriage and other acts relating to citizenship do not survive and were presumably in the lost section at the beginning of the law (there is a brief reference to the rules about marriage in the subscript of the emperor Domitian at the end). Similarly, we have lost the regulations about religion and games, such as occur in the *lex Ursonensis*.[46] The first preserved section (chs 19–20) deals with the duties of magistrates – the aediles and quaestors (the rules for duumvirs, the senior local magistrates, are lost). The text moves on to the right of magistrates to acquire Roman citizenship on leaving office, with all its qualifications (chs 21–3), the appointment of *praefecti* to replace duumvirs (chs 24–5), the magistrate's oath and the rules about appeal (ch. 27). Attached to this are two chapters about the duumvir's powers in two aspects of civil law – manumission of slaves and the granting of guardians (chs 28–9). There follows a section on the local senate. This begins in the preserved chapters 30–1 (senators are to have the same status as those in other *municipia Latina*; the number of sixty-two is to be maintained). A whole tablet with about ten more chapters presumably also relating to the senate is lost; then on the next tablet we have details of senate procedure (chs A–E), provisions about embassies (chs F–I), the letting of public contracts (ch. J) and public holidays (chs J–K). The majority of the section on elections only survives on the Malaca bronze (chs 51–60). After two chapters on the co-option of patrons and the demolition of buildings (chs 61–2), the law moves on to a series of regulations which are in some way financial – the letting of contracts (chs 63–5), appeals against magistrates' fines (ch. 66), the rendering of accounts for the handling of public money (chs 67–8) and trials to recover money due to the community (chs 69–71).

The organisation of the law now becomes more fragmentary. There is a section on personnel – the manumission of public slaves, the pay of free public servants (*apparitores*) and the oath of the scribes (chs 72–3). The draughtsman then interjects three chapters about unlawful associations and assemblies, hoarding and price-rings, visits to borders and public lands (chs 74–6), before returning to financial matters – rules for public expenditure, the use of public slaves, the raising of public loans, the organisation of spectacles and public works (chs 77–83). There follows a long section on the procedure in private lawsuits, including the limits to local jurisdiction, the selection of single judges and panels of *recuperatores* and forms of adjournment (chs 84–93). Finally, we find a brief item stating that the *incolae* (resident non-members of the citizen-body) are to be as subject to the constitution as the *municipes*, who are local citizens; then the customary clause ordering the engraving and publication of the text, an enforcement clause (*sanctio*) and what is obviously a postscript regarding freedmen of those who are elevated to the citizenship (they are still to be clients of their patrons). After the law itself has been concluded, there is engraved a note from Domitian concerning marriages which had been taking place contrary to the provisions of the constitution.

Many provisions can be recognised as having a long tradition behind them. The replacement of the chief magistrates by *praefecti* (chs 24–5) appears in the Oscan law from Bantia (line 23) as well as in the *lex Ursonensis* (chs 94–5). The rules for the granting of guardians (ch. 29) must have been in *lex Ursonensis* 108–9 and enable us to restore this fragmentary text. Regulations about embassies (ch. G) have been expanded from those in *Ursonensis* 92, as have the qualifications for election to magistracies (ch. 54; *Urs.* 101).[47] The security to be taken from successful candidates against their future handling of public money (ch. 57) has a precedent in the law from Tarentum (lines 14–25). The chapter regarding the adoption of patrons (61) is similar to the first provision in *lex Ursonensis* (97), but there is no sign of the extra rule (*Urs.* 130) that patrons must be private citizens in Italy without *imperium*. As we have seen, the ban on the demolition of houses (ch. 62) can be traced back through the *lex Ursonensis* to the *lex Tarentina*, while the rules about rendering accounts for public money also had their precedent at Tarentum.[48]

On a broad view we have the impression of an attempt to simplify, where possible, and to maintain a degree of local discretion. We cannot tell, thanks to the loss of a tablet, whether the Flavian law strictly limited the initiative of magistrates without consultation with the senate, as the Urso constitution did.[49] However, there are no equivalents in the surviving text of the Flavian municipal constitution to the chapters about exacting corvées for road-building and about public water-supplies in *Urs.* 98–100, nor to other chapters about use of land and public works (*Urs.* 73–4, 78–9 and the tralatician chapter in 104), and such matters do not naturally belong in the lacunae in the Flavian law.[50] Moreover, the duties of the aedile at Irni, for example, are sketched in a very general way (ch. 19), expenditure on games and festivals is briefly provided for in a single chapter (77), by contrast with the four elaborate chapters at Urso (69–72), and the chapter at Irni (71) about visitations of boundaries and sources of rent each year is not specific about details.

There is no mention of *curatores rei publicae* in the financial section, but this may merely reflect the fact that in this period such men were not regular appointees but created to deal with particular problems.[51] Equally, the provincial governor and his quaestor are not mentioned at Irni, but the only references to Roman magistrates in the Urso text come in the chapters about seating arrangements at the games and the adoption of patrons or guest-friends.[52] It is of course implicit in the limits laid down for local jurisdiction at Irni that those lawsuits which it was illegal to try locally – that is, private cases worth more than 1,000 sesterces, those creating *infamia* or those which might predetermine the guilt of a free man in a capital case, where both parties were not prepared to accept a local decision – would be

referred to the Roman proconsul or his *legatus*, either for investigation themselves or for submission to a judge or panel of judges.[53]

We do not find any evidence in the Flavian constitution of criminal
jurisdiction – cases of treason, murder and brigandage, for example –
which must have been reserved for higher authority (although the
creation of membership of an illegal association is punished locally by
a fine).[54] The aedile (ch. 19), and so *a fortiori* the duumvir had powers
to exact fines and take pledges up to a limit of 10,000 sesterces, but
this is probably more in the field of what we would call administrative
law. These punishments enable them to exact obedience from
members of the community in the execution of their public duties and
to ensure respect for the rules set out in the constitution itself (the
latter could also be enforced by legal actions by any *municeps* who
wanted – the so-called *actio popularis*).[55]

By contrast, the Oscan law from Bantia provided for capital trials in
an assembly, the Table of Heraclea later envisaged condemnations in
a *iudicium publicum* held in colonies, *municipia, fora* and *conciliabula*
in Italy, while the law from Urso shows that a magistrate there could
hold a *quaestio* (a term for a criminal enquiry).[56] It seems that the
local criminal jurisdiction permitted in towns in Italy in the late
Republic was extended to Caesarian colonies (including perhaps
jurisdiction in some capital cases). It is interesting that the decree
about the altar for the imperial cult at the colony of Narbo
commended Augustus for linking the courts of the plebs with the local
senate.[57] The fact that this sort of criminal jurisdiction was not
conceded to a Latin *municipium* in the provinces would mean that
magistrates in colonies had more delegated jurisdiction than those in
municipia. The latter, however, had more discretion in administrative
matters, whether secular or religious, and were not subject to so many
rigid prescriptions as magistrates in a colony. This comparative
freedom provides some justification for Hadrian's reply to the people
of Italica (see p. 141), even if we may not be entirely convinced of the
emperor's sincerity.

The documents we have considered so far represent the extreme of
Roman intervention in local government. How widespread intervention on this scale was is hard to assess. The implication of Hadrian's
reply to Italica is that every community which became a Roman
colony, no matter where, had *ex hypothesei* a rigid constitution
imposed on it. The probability is that towns which were *municipia*,
like Malaca and Irni, would be required to adopt a constitution which,
first, compelled them to adopt Roman civil law and subjected them in

part to Roman jurisdiction, and, second, enforced a standard pattern of magistracies and arrangements regarding the local senate, even if it allowed them some choice in the duties they were to perform. A town or other settlement with a dominant body of Roman citizens, even if it had no municipal status, would also have been subjected to Roman private law and jurisdiction, while its administrative arrangements would have tended to imitate closely those of *coloniae* and *municipia*, even if this was not enforced from above. In the western provinces before AD 212, where there were simple *civitates peregrinae* (communities with neither Roman nor Latin status), our evidence suggests that their constitutions had the same general pattern as those of Roman and Latin communities.[58] The centre of the community was the *decuriones* – a fixed body who held office for life; there were magistrates who performed jurisdiction, like *duumviri*, others concerned with the fabric of the city (*aediles*) and financial magistrates (*quaestores*). There were also five-yearly magistrates (*quinquennales*) who fulfilled the function of Roman censors.[59] Sometimes magistrates retained their local titles: we find *sufetes* in formerly Punic Africa and a *vergobretus* in Gaul.[60] How far this pattern was the result of Roman pressure or a desire to imitate by the provincials themselves is impossible to tell. We may suspect that in any case much depended on the attitude of the leaders of the local community.

Even if conformity with Roman models decided matters like the size of the senate in *civitates peregrinae*, there would have been room for local tradition and initiative in financial arrangements, public works and the organisation of festivals (this does not exclude the provincials seeking Roman approval for their policies, once they had been devised). Jurisidiction in these communities may also have had a strong local element (though this raises problems over discrepancies between legal systems, which will be dealt with in Chapter 9). It is in any case likely that the Romans would have imposed limits on this according to the type of case and its financial value, which would have removed lawsuits of significance to the jurisdiction of a Roman magistrate.

THE GREEK EAST

Much of what has been said at the end of the last section is equally valid for the non-Roman communities in the hellenised provinces of the Greek east. The existing Greek cities there provided the Roman empire with ready-made urban centres, but some sort of accommodation was required between Roman expectations and the long tradition of Greek city politics. Since the seventh century BC, if not earlier, these cities tended to have constitutions based on annual magistrates, one or more councils and an assembly. Depending on the qualifications for magistracies and membership of council and assembly, and on the relative powers of these three organs of the constitution, the city could be assigned a place on the spectrum of grades between extreme oligarchy and extreme democracy (in Aristotle's *Politics* Book IV there are two spectra which overlap); otherwise it would be a monarchy, tyranny or *dunasteia*, i.e., ruled by a small oligarchic junta.

From the time the Romans began to exercise power in Greece, they had tended to favour oligarchic constitutions, without trying to eliminate entirely any of the three main elements, which were the foundation not only of Greek constitutions but of their own republican system.[61] Indeed, when they first intervened in a Greek city's internal affairs, they may have done little more than ensure that the effective participants in its government were their own partisans.[62] After the sack of Corinth in 146 BC, when a considerable amount of Greek territory was subjected to the governor of Macedonia, we begin to have evidence of more fundamental limitation of Greek freedom. There is a letter of Q. Fabius Maximus to Dyme, probably of 145, which reveals that there had been an uprising against the Roman constitution and the drafting of a new one to replace it. The language of the letter strongly suggests that certain Dymaeans had tried to replace an oligarchy with something more democratic (though it must be admitted that we do not know how much, or how little, support there had been in Dyme for the constitution with the Roman imprimatur).[63] In any case, councils and assemblies still survived in cities subjected to Rome,[64] while in the early first century BC the assembly of the independent city of Athens retained sufficient of its old anti-aristocratic spirit to create a tyrant for itself and join Mithridates against Rome.[65]

When Bithynia was made into a province *c*. 65 BC, Pompey's regulations governed the qualifications for membership of the councils in the cities and we may reasonably assume that they extended to matters such as elections and qualifications for membership of the assembly.[66] References to a *lex Cornelia* governing elections and financial arrangements in two decrees of the Augustan period – one of the *koinon* of Asia and one of Thyateira – seem to me more likely to describe a regulation imposed on Asiatic cities by Sulla in 85–4 BC than a law passed at Rome about that province, but for the provincials the effect was the same.[67] We also have evidence of a law regulating assemblies and election procedures in Lycia–Pamphylia during the second century AD (perhaps a *lex provinciae* of general application, perhaps a constitution given to an individual city).[68]

By the end of the Roman Republic it must be doubtful if a city assembly remained which was still democratic by classical standards, in the sense that it represented the majority of adult male citizens.[69] Nevertheless, the existence of assemblies which passed decrees makes a contrast with the situation in colonies and *municipia* with constitutions provided by Rome, whose assemblies were significant only for elections.[70] The similarity of constitutions of colonies in the east to those in the west is shown by the appeal from Pisidian Antioch to Antistius Rusticus in AD 93, which was dispatched by the *duumviri* and *decuriones*.[71] In a Greek city, on the other hand, legal enactments required approval of both the council and the assembly, even if the latter might do little more than formally ratify the council's decisions. This is well illustrated in a decree of the city of Gazorus in Macedonia of the second century AD about the lease of public land, which encouraged the plantation of vines, olives and fruit-trees. Almost the whole text of the public record concerns the proposal in the council, which was approved and voted through *nemine contradicente*: the comment that the people ratified this is briefly added at the end.[72] Yet the importance of the *dêmos* in the political life of the cities of the east about the end of the first century AD is patent in the speeches of Dio of Prusa, while an underlying theme of Plutarch's *Precepts of Political Life* is how to maintain the common people in order and tranquillity (by education and moral improvement, if possible) and not to let yourself be carried away by their sort of passions.[73]

One city in which the Romans did take a special interest was Athens. From the time of Athens' capture by Sulla (86 BC) the traditional elements of the Athenian constitution seem to have been adapted to ensure an oligarchic society.[74] During the late Republic some Romans became citizens of Athens and actually were elected to the Areopagus – something for which Cicero showed strong disapproval in 65 BC, on the ground that it implied holding another citizenship concurrently with Roman citizenship, but which seems to have been legitimised at Rome by the time of Caesar's death[75] (Athens' own qualifications for high office were also modified so that three generations of free birth were substituted for the requirement to have three generations of citizen parents).[76] By the first century AD the Areopagus had returned to its position of bygone years, with political powers as well as an important judiciary function, while the council of five hundred (or six hundred) had taken on a judiciary role.[77] It is likely that this development had been encouraged by the Romans as a way of ensuring that the wealthier and more aristocratic section of society dominated politics and the judiciary.[78] In addition, the organisation called the sacred *gerousia*, apparently invented in the early Hellenistic period as a supervisory body concerned with finance and perhaps cult, was revived and expanded in the Roman period: it has been argued that it was established at Athens by Marcus Aurelius as a kind of academy of culture.[79] Moreover, Hadrian and subsequent emperors fostered a new organisation based in Attica called the Panhellenion, which was to be a meeting-place for the wealthy and cultured throughout the Greek world and a focus for Hellenism.[80]

The example of Athens shows the impact that Roman power could have on a Greek city, but also how this was mediated by the use of Greek institutions: the political vocabulary, as it were, had to be Greek. There was no question of the imposition of a structure developed for a colony or *municipium*. Nevertheless, certain legislative items, characteristic of western local constitutions, were imported into Greek cities. For example, we know that Hadrian introduced to Athens a ban on members of a council undertaking tax-farming – something which formed part of the Flavian municipal law in Spain.[81] The injunction in Trajan's *mandata* to Pliny that he should not permit public money to be given to individuals can be found in the *lex Ursonensis*.[82] The Roman opposition to all *collegia*, except those specifically legitimised, which formed part of public law at Rome and local constitutions in the west, was applied in Greek cities: only when the city was free, had care to be taken to reconcile this with the existing Greek constitution.[83]

CITY CONSTITUTIONS AND THE GOVERNOR: THE BITHYNIAN EVIDENCE

The Flavian municipal laws show both the autonomy permitted to *municipia* and at the same time how much it was limited by these laws themselves. The inferences they permit about what matters were reserved for the provincial governor or his legate (see pp. 143–4) can be supplemented by the direct evidence of inscriptions on this topic. For example, in the emperor Titus' letter to Munigua he states that their dispute with the tax-collector should have been first referred to the governor, while Vespasian in a letter to Sabora similarly refers to the governor a matter relating to the city's own tax-revenues.[84]

In Bithynia the cities' constitutions, as we have seen, had been regulated by Pompey during his establishment of the province. We have no texts from these constitutions, but we can exploit the implications of Pliny's correspondence about them: indeed the correspondence itself is direct evidence of the governor's capacity to intervene. Like a municipal law, the *lex Pompeia* dealt with magistracies and admission to the senate, the latter being dealt with by censors (the Greek title for them was *timêtai*). If a candidate for the local senate had held one of the magistracies, he seems to have had a prescriptive right to be made a member; if he had not, he might still be chosen by the censors.[85] There were, as in the municipal laws, a limit to the membership of the senate and provision for expulsion. This basic position had been modified by an edict of Augustus, which lowered the qualifying age for candidacy for magistracy, and Trajan had permitted cities to admit senators above the number prescribed in the *lex Pompeia*.[86]

It appears that in a number of cities it had become customary to ask for a *summa honoraria* (a financial contribution to the city associated with elevation to office or rank) from those entering the local senate. This applied originally to supernumary senators, but later, after a ruling by the proconsul Anicius Maximus, to those who were chosen according to the *lex Pompeia*, the sum varying from city to city. Though the situation obtaining at the time of Pliny's correspondence had been ratified by Anicius Maximus, it had been first enacted through a law in each city (*cuiusque civitatis legem*). Thus the cities had possessed within the *lex Pompeia* a certain room for manœuvre, which Pliny was now seeking to restrict with Trajan's help.[87]

We also find a provision in the *lex Pompeia* permitting a city to enrol as honorary citizens those who were already citizens of another city, provided that this city was not also in Bithynia – something for which there is no equivalent in what survives of the municipal laws of the west, but which was to some extent parallel to grants of *hospitium* and *patrocinium*.[88] Pompey had made concessions to a Greek tradition, which was beginning to have its effect on Rome itself but at the time was still contrary to a fundamental Roman principle. The ban on the admission of men from other cities of Bithynia may have been an attempt to prevent a few men becoming dominant throughout the province, but this prohibition was later ignored to the profit of those like Dio of Prusa, who was also a citizen of Nicaea, Nicomedia and

Apamea.[89] Trajan's solution was to return to the *lex Pompeia* for the future, but to take no action against past violators of the law.[90]

So far I have been dealing with the explicit provisions of the *lex Pompeia* known to us. More generally, it must have regulated the citizenship of the cities and the elements of their constitutions, including the local senate (*boulê*) and assembly (*ekklêsia*). Similarly, the *lex Cornelia* had regulated the holding of elections in Asia.[91] However, the *lex Pompeia* was not so developed and refined as to have incorporated detailed rules about administration and justice such as are found in the municipal laws of the west. When there had been a general enactment at Rome about government or administrative practice (as opposed to private law), the governor was evidently expected to enforce it, as far as his writ ran. The *eranoi* (welfare-associations) at Amisus came under the prohibition of the Roman *lex Iulia de collegiis*, or would have done, had not Amisus been a free city (its freedom consisted not in exemption from any intervention from the governor, but in the possession of a constitution and laws which were not overridden by relevant Roman laws). Hence Trajan instructed that in Amisus the legitimacy of *eranoi* should be judged in the light of the city's own constitution, while in other cities the general Roman ban on associations among the plebs – one that we find translated into the municipal constitutions – should prevail.[92] Another case from Amisus was referred to Pliny by the city's *ecdicus* (a sort of district attorney). The issue was a gift from public funds to a private individual, apparently as recompense for his services, which had been voted into effect by decrees of the local senate and assembly. Pliny points out that such gifts were forbidden in Trajan's *mandata*. We know of no general Roman law, like the *lex Iulia de collegiis*, relevant to this case, but we find in the *lex Ursonensis* a chapter forbidding any proposal to the local senate that a man should receive public money for holding office, giving or promising a show or setting up a statue. It seems then that a rule, originally incorporated in this and, no doubt, other colonial constitutions, was in due course enforced elsewhere by a proconsul on the emperor's authority.[93] On another financial matter, the priority of the community over other creditors in recovering what was owed to it (*protopraxia*), proconsuls seem to have enforced this in accordance with general Roman principles, which applied to both provincial and municipal treasuries (though a later jurist argues that a municipal treasury had only priority in claims if this had been specifically conceded by the emperor).[94] The priority of the community as creditor was implicit in the Flavian municipal laws which assimilated procedure in such matters to that in Rome.[95]

Questions of personal freedom, though a matter of private law, were considered so important issues that they were normally reserved for the jurisdiction of the governor. Yet in the Flavian municipal laws permission is given for them to be tried locally, if both sides agreed.[96] Roman law would have been applied, whether a case was sent up to the governor of a Spanish province from a *municipium* or it was tried in the *municipium* itself. Pliny, however, though his authority was parallel to that of a governor in Spain, was not apparently in such a clear-cut situation. Regarding the restoration to freedom of those illegally enslaved, he did not know whether he was permitted to investigate and judge (*cognoscere*) the case himself. It is not clear whether the alternative envisaged was to refer the case to a judge chosen by himself after a preliminary hearing, or to leave it to local jurisdiction, or if indeed both possibilities were open. Trajan seems to have assumed that Pliny was permitted to judge the case himself but wanted to check the *senatus consultum* that had worried Pliny.[97] As for the *threptoi* (foundlings) – that is in this case, freeborn children exposed and brought up by others in servitude (other categories of *threptoi* were freeborn foster-children, house-slaves and adopted children) – the Romans had not been systematically applying the rules of Roman civil law for *alumni* in the east; edicts and letters of varying effect had been sent by previous emperors in response to petitions and enquiries.[98] Trajan's solution was that actions to liberate foundlings should not be denied in principle, but one should not be allowed to buy liberty itself by paying the price of maintenance. It has been argued that this was closer to the Greek legal position, where it was not usual for *alumni* to be freed by the payment of their maintenance costs, but Trajan's point may have been that Pliny had to be sure that it was a freeborn child that had been exposed and that the action was not a form of concealed manumussion: if he was, then the Roman rule on the subject could be applied.[99]

It is an open question whether any local criminal jurisdiction was permitted in the Flavian municipal law, as it apparently was in Italian *municipia* and in Caesar's colony at Urso (see p. 144). In Bithynia it was certainly permitted, at least in some cases perhaps not involving Roman citizens. Pliny was horrified at the liberal penal regime obtaining at Nicomedia and Nicaea, where those who had been condemned to public service, probably in mines or quarries, or to serve in the amphitheatre as animal-hunters (*venatores*), were being treated like public slaves and had been paid an annual salary.[100] Whatever we may think of his zeal for severity, he had a valid point, that the cities should abide by their own laws, and this point was accepted by the cities themselves, in so far as they alleged that the release of such criminals had been a response to pleas by Roman officials. Pliny's attitude here is consistent with the general Roman policy that granted a *municipium* or colony autonomy, provided that it followed the rules laid down in its carefully drafted charter.

Pliny's chief assignment as Trajan's legate in Bithynia was to investigate local finance.[101] This kind of intervention in local govern-ment was not a new departure: the post of *logistês* or *curator* seems to owe its origin to the Flavians, but before this there are examples of governors undertaking similar tasks – Paullus Fabius Persicus in relation to the temple of Artemis at Ephesus, when Claudius was emperor, and even Cicero during his governorship of Cilicia.[102] Such *ex post facto* remedies for local insolvency are the counterpoint to the strict rules about local public spending in the *lex Ursonensis* and the more relaxed but still restrictive rules in the Flavian municipal law.[103]

A comparison between the colonial and municipal laws and the activity of Trajan's legate in Bithynia shows that in Spain and Bithynia the Romans were trying to inculcate similar behaviour, though not to impose identical legal rules. In one case local autonomy on a Roman model was conceded, but precisely defined so as to prevent financial irresponsibility and to suppress any temptation for a local magistrate to promote his own popularity through providing benefits at the public expense. In the Greek world the Roman aim was, first, to ensure that the cities obeyed any general rules laid down for the province, whether in an all-embracing *lex provinciae* or on separate occasions, and further to apply through proconsular auth-ority both laws that the Romans applied to themselves (such as the *lex Iulia de collegiis*) and other regulations devised by emperors or the senate for the provinces. Initially, this still left the local aristocracies in the east considerable room for manœuvre, but they did not always handle this satisfactorily and their financial embarrassment was an excellent excuse for Roman intervention. At Amisus Iulius Piso seems to have bankrupted himself through spending money on the city.[104] The people of Prusa seem to have expected the same of Dio but received long hortatory speeches instead.[105] In addition, there were of course, as Plutarch pointed out, those who sought personal advantage by themselves drawing in the Romans.[106] In the end, governors operating like Pliny must have instilled in the local senates a wariness and a tendency to watch their own backs, which was to result in an excessive eagerness to refer local policy decisions to the governor or the emperor in succeeding years.[107]

9

ROMAN AND INDIGENOUS LAW

As a preliminary, let me briefly summarise Roman provincial jurisdiction as discussed so far (Chapters 4 and 8). First, there are the practical limits of time and space on a governor's jurisdiction, to some extent relaxed by the presence of a *legatus* who could deputise for him in certain cases, and less severe than is sometimes thought, if we accept that a governor in civil cases normally acted as a magistrate in Rome would have done – accepting or rejecting the suit initially, defining the issue in a formula and remitting it to a judge or judges for judication. The second main feature is the recognition of the importance of local jurisidiction. In a comparatively few 'free' cities, the independence of the local jurisdiction was specifically established by senatorial decree. Otherwise it seems to have been normal for matters involving local residents who were not Roman citizens to be judged locally, even if there was a preliminary hearing by a Roman magistrate and this magistrate might decide to take over a case himself or use a Roman court. Third, there is this pervasive authority of the governor, summarised in his edict, which was fundamentally articulated in the forms of Roman law and included much of its substance as well.

This somewhat fluid situation may well seem characteristic of the Republic. Under the monarchy of Augustus and his successors, it may be thought – when the emperor was ultimately the authority for all matters outside Italy and appeals and referrals were made to him – Roman law spread throughout the empire, and although local jurisdiction was maintained, it was jurisdiction on Roman lines. However, it is not so simple as that. Only after Caracalla gave Roman citizenship to almost all the free population of the empire (in AD 212 on the usual view), can Roman law be said to have been, at least in theory, the law of the empire. There is a period of evolution and

154

compromise before this date, and this continues beyond it. Furthermore, there is the question of how far even in a Roman context allowance was made for the local law of the peoples of the provinces. This was the subject of Ludwig Mitteis' epoch-making book, *Reichsrecht und Volksrecht in den Östlichen Provinzen des römischen Kaiserreich* (Leipzig, 1891). He stressed the persistence of Greek and demotic Egyptian law in Egypt, and of Greek law in Syria, Asia Minor and Greece itself. If anything, that powerfully argued book encourages us to overestimate the influence of non-Roman law. However, some important pieces of new evidence provide a useful control and it may be possible now to take a more balanced view.

The *Tabula Contrebiensis*, which contains a decree made in 87 BC by the governor of the Spanish provinces C. Valerius Flaccus, provides a strong warning that we should not underestimate the early impact of Roman private law in the provinces.[1] The governor is entrusting to the local senate of Contrebia Balaisca an arbitration over boundaries and water-rights between two communities in its neighbourhood, the Salluvienses and Allavonenses. The issue is presented to it in a formula which resembles a Roman private law *formula*, such as a Roman magistrate would use with a Roman judge or *recuperatores* in Italy. This includes the use of a fiction (line 6) presuming the existence of a third community, the Sosinestani, as an independent legal entity, the fiction being expressed, as normal in Latin, in an imperfect subjunctive tense.

What are the implications of this? The Spaniards are expected at this time to understand the way that Romans conceptualised and verbalised issues in litigation, including the use of the imperfect subjunctive to express a fiction; they are not expected to know the substance of Roman private law. The right of the third party, the Sosinestani, to sell land to the Salluvienses and the right of the Salluvienses to dig a water-channel there are to be decided by the Contrebian senate with no further guidance from the Roman magistrate, presumably according to their own law. It may be that, by his fiction that the Sosinestani are a community, Valerius Flaccus had assumed the really controversial point and so biased the issue in advance, but that is not our concern here. It is clear that he is operating within the context of local tradition. By the same token, we can draw no inference from the *tabula* that native Spanish law in, for example, matters of marriage and the status of children had been abandoned, where it conflicted with Roman law. Certainly, Greek family law survived under the Roman empire, both in cities declared free and those more directly subject to Rome.[2]

In Spain 170 years later, when the Flavian municipal laws were adopted, this situation had changed radically. The text of the *lex Irnitana* (see Chapter 8, pp. 141–4) shows that even a small *municipium* with Latin rights, like Irni, might adopt Roman law wholesale – the fact that similar charters have been found in a number of towns in Spain suggests that this was a Roman policy, though it probably worked not through compulsion but through diplomacy and pressure towards conformity.[3] The details of both administrative law and private jurisdiction specifically prescribed are Roman and, apart from this, the magistrates are instructed to conform to the edict of the provincial governor (ch. 85). Further, where no specific prescription has been made in the law or the governor's edict, actions between the members of the *municipium* must be in accordance with Roman civil law (ch. 93).

It is reasonable inference that, in the time of the Flavian emperors or soon afterwards, other Latin *municipia* were required to use Roman procedure and substantive law.[4] However, it remains a question how far this conformity extended among communities which were simply foreign (*civitates peregrinae*), that is, those with neither Roman citizenship nor Latin rights. From the period before AD 200 we have surviving a scatter of documents showing Roman procedure in use in the provinces. If we leave aside Spain (whence comes the *formula Baetica*, a model contract for taking real security, *fidei fiduciae causa*), we have contracts and other legal documents in Roman form from Britain, Frisia, Dacia, Seleucia Pieria in Syria and Side in Pamphylia.[5] The most astonishing evidence is the appearance of Roman formulary procedure among recently published documents from a cave by the Dead Sea, belonging to a Nabataean Jewish lady called Babatha, who had fled there at the time of the Bar-Kochba revolt.[6]

Evidently, forms of Roman law, albeit perhaps vulgarised, that is, modified for local use,[7] spread to the ends of the empire. However, this does not mean that they drove out non-Roman forms. At Dura-Europos in Mesopotamia no Roman influence is detectable on Greek forms of law until AD 227, some fifteen years after Caracalla gave citizenship to the empire.[8] In Egypt Greco-Egyptian forms and rules still prevailed in private law, while the Romano-Syrian law book of the Byzantine period (fifth century AD) has elements within it which are not Roman (see below). Even in Italy in the first century AD a sea-freight contract for a voyage from Puteoli to Athens involved both Roman *stipulationes* and a Greek literal contract (*suggraphê*).[9] It would have been in any case improbable that the substantive law of non-Roman communities generally gave way to Roman law before the universal spread of Roman citizenship, and there is now more evidence to buttress this conclusion than when Mitteis wrote.

Documents from the Babatha archive in Greek follow a mixture of Roman law, the Hellenised law of Nabataean Arabia and Jewish law, while Aramaic documents followed Jewish law.[10] Babatha, who was the second wife in a polygamous marriage, after the death of her husband summoned the other wife Miriam (Mariame) before the governor Haterius Nepos over her seizure of the property in her dead husband's house, using a legal instrument similar to a Roman *vadimonium*. Other documents attest her concern for the maintenance of her orphan son Jesus. Among these are three copies of the formulas for the Roman *actio tutelae*. It looks as if she resorted, or at least considered resorting, to a Roman form of action, which was carefully copied out for her, as the best way of winning her case before the governor.[11]

When Mitteis was making his case for the survival of native law (*Volksrecht*), his most obvious example was Egypt. Here papyri revealed legal procedures which were indeed different in some respect to those of the Ptolemaic period, but which nevertheless were not those standard in Roman civil law. Although we find issues submitted to a judge by a magistrate's decree as in Roman private law,[12] suits are usually made by *libelli* or requests to a magistrate to summon one's opponent.[13] Contracts were concluded in a Greco-Egyptian form (marriage contracts, in particular, had a provision for an experimental year),[14] and the underlying substantive law was Egyptian, which differed significantly from Roman in matters such as marriage, guardianship, paternal authority, sales and debts.[15] That the Romans accepted such discrepancies is not surprising, when they tolerated there, at least in the pre-Christian period, endogamy, especially brother–sister marriage – a fundamental breach of their own law and tradition.[16]

Egypt may be set aside as a peculiar country, for which the Romans made a special exception. Yet Mitteis was also able to exploit the Romano-Syrian law book to show that there persisted in the law of that province in the Byzantine period principles which were not Roman: for example, the rights of inheritance in intestacy and the rules relating to dowry and gifts by bridegrooms resembled more those of Greek law than those of Rome.[17] It is possible that this arose from an original Roman recognition of local traditions about paternity and inheritance and a blending of these with Roman principles over centuries. The evidence from Dura-Europos in Mesopotamia points in the same direction. A sale of AD 180 is still in Greek form, similar to that found in Egypt, while as late as AD 232 a marriage contract between a soldier and a widow with a Latin name resembles marriage contracts known from Roman Egypt in the preceding period.[18]

A similar tolerance was extended to the Jews. Even after the destruction of the temple and the Jewish state, they were accepted as a nation with their own religion and forms of private law until late in the fourth century AD. Among the Greek documents in the Babatha archive is a marriage in fundamentally Jewish form, while among the documents from the Murabba'at cave are a loan made in Nero's reign – in a form very different both to those of the contemporary Pompeii tablets and loans by Jews in Greco-Roman Egypt – and a divorce of AD 111 in accordance with Mosaic law.[19]

In Greece we do not have the detailed documents which the deserts provide. At Athens it can at least be seen that, where the city was permitted to use its own jurisdiction, it did so through courts in Athenian form (the *dikasteria* of the classical era no longer existed; their functions belonged to the Areopagus, the Council of Five Hundred or Six Hundred and the assembly). In Hadrian's oil law the council is to judge by itself suits up to a limit of fifty amphorae; beyond this limit it is to judge in conjunction with the assembly.[20] In the letter about Eleusinian fishermen we hear of *endeixis* to the herald of the Areopagus, which must decide 'what the defendant must suffer or pay' (an old Athenian formula).[21] Outside Athens it is worth noting that a Thessalian inscription refers to manumission occurring according to the laws of the Magnesians.[22] Against his background it seems unlikely that the engraving of the laws of Gortyn in a portico at the rear of the *cavea* of the *odeion* was simply an historical memento or tourist attraction, but an affirmation that these local Cretan rules of private law had still some validity, even though Gortyn was the residence of the Roman governor of Crete. We also have glimpses of the importance of local law in the Greek provinces of Asia Minor. Gaius cites the law of the Bithynians as an example of a foreign law whose treatment of the guardianship of women, while recognising the principle, differs in detail from the Roman.[23] An inscription from Tralles defending the inviolability of a grave refers to the 'the rules and the ancestral laws'; the age of majority varied from city to city; it was permitted under the local Greek law in Phrygia to sell children into slavery.[24] This last Greek tradition was probably a relevant factor in the case of the *threptoi* (foster-children) which Pliny the younger was called on to adjudicate (see p. 151). It is a moot point whether the ruling prescribed by Trajan was closer to Roman or Greek law (a major problem is that we have nowhere a clear statement of the Roman rules about *alumni*). However, it was evidently a matter where Roman and local law had been found to conflict and Trajan's reply shows that no universal ruling had been made by any previous emperor on the topic.[25]

In the Greek provinces a large number of cases were referred upward to the governor or another Roman magistrate or indeed to the emperor. Plutarch complained:

> The chief cause of this is the greed and combative spirit of the leading men. For either by their injuries to their inferiors they force them to go outside the city or, through thinking it unacceptable to be worsted in contests with their equals, they bring in the ruling power. As a result of this, council and assembly and courts and every magistracy lose their authority.[26]

However, it is worth stressing Plutarch's implied point, that, if cases and problems were not referred upwards, politics and jurisdiction could have proceeded in an autonomous fashion, without intervention by the Romans. Plutarch's complaint is illustrated in Marcus Aurelius' long edict to the Athenians about cases appealed to his jurisdiction. Those that are referred back to Athens are sent to particular magistrates or judges nominated by Marcus and not to any Athenian court (in this respect Marcus is behaving like a Roman civil magistrate who selects the judge to hear each case). At one point we hear of an arbitrator, but even he was to be appointed by Roman officials, the Quinctilii.[27]

However, this document, which deals with the quarrels of the rich, may give an exaggerated impression of the depth of Roman penetration into Athenian legal procedure. In fact, the Romans had refrained from trying to strip Athens of her individuality. We can apply more generally a principle derived from the charter from Irni – that, if both parties are willing, a dispute can be settled locally, except when the result might predetermine a capital sentence (ch. 84). There the machinery of local jurisdiction was supported as far as possible, while at the same time, in all but minor cases, the way to the Roman magistrate's tribunal was left open. In the majority of provinces (Egypt being the certain exception), if a Roman magistrate chose to investigate a case referred to him, he could decide himself not to apply all the rules specifically created by law, *senatus consultum* or other means for Roman citizens. For example, a child born to a free woman and a slave father, who would be a slave according to the *SC Claudianum*, was only a slave in communities which had the same rule as Rome: elsewhere, according to *ius gentium*, this child was free.[28] However, the magistrate would not necessarily follow local law either. That is implicit in the episode of Pliny and the *threptoi*. If the Roman magistrate referred a case to a local judge or a court native to the province, then the judge would probably have been able to give a verdict in the light of local law.[29] At the highest level, that of the jurists who advised the emperor on his responses to submissions and appeals, it would not have been always the strict interpretation of Roman law which would have prevailed (though, once made, an imperial rescript was held to override any local law).[30]

It would be satisfying to think in terms of creative tension between differing systems of law. That indeed may have been what created the Roman law of Syria. However, it looks as if cases of real importance tended to be handled by Roman magistrates, and litigants may have often found Roman methods and legal principles more attractive. The Romans were certainly ready to create uniformity or near-uniformity when it was opportune, but could tolerate diversity. It is hard to judge which of these two solutions was the more satisfactory. Conformity with Roman law can be seen as the suppression of local identity and initiative. However, if we seek to investigate the degree of political and social coherence in the Roman empire, the acceptability of Roman law to the dependent peoples is an obvious yardstick.

10

ROMAN CITIZENSHIP

By the time of the Second Punic War the Romans had obtained a reputation among the Greeks for generosity with their citizenship, sufficient for Philip V of Macedon to commend their example to the Thessalian city of Larissa.[1] There were at that point two main forms of this generosity. One was the manumission of slaves into a condition of citizenship (even if there were some political and legal disadvantages in being an ex-slave). This will not be our concern here, but it is worth remarking that the Romans were concerned at more than one time in the Republic with foreigners who fraudulently took on the status of slaves for a short time in order to use manumission as a route into Roman citizenship.[2] The second was the full enfranchisement of whole Italian communities after a period in which they were citizens without the vote. These mass enfranchisements seem to have ceased in the first half of the second century BC (we hear of Fundi, Formiae and Arpinum getting full citizenship in 188), and there was then a lull (not without abortive proposals) until citizenship was offered to all Italians south of the river Po by the *lex Iulia* of 90 BC, passed at the end of the first year of the Social War.[3] The Romans also gave some communities and individuals Latin rights, which in effect meant having the private rights of a Roman citizen – including intermarriage with Romans, inheritance from them and the right to own Roman land – but no political rights except symbolic participation in Roman assemblies when present in Rome.[4] Originally these included the right to migrate to Rome and take up Roman citizenship at the expense of losing that of their original community, but this privilege was suppressed early in the second century BC at the request of the Latins themselves, concerned at their depopulation. If we believe Asconius, by 89 BC they had obtained the privilege of full Roman citizenship for their ex-magistrates.[5]

The evidence for the enfranchisement of individual free foreigners, whether from Italy or outside, is comparatively small in the Republican period. There are some Carthaginian deserters who profited from this in the Second Punic War. Under legislation which originated with C. Gracchus' *lex repetundarum* of 123–2 (see pp. 100–2), a non-Roman who had conducted a successful prosecution *de repetundis*, could, if he so wished, become a Roman, conferring this status on his sons and descendants after him. We know of two men of former Latin status from Tibur who benefited from this.[6] More numerous are those rewarded for military service, of which the most spectacular are the cohorts of Umbrian infantry given citizenship by C. Marius on the field of battle in the Cimbric War and the Spanish cavalry similarly rewarded by Cn. Pompeius Strabo in December 89 BC, this last procedure stated to be in accordance with the provisions of the *lex Iulia*.[7]

The particular distinguishing factor of a new citizen was his enrolment in a Roman voting district (*tribus*).[8] This *tribus*, written in abbreviation after the patronymic was an essential part of a Roman male's official name, for example, L. Cornelius L.f. Ouf(entina) Balbus. Without this distinguishing mark, a man with apparently Roman names might in fact only have Latin rights or be simply a foreigner who fancied this kind of nomenclature. (Some of the Spanish cavalrymen listed as receiving citizenship from Pompeius Strabo had already Roman-looking names before they received it.)

In the late Republic we have attested examples like those of L. Cornelius Balbus from Gades, who received citizenship from Pompey by virtue of the *lex Gellia Cornelia* of 73 BC, and Cn. Pompeius Theophanes. Other cases are deducible from the names carried by themselves or their successors.[9] There was a crescendo in the period of the civil wars and Caesar's dictatorship, with the protagonists ready to express their gratitude to partisans: hence C. Iulius Artemidorus, C. Iulius Hybreas and many others.[10] The area of Cisalpine Gaul north of the Po, which had as a whole been given Latin rights by Pompeius Strabo in 89 BC and already contained cities with Roman citizenship, was completely enfranchised at Caesar's instigation.[11] Julius Caesar conferred Latin rights on Sicily and Mark Antony increased this to full citizenship, but after the recovery of the island from Sextus Pompeius in 36 BC these privileges seem to have been forfeited.[12] Thus, while by Augustus' time Italy south of the Alps was unified under Roman citizenship, in the provinces, where a number of Roman citizens were to be found, this was not through enfranchisement of foreigners but the settlement of demobilised legionaries who were already Roman, especially in Gallia Narbonensis and Spain. Rewards for communities in the Greek world tended to take the form of the grant of a treaty or recognised autonomy, combined with freedom from tribute and corvées (see Chapter 3, pp. 36–40), and until Caesar's dictatorship privileges short of Roman citizenship were given to individuals such as the sea-captains honoured by a *senatus consultum* of 78 BC.[13]

Until Caesar's dictatorship acquisition of Roman citizenship was not regarded as compatible with the retention of another citizenship. This contrasted with the Greek practice of rewarding members of other cities with honorific citizenship grants. A compromise between the Roman and Greek principles can be seen in Pompey's rules for Bithynia, which allowed the Greek cities there to create honorary citizens from other cities, provided these people did not come from within Bithynia.[14] In 56 BC when speaking on behalf of Balbus, who had been accused of exercising Roman citizenship illegally, Cicero illustrated current laxness on duplication of citizenship by referring to men who had become members of the Areopagus after individual grants of Athenian status, but still claimed to be Romans.[15] Thus, when the Romans had offered their citizenship as a reward in the Republic, it would have been in the expectation that the men so honoured would become members of the Roman community. One of the Spaniards given citizenship by Pompeius Strabo has appeared again in an inscription – as a municipal magistrate of the town of Casinum (Cassino).[16] While it was hardly compulsory for a new citizen to acquire a house in Roman territory, it would have been attractive to do so, since in what had been his former domicile he was now legally a foreigner. By contrast, for those who wished to stay in their homes rewards of immunity from tribute, corvées and public service, together with access to Roman law, would have been more appropriate and valuable, as they presumably were for the sea-captains in the *senatus consultum* of 78 BC.

However, in the communities beyond the Po given Latin rights in 89 BC ex-magistrates became Roman citizens but remained in their original homes and probably were politically active there.[17] Their similarity to communities south of the Po, which by now were fully Roman, would have made this break with Roman tradition less glaring, and, of course, at the same time migrating Romans at Athens were seeking to be both Athenian and Roman at once. After Caesar's dictatorship it seems that the Roman had accepted the Greek principle that one could hold two citizenships at once: Cicero no longer finds it objectionable that Roman citizens are members of the Areopagus.[18] In the triumviral period we find attested grants of Roman citizenship in which it is clear that the recipients are expected to stay at home. Octavian's edict about veterans includes immunities from tribute, local taxes, public duties and corvées, including the billeting of Roman officials[19] – appropriate to men living among provincials, not as Romans on Roman territory. Citizenship is also extended to parents, something not found in the Gracchan *lex repetundarum* or the edict of Pompeius Strabo,[20] but which is an understandable extension, if the whole family was to continue living together in their old domicile. The same provision can be found in Octavian's edict granting Seleucus of Rhosos citizenship in accordance with the *lex Munatia Aemilia* of 42 BC.[21]

A further stage of development is revealed by Augustus' third Cyrene edict of 7–6 BC. The emperor here lays down that the grant of Roman citizenship should not constitute a dispensation from paying taxes and performing duties in a man's own city: it should not pluck him legally out of the community in which he lived.[22] Freedom from local taxation and *munera* is regarded here as a special privilege over and above that of Roman citizenship, not ordinarily granted in the past and, the implication is, unlikely to be granted in the future. Even those granted exemption from taxes are only to enjoy this on the property they held at the time, not on that acquired subsequently. Similarly, those members of Latin communities who acquired Roman citizenship by holding a magistracy there were not removed from public duties, as can be seen in the later Flavian municipal law.[23] The principle has become established that citizenship grants should not infringe on the laws of the local community. This is later illustrated in the donation to the chiefs of the Mauretanian Zegrenses (*salvo iure gentis*) on the *Tabula Banasitana* and ultimately in Caracalla's enactment of universal Roman citizenship.[24]

From the beginning there had been two aspects to Roman policy. The first was reward for services rendered, the second was the strategic incorporation of communities within the Roman body politic for the purpose of security or imperial expansion. Both aspects were not necesssarily present together when a community was made Roman. The people of Campania, for example, were first given citizenship without the vote and then full citizenship in spite of their record of hostility to Rome.[25] By the beginning of the Principate strategic incorporation had unified Italy under Rome and extended it to the Alps (after the Social War this had clearly not been a matter of rewarding the virtue of the rebels): Italy was thus visibly privileged over the rest of the Roman empire. Augustus, the leader of *tota Italia* against the decadent power of the east, surrounded by men with Italian origins, kept it so. Conveniently, there was no further political or military need for the large-scale incorporation of communities. What remained for the emperors down to AD 200 was the exploitation of selective privilege, which of course needed to be selective in order to be a real privilege. This might take one of two forms: the elevation of individuals or grants to communities of either colonial or municipal status.

Grants of full citizenship to communities are comparatively rarely attested. According to Dio, Caesar gave Roman citizenship to Gades (Cadiz) and Octavian did the same for Utica in Africa and Tingi (Tangier) in Mauretania.[26] There is also a considerable number of towns of Roman citizens (*oppida civium Romanorum*) recorded by the elder Pliny, especially in Spain, Africa and Dalmatia, which may represent communities composed in whole or part of enfranchised provincials, but it is hard to extract greater precision from the evidence.[27] Later, under Claudius, Volubilis in Mauretania was recompensed for its services in a war against the rebel Aedemon by the status of a *municipium* of Roman citizens, while Iol and Rusucurru received citizenship with colonial status.[28] However, we do not hear of communities directly promoted to Roman citizenship later. Instead, as we have seen in the discussion of local constitutions (Chapter 8), they were given the rank of *municipium* with Latin rights, from which further promotion to the status of Roman colony was possible. Many *municipia* were advanced to colonial status in the second century AD and an enhanced form of Latin status was invented (*Latium maius*), whereby all the local senators (*decuriones*) became automatically Roman citizens, not ex-magistrates alone (though, given the recruitment of magistrates in this period solely from the *decuriones*, it is hard to see that this would extend Roman citizenship greatly: it would merely have accelerated its receipt).[29] Such privileges had to be requested and were not necessarily granted by the emperor. They were available as a reward for co-operation, for example, in a military emergency, or as a more gratuitous display of imperial favour.

As for grants of citizenship to individuals, the rewards for special services made by the leaders in the civil wars, discussed earlier (p. 162) were a natural precedent for Augustus and his successors.

Services in peace were as deserving as those in war for men like
C. Iulius Xenon of Thyateira, Nicanor and Theon from Alexandria
and Pardalis from Sardis.[30] This honour may have fallen almost
automatically to high-priests of the imperial cult like Xenon, Hybreas
and the Gauls, C. Iulius Magnus, son of Eporedirix, and C. Iulius
Vercondaridubnus.[31] The German chiefs, Arminius and Segestes,
profited too – with differing consequences for Rome – as did a man
from Noricum.[32]

However, these impressive clusters of names are not testimony to
any wholesale generosity. Augustus apparently refused petitions from
his wife Livia on behalf of a Gaul on the ground that he did not wish
to cheapen Roman citizenship, granting the man immunity from
tribute instead.[33] Suetonius perhaps tries too hard to convince us that
Augustus was mean with Roman citizenship. How could he have
been, with so many partisans to reward? The implication of the third
Cyrene Edict is that he knew that there were a number of beneficiaries
of enfranchisements by himself or his father in the Cyrenean cities
(the inscription from Banasa refers to a catalogue (*commentarius*) of
those individually granted Roman citizenship from Augustus' time
onwards, so he should have been able to check his own awards).[34]
Nevertheless, the point remains that Roman status served to distinguish an elite in the non-Roman cities and to tie these as closely as
possible to the emperor.

This attitude does not substantially change under later emperors,
although there were variations in the quantity of individual awards
depending on the atitude of the emperor and the force of the claims
that could be made on him. Claudius was accused in Seneca's
Apocolocyntosis of wanting to see all Gauls, Spaniards and Britons in
togas. It is hard to assess fairly the policy which provoked this
reaction, if policy indeed there was. Claudius himself in the speech of
AD 47 to the senate about the expansion of its own catchment area
claims that Augustus and Tiberius wanted to see the flower of colonies
and *municipia* everywhere in the senate, but, whether truthful or
disingenuous, this is not a statement about enlarging the elite of
Roman citizens in the provinces but about admitting existing
members of it to the senate on as broad a basis as possible.[35] The grant
of Roman status to Volubilis was spectacular, because out of the
ordinary, but arguably a deserved reward for special services, for
which precedents could be found.[36] It is plausible that it was Claudius
who devised the right of demobilised auxiliary soldiers to obtain
Roman citizenship for themselves, their wives and children after their

discharge. This may have been motivated as much by the need to stimulate recruitment of auxiliaries as by the desire to spread Roman citizenship among the non-Roman peoples of the empire.[37] A last and important piece of evidence is the number of notables from the provinces who took the names Tiberius Claudius, not all of whom can be certainly assumed to owe their citizenship to Claudius (on our evidence no enfranchised provincial took his name from Nero).[38] However, these are precisely the sort of people that we would have expected an emperor to honour as a personal choice – Claudius' doctor from Cos together with his relatives, another doctor, an Alexandrian friend, political leaders and men of culture from Greek provinces.[39] More indicative of Claudius' general attitude is his recorded hostility to those proved to have usurped citizenship, who were executed on the Esquiline.[40]

Even if Claudius gave an impression to his contemporaries that he was generous with citizenship – and much of this may have sprung from his own insecurity and his desire to reward anyone who had been helpful to him – there was no major change in imperial policy then or later towards grants to individuals. Such grants had the object of binding the loyalty of important men in the empire not only to Rome as a whole but to the imperial house. It was also useful to single out these men as an object-lesson and a focus of attention in their own communities. These men were friends of Caesar; they and their descendants were obvious choices for embassies to the emperor and for mediation with governors and other Roman officials. Granting them citizenship does not seem to have been a contribution to a policy of raising the status of provincials: rather, they formed channels of communication with the allies for emperors and other Roman authorities. As such, they were an important part of the system of patronage which created and sustained the ruling class throughout the empire, making it manageable and useful in the service of the emperor. The final integration of the free members of communities throughout the empire in Roman citizenship by Caracalla was a monstrous piece of patronage, whose purpose may have been to create more integration and uniformity or, as Dio alleges, to increase revenues from the empire.[41] In any event it constituted a spending-spree which exhausted for the emperors one of their most useful ways of obtaining and publicly acknowledging devotion.

11

THE WORKINGS OF PATRONAGE

The importance of patronage in Roman society is a commonplace of modern historiography, though one which has been subjected recently to close analysis and criticism.[1] It is not the place here to discuss how far the domestic politics of the Republic were determined by patronage or how important it was for individuals seeking official promotion under the Principate. We are dealing with patronage as a link, or series of links, between the rulers of the empire and the ruled. It was shown in the account of the structure of the empire how both free and subjected allies under the Republic used Roman patrons in order to further their claims at Rome, whether this was preparatory to an appearance in the senate or to the mounting of a prosecution in the forum.[2] Cicero's quaestorship in Sicily made him a prime candidate for the task of prosecuting Verres and his success secured him a position as one of the province's patrons. However, such patronage was rarely exclusive: Cicero joined the Claudii Marcelli, descendants of the man who recaptured Syracuse for Rome in the second Punic War, and Pompey, who had made friends there during his operations against the Marians. His opponent P. Clodius claimed later to be joining the number.[3]

Nor were attachments necessarily secure. Transpadane Gaul was indebted to Pompey's father, Cn. Pompeius Strabo, for its acquisition of Latin rights and Pompey continued to have some influence there. However, from 69 BC onwards Caesar had agitated in favour of full citizenship for the area, and he built on this foundation of goodwill during his proconsulship of Gaul to the extent that there were no Pompeians visible in 49 when he crossed the Rubicon, and the region's loyalty was confirmed by the long-awaited grant of citizenship that same year.[4] Most Pompeian influence in southern Transalpine Gaul (Narbonensis) had also been eclipsed, except in the old Greek colony of Massilia, but the effect of Pompey's long stay in Spain in the 70s and the friends he had made there stood him and his sons in good stead during the civil wars.[5]

Patronage on a grand scale like this was monopolised by the emperors. However, there was a tradition of formal pacts between cities and patrons, that can be glimpsed in Italy in Republican times and is well attested in Italy, Spain and Africa under the Principate. One fragmentary inscription from Fundi has been recorded, belonging to the third or late second century BC, in which the *praefectura* put itself in the *fides* (good faith, protection) of a patron officially, that is, by decree of its local senate.[6] That this had been a common practice among communities in Italy is suggested by the rules for the adoption of patrons inserted into municipal legislation. Chapter 97 of the Caesarian *lex Ursonensis* forbids the adoption of a patron, other than the founder of the colony or the man who presided over the allocation of its land and their descendants, except by secret ballot in the local senate with a quorum of fifty members. This, like other features of the *lex Ursonensis* (see pp. 137–9), is likely to be a tralatician provision from charters created for Italian colonies. Later chapters (130 and 131) apparently substitute for this two new provisions, one about adoption of patrons and the other about the conclusion of *hospitium* (public guest-friendship). A quorum of three-quarters of the members is required in the senate for the secret ballot and the choice is confined to private citizens without *imperium* living in Italy. There is no longer any mention of the founder or land-commissioner, presumably because the time when the colony could have decided whether to make them and their descendants patrons was now past. In the Flavian municipal law (ch. 61) there is simply a rule requiring a two-thirds majority in the local senate for their election.

Taken by itself, this evidence might suggest that Rome exported the tradition of making formal guest-friendship and patronage links from Italy to Roman and Italian communities in the provinces. However, we also have to consider twenty-eight surviving records on bronze of such agreements from the provinces – ten from Hispania Tarraconensis, three from Baetica, five from Mauretania, eight from the province of Africa, one from Sardinia and one from Thrace.[7] In the majority of these the transaction is described as a reciprocal agreement.[8] *Hospitium* is clearly an important and separate notion in about half of them and three tablets refer to *hospitium* alone.[9] It is therefore arguable that there was a tradition in some provinces of a more equal relationship between communities and respected outside parties, whether individuals or communities.[10] This is the more probable in that we find in Hispania Tarraconensis agreements between a community and an individual who is not Roman.[11] We have no other evidence for a native tradition of guest-friendship and patron–client relationship in Spain, but there clearly was one in Gaul, albeit a one-sided one. Caesar attests the existence there of patronage both by individuals of their inferiors and by one tribe of another, while the ethnographic fragments of Poseidonius suggest a system of patronage between the leading chiefs and less exalted aristocrats.[12] Although we have no tablets recording patronage from Gaul, it is clear that Roman colonies and other towns adopted patrons.[13]

No bronze tablets of this kind survive from the Greek world (the single example east of the Adriatic is from a Roman colony in Thrace). This is not to say the Greek colonies did not have patrons, only that the same formalities do not seem to have been used. An early reference is in the decree of Abdera honouring their embassy to Rome, which states that they had solicited the assistance of the patron of their community.[14] In the First Mithridatic War the city of Aphrodisias sent an embassy to the proconsul Q. Oppius, assuring him of their military support. The embassy also asked him to be their patron, and in his reply he signified his acceptance of this position as well as his intention to inform the senate and people of their services to Rome and to give them general assistance.[15] It has recently been argued that some recorded patrons under the Republic attained this status through being chosen as a *patronus* in court to assist in the conduct of a prosecution *de repetundis* (cf. pp. 99–104).[16] In any case there may well have been more practical necessity than tradition in the development of the institution in the Greek east. 'Patrons' are attested in numerous inscribed dedications,[17] but the honorific title might vary: a person could also be declared a benefactor of the city,[18] and this title, whether or not it was linked, as it often was, with that of patron, effectively placed the honorand in a position of patronage.

The practical value to the peoples of the empire of the formal creation of patron–client links will have varied with political developments at Rome. Under the Republic, whenever a community sent an embassy to the senate with pleas or complaints, it may well have thought it especially desirable to have on its side Roman senators, who could guide the delegation through technicalities of procedure, secure hearings in the senate and induce other senators to take a favourable view of the community's submissions. The senators for their part might be content with the prestige conferred by being chosen, but they could also exploit the relationship to their advantage, when they or their relatives or friends happened to be visiting the province. During the civil wars the community needed influence with the commanders of the faction currently victorious; the mere possession of patrons in the senate was of comparatively little value. Conversely, the community itself might be exploited as a base or source of supplies in a military coup.[19] This is presumably the explanation of the chapter later added to the *lex Ursonensis* limiting the choice of patrons to those who were private citizens in Italy without *imperium*.

Under the Principate the importance of friends in high places continued, as Plutarch pointed out (though his examples were not from the Principate – Scipio Aemilianus and Polybius, Caesar and Arius).[20] The advantages to patrons returned to the Republican level, except when there was again civil war. Although the strict enforcement of the *lex Iulia repetundarum* would have made it dangerous for a visitor to a province to recover the material rewards which might otherwise have been a natural response to patronage from the relevant communities, the law does not seem to have changed practices or attitudes. Iulius Bassus, who had made friends in Bithynia as quaestor, seems to have been surprised that the gifts he received from them when he returned as proconsul led to a prosecution – and the younger Pliny sympathised with him.[21]

As for the provincial communities themselves, the change in criteria for selecting a patron, which commenced during the civil wars, was perpetuated under monarchy. An ordinary senator, even a *consularis*, was not so valuable as a guide, counsellor and friend in a system where most requests and appeals went in the first instance to the emperor and where the *concilium provinciae* had become important as a springboard for access to him. Instead it was desirable to forge links with those who had access to the emperor. This was foreshadowed under the triumvirate: M. Antonius, when writing to the Guild of Victors in Sacred Contests and Crown-Winners, refers to the intercession of his trainer M. Antonius Artemidorus; Octavian claims that he is eager to give privileges to Aphrodisias because of his freedman C. Iulius Zoilus.[22] In the same vein the emperor Claudius tells the citizens of Alexandria of the efforts of Ti. Claudius Balbillus and Archibius on their behalf.[23]

Another sort of patron, who offered special advantages, was a *patronus* in the special sense of court orator. We have already seen that the route from pleading to permanent patronage was first laid down under the Republic. The same connection can be seen, when the Baeticans want Pliny to be their *patronus* (advocate), pleading the bond of his previously existing *patrocinium*.[24] Fronto had friends in Cilicia because he had been a regular advocate for the province. 'What', says the character Aper in Tacitus' *Dialogue about Orators*, 'is more secure than to exercise that art through which you can always have arms to protect your friends, lend aid to foreigners and bring safety to those in peril . . . ?'[25]

There was, however, no longer any special magic about senatorial oratory as a medium for provincial pleas. Instead of an advocate drawn from the elite of Rome, a community might find better value in one of their own people who was a friend of the emperor. Under Augustus we hear of Athenodorus of Tarsus and Arius of Alexandria.[26] These learned men are the outriders of a cavalcade of sophists who pass successively through the court-history of the Roman empire, adding lustre to their art and securing desirable favours for their home city.[27] Under Claudius there was Balbillus of Alexandria, under Hadrian Dionysius of Miletus. Dio of Prusa's maternal grandfather and grandmother got Roman citizenship from an emperor and thus placed him among those who might be able to secure access to the emperor's ears. With this background and his own oratorical powers, Dio fell foul of Domitian on a visit to Rome and then, after his exile, was sent by his city on an embassy to his old friend Nerva, which was unfortunately abortive, though it brought no harsh consequences to himself. Trajan is said to have placed him in his golden car with the words, 'I do not know what you are saying, but I love you as myself.'[28] The story may be *ben trovato* but it illustrates the status that a sophist like Dio might possess.

Another sophist was more successful with Domitian: Scopelian of Smyrna led a delegation of the *koinon* (provincial assembly) of the cities of Asia to protest about Domitian's edict forbidding the planting of vines in Asia. His compatriot Polemo obtained a gift of 10 million drachmai from Hadrian for the rebuilding of Smyrna.[29] There were also men like Q. Popilius Python from Beroea in Macedonia, who relied more on their wealth and connections. We do not know wherein lay the influence of Q. Cornelius Zosimus, a *sevir Augustalis* of the colony of Arelate (Arles), but the inhabitants of a nearby parish (*pagus*) thanked him for conveying a complaint of theirs to Antoninus Pius; similarly, Tergeste (Trieste) passed a motion in honour of a senator from that city, L. Fabius Severus, who had represented it before the emperor.[30]

Patrons, in addition to assisting cities, might work for individuals. Voconius Romanus was an eminent Spaniard, who had become priest of the imperial cult in his province. The younger Pliny had been educated with him and prided himself on his services to him since that time: he ensured that Voconius acquired equestrian status from Trajan and the privilege normally associated with having three children (*ius trium liberorum*) and he is found begging an imperial legate called Priscus to give Voconius a position on his staff. He also passed on a letter from Romanus to the emperor's wife, Plotina.[31] A similar relationship is implied by Fronto's letter to the proconsul Lollianus Avitus on behalf of Licinius Montanus, whose origin was Fronto's own native Cirta and was Fronto's guest on his visits to Rome. Further inferences may be made about the identity of certain friends of Fronto with men known to have obtained the consulship, a position which for men other than imperial protégés was only attainable through the recommendation of powerful senators.[32]

The life of Fronto illustrates another phenomenon – the entry of provincials into the highest political and social ranks at Rome. At the time when the emperor Claudius urged the admission to the senate of Gauls from among the Aedui, there already were, or had been, leading senators from Gallia Narbonensis. These included Domitius Afer, Valerius Asiaticus and Agricola's father Julius Graecinus. (Shortly after this speech of Claudius' senators from Narbonensis were given permission to leave Italy to visit their properties in the province.)[33] Once a city had seen one of its own sons become consul (Fronto was suffect in AD 143, the year that the Athenian Ti. Claudius Atticus Herodes was ordinary consul), the need for patrons from Rome was less serious, though it must be remembered that a promoted provincial or his family might not continue in imperial favour. A man who had succeeded in an official career might combine the obtaining of imperial favours for his city with the exercise of the wealth and influence he had gained himself. C. Iulius Demosthenes from Oenoanda had been raised to equestrian status and held a series of military posts as prefect and tribune of the soldiers under Trajan before moving on to a procuratorship in Sicily. After contributing various public buildings to Oenoanda, he secured in AD 124 Hadrian's approval for the founding of a music festival in his home town, to be financed from a fund of 15,000 *denarii* provided by himself – one which in its final form was also to have elements of the imperial cult. The decree of the Termessians at Oenoanda welcoming this proposal appropriately terms him 'a most distinguished man and leading man of the province, a friend of the emperors and recognised by them through the finest achievements'.[34]

The general aims pursued by patrons and clients in the relationship between the governing circles of the empire and their subjects do not radically change with the transition from Republic to Principate. However, there is a new focus, as the emperor first complements and tends to replace the senate as the source of benefits, and consequently new criteria arise for choosing a useful patron. In addition, the vertical connections between ruler and ruled become much more complex with both the elevation of provincials into the senate or the emperor's service and the exploitation of local men as ambassadors to the emperor. The texture of these relationships is dense, but the basic material, that of personal acquaintance and affection, is in principle impermanent. The evidence of contacts between Rome and the provinces gives a powerful impression of the unity of the empire, where it exists, but we cannot with any certainty extrapolate from this evidence to other areas, for which such documentation is weak or non-existent.

Ultimately, if there were no patron–client links to exploit, a community would have been obliged either to rely on its official superior or to take direct action. Let me take two pieces of evidence from beyond my designated period. The farmers of the *saltus Burunitanus* appealed to the emperor Commodus against the contractors who managed this imperial estate, with some aid from the supervising procurator Lurius Lucullus. Later, the villagers of Scaptopara presented their petition to Gordian III through a villager who happened to be a veteran of the praetorian cohorts.[35] Those who lived in villages or on imperial estates were unlikely to acquire the assistance and patronage available to those in towns, especially to the towns in the more urbanised areas of the empire. Yet, even a well-connected region might suffer if emperors were uninterested and few representatives of the locality existed in governing circles at Rome. Under the Republic, thanks to the continuity of the senate and the permanence of certain noble families, the patronage of the Scipiones or Claudii Marcelli over a city or province could last for centuries; no equivalent to this could be guaranteed under the Principate.

12

PUBLICITY, THEATRE AND CULT

The evidence considered in the last four chapters has tended to suggest that in the empire of the first two centuries AD the Roman presence and Roman influence was very uneven. Strong links between rulers and ruled might be forged permanently through the adoption of Roman local constitutions and law and rather less permanently through the personal relationships of patronage and the accessibility of the emperor to leading provincials. However, although the documented Roman connections are striking, they must be seen against a background of an empire where for the most part the impact of central authority was intermittent and localised and a great deal of cultural diversity persisted. We have evidence for the survival of non-Roman local constitutions and legal rules. The very nature of the grant of Roman citizenship reveals it as a special privilege. Patronage and personal contact with the emperor depended on human circumstances which could not be infinitely reproduced. It is important, therefore, to consider factors which contributed to a perception of Roman authority and of the congruence of the empire, which reached outside the circle of provincials with strong political or social ties to Rome.

From the very beginning of Rome's overseas empire, her subjects would have been conscious of the *fasces*. They might have found it hard to visualise the consuls and the senate at Rome,[1] but the magistrate abroad seated on his tribunal, with the Roman symbols of power about him and a glint of legionary armour in the background, was a powerful image which would have impressed even those who could not understand the niceties of *deditiones* and the restorations of autonomy. They could not pursue their local concerns without thought for what lay beyond. This consciousness was magnified under the Principate by its focus on a single monarch, who loomed behind the provincial governor or the dynast in the allied kingdom. The ordinary people of Judaea in the first century AD knew of the ultimate authority of Caesar and that it was his head on the money that they payed him in tribute.[2]

Furthermore, from an early point in their period of overseas expansion we find both Roman actions and responses by others to Roman power (some orchestrated, some apparently unsolicited), which served in various ways to bring home the fact of Roman domination but at the same time to present it in the most acceptable form possible. It was Roman contact with Greek civilisation that seems to have stimulated this process first. Flamininus' dramatic announcement of the freedom of Greece at the Isthmian games of 196 BC is a fine example of the extraction of maximum publicity from a political act.[3] Rome's public credit did not, however, merely rest on her being a liberator: as the praetor Messalla remarked in his letter to Teos, the Romans thought that their phenomenal success was a reward for their piety towards the gods and this piety is stressed by another praetor in a letter to Delphi.[4] About this time or a little earlier a friend of Rome on Chios was honoured for having engraved a genealogy of Romulus and Remus on a commemorative stone and having portrayed myths from Roman history on shields given as prizes in games in honour of Rome.[5]

This last action must be fitted into the wider context of the Roman creation of their own history – a process which seems to have been equally designed to satisfy their own pride and curiosity and to impress and enlighten foreigners. The tradition of the foundation of Rome by Aeneas was an ancient one in the Greek world, attested in Hellanicus' work in the fifth century BC and arguably beginning earlier.[6] There is evidence that the Romans themselves knew the Aeneas legend by the fourth century BC, while at the same time being attached to their local myth of Romulus and Remus, which was illustrated by the placing of statues of the twins and the wolf under the fig-tree of Rumina in the last years of the century.[7] Early attempts to make the twins grandchildren of Aeneas could not stand up in the critical light of Hellenistic scholarship and chronography. Hence about 200 BC, between the publication dates of the epics of Naevius and Ennius, the story of the kings of Alba Longa conveniently emerged – perhaps an invention of Rome's earliest historian Fabius Pictor, but also found in the chronographer Diocles of Peparethos.[8] It is possible that the friend of Rome on Chios had managed to publicise this revised standard version. What was at stake was not merely intellectual respectability for the stories of Rome's origins but their secure integration into Greek mythography, so that they could be naturally introduced in Greek drama and poetry. It is for this reason that Lycophron's *Alexandra* – for whose date it is hard to find sound objective criteria – would fit excellently into the early decades of the second century BC. With Aeneas established as the founder of Rome, Cassandra could be made to prophesy the ultimate revenge for the wrongs inflicted on the Trojans by the Greeks, that the Trojans' Roman descendants were about to accomplish.[9] Appropriately, in the first decade of the second century Argos, Sparta and Macedonia felt the strength of Roman arms. For reasons which we will shortly see, it is highly unlikely that the *Alexandra* was the last Greek drama in which the Romans were mentioned.

Another mode of glorification of Rome, which did not necessarily owe anything to the literary stabilisation of the origins of Rome, was the praise-song. Flamininus was honoured at Chalcis in a paean, whose last verse is preserved by Plutarch (he did not retail the whole paean because of its length):

> We worship the good faith [*pistis* = *fides*] of the Romans, the most sought in prayer for protection through oaths. Sing, maidens, of great Zeus and Rome and Titus and with him the good faith of the Romans. Hail, Paean. Hail, Titus our saviour.[10]

Rome's military might was also hymned by an otherwise unknown poetess, Melinno. In this work Rome was the offspring of Arês (Mars) whose own progeny were the finest spearmen; Rome's home was an untroubled Olympus on earth. For Rome alone had been granted by Fate the royal glory of uninterrupted empire, which was even proof against the changes and destruction wrought by time.[11] Such poems had prose equivalents: the Delphians voted the honour of *proxenia* to a history writer who had read publicly encomia about the Romans, 'the common benefactors of Greece'.[12] This description of the Romans first appears in 182 and is frequent in Greece during the second century BC, though instances taper off in the late Republic and ultimately the title is taken over by Julius Caesar and the emperors.[13]

Hymns, encomia and plays required public occasions for their performance. Chalcis' paean to Flamininus was sung at a festival. We also hear of festivals in Flamininus' honour (Titia) at Argos and Gytheion.[14] Other Roman commanders were to have festivals in their honour elsewhere; the Marcellia and Verria at Syracuse, the Mucia and Luculleia in Asia.[15] More important and widespread were the festivals of Greek cities in honour of Rome itself, Romaia, for which in some cases an early origin is attested. We have already noticed the festival in honour of Rome at Chios; Romaia are in evidence at Delos in 167–6, at Araxa in Lycia probably by 150, at Athens by 150, while an early date is plausible for the Romaia at Chalcis. We find this festival sometimes linked to another local festival – Pythaia and Romaia at Megara; Dia, Aianteia and Romaia at Opus in Locris; Poseidaia and Romaia at Antigoneia (Mantinea).[16]

Two features of these festivals were to have lasting importance: the emergence of Roma as a figure of cult and Roman concern for the performers, on whose work the quality of festivals depended. Actors, singers and musicians in the Greek world had organised themselves into professional associations since the early third century BC: they called themselves *koina* or *synodoi* of the Dionysiac Artists. There were four associations related to the location of festivals, one based on the Isthmia and Nemea, one in Athens, one in Egypt and Cyprus and one in Ionia and the Hellespont.[17] The performers in Egypt and Cyprus combined the cult of Dionysus with that of the reigning Ptolemies, as Athenaeus' account of Ptolemy Philadelphus' Dionysiac procession shows (Alexander the Great, too, had made great use of the performers, though not, as far as we know, to develop a cult of himself).[18]

The Ionia–Hellespont association was given a headquarters on Teos in the third century, whose status was confirmed by Antiochus III in 204–3, at the time when he and his wife Laodice were given a share in the cult and temple of Dionysus at Teos (the Dionysiac Artists would surely have been involved in the celebrations there).[19] Eumenes II, when he took over the dominance of this city, linked the Dionysiac Artists to his own royal cult of Dionysus Kathêgêmon at Pergamum.[20] It was a natural development for the Dionysiac Artists in Asia to take over the cult of Rome. In fact on a stone found at Elaea (which should relate to this city, although it has often been assumed to relate to Pergamum by scholars in the past), there is a decree concerning a treaty with Rome of *c.* 130 BC, in which are mentioned both the artists devoted to Dionysus Kathêgêmôn and sacrifices to Roma among other deities.[21]

In Greece, although the artists had sung in praise of Aratus, after he died,[22] there had been no such tradition in relation to the Macedonian kings. The celebration of a living man like Flamininus was unusual, the adoption of a new goddess like Roma even more so. However, as we have seen, Romaia were founded, and it is striking to see the care lavished by the Romans on the Dionysiac Artists themselves. Within a year of the destruction of Corinth measures were being taken to protect the artists in the Peloponnese, where the association based on the Isthmia and Nemea may have felt itself specially threatened (a further fragmentary letter of a proconsul to this association has been found at Thebes).[23] Moreover, an enormous dossier engraved at Delphi reveals how the Romans later promoted the interests of the Athenian association, when it appears to have been claiming that it was being excluded from participation in festivals with the Isthmia–Nemea group. In spite of its successful participation in the Pythia and the recognition of its privileges by Delphi, the Athenian group found itself in a bitter quarrel with its Isthmian–Nemean rivals, which led to two Roman *senatus consulta* and, in between these, a hearing and temporary reconciliation before the governor of Macedonia at Pella.[24] The labour expended by the senate and Roman magistrates and the close contacts that developed between them and representatives of the artists are evidence of Roman concern for good relations with them. This concern cannot have been entirely disinterested.

The celebration of Roma took a more permanent form than festivals. The people of Smyrna were to claim in Tiberius' reign that they had set up the first temple to Roma in the consulship of Cato (195 BC), a claim which does not seem to have been contested by other Asiatic cities.[25] However, a number of other cities were not far behind Smyrna in such foundations. An embassy to Rome from Alabanda in 170 BC could point to an existing shrine to *urbs Roma*, and there are also a number of inscriptions attesting shrines or cult-statues of Roma, which can plausibly be dated to the period before 133 BC – the date of the creation of the province of Asia.[26] Cibyra in Lycia had a treaty with Rome, which, according to the text, was engraved on the base of the statue of Roma.[27] Aphrodisias with Plarasa made a treaty with Cibyra and Tabae, that was to be based *inter alia* on doing nothing against the Romans or each other and was sworn by Zeus Philios (Zeus of Friendship), Homonoia (Concord) and Thea Romê (the goddess Roma).[28] The stone honouring Orthagoras of Araxa shows that the Lycians held a five-yearly festival to Thea Romê Epiphanês (Appearing at the Right Time).[29] An inscription at the Hêraion on Samos regarding territorial reorganisation at Antioch-on-the-Maeander provides that offences should be punished by a fine paid to the goddess Romê at Antioch.[30] Thus we are not dealing here merely with celebrations or portable cult-images, but shrines with permanent cult-images and funds to support them.

There is a related phenomenon in the city of Rome itself. A series of dedications has been found on blocks of stone, which seem to belong to a single monument on the Capitol, perhaps a wall, and probably once had pegs on which wreaths could be hung.[31] On the most plausible interpretation, the monument was constructed in the Sullan era, but earlier dedications were re-engraved on it before it was used for new ones.[32] The dedications are from Asiatic peoples and kings to the *populus Romanus*, whose name is sometimes joined with that of Jupiter Capitolinus or Jupiter Optimus Maximus. To judge from the texts, these were marks of genuine gratitude for special favours. For example, the Lycians twice thank the Roman people for their recovery of their ancestral *dêmokratia* (the first occasion was probably their liberation from the power of Rhodes and the second after the end of the Roman war with Aristonicus); the Ephesians thank the Romans for their liberty, the people of Laodicea-on-the-Lycus for their security.[33] A different religious language was being used at Rome to that found in the cities themselves, but what is being enacted is closely akin. It was inappropriate to make Roma a goddess at Rome; Jupiter Optimus Maximus protected Rome, as Roma protected the Asiatic cities. However, we should not make the dedications to the Roman people at Rome a reason for devaluing the creation of shrines to Rome in Asia. If anything, the shrines in Asia show how seriously we should take the dedications at Rome.

So many pages have been devoted in recent literature to the interpretation of ruler-cult in antiquity that it would be otiose to discuss this at length.[34] If we leave aside any speculations by Alexander the Great about his own relationship to divinity (even if he really did believe that he was a god, it was not this that affected later generations), the honours given to Hellenistic kings in the form of cult are best ascribed to gratitude, hope of fresh favours and the representation of their superior power in a way that offended neither those who gave, nor those who received such honours.[35] When the power of Rome overshadowed that of the kings, it was a natural step to honour her commanders and the city itself in similar ways. After a few early examples, such as that of Titus Flamininus discussed above, the celebration by cult of individual Roman magistrates became common from *c.* 100 BC onwards.[36] By the late Republic it was considered so natural for a Roman magistrate abroad to have a temple in his honour, that under the *lex Cornelia de repetundis* (of 81–80 BC) those magistrates who took money for this purpose from provincials were exempted from the penalties of the law. Cicero himself and his brother Quintus might have had a shrine constructed for them in Asia; so might Cicero himself in Cilicia.[37] We have no epigraphic evidence of shrines dedicated solely to a Roman magistrate and it may be that what the *lex Cornelia* envisaged was in fact a temple to Rome commemorating the achievement of the man in question.[38] In any case, against this background the form of ruler-cult that developed for Julius Caesar and his successors is in principle nothing surprising. However, we cannot do justice to its extent and ramifications by simply referring to tradition: there were other forces at work.

After Pharsalus, temples were set up to Caesar in cities in the east and, more remarkable, in some of them he was given the title *theos*. At Ephesus he was *theos epiphanês*, a god who had manifested power to assist his worshippers, and *sotêr* (saviour) of humanity;[39] at Alexandria he received divine honours as Caesar Epibatêrios (Caesar of the Happy Landing). He commenced the building of a shrine (Caesareum) to himself both at Alexandria and Antioch-on-the-Orontes, the second of which had statues not only of himself but of Dea Roma.[40] Whether Caesar was actually voted divine honours and a priesthood at Rome in his lifetime, as Dio suggests, is a problem beyond the scope of this book: conceivably, there was a *senatus consultum* to that effect. What is certain is that a law was passed in a Roman assembly establishing a priesthood and making provisions for Caesar's cult before the composition of Cicero's Second Philippic in autumn 44 BC. A fragment of this is preserved in an inscription from Ephesus.[41]

This last text illustrates how the news of the cult of Divus Iulius was transmitted to the provinces. Its establishment there is attested in a number of ways. A bronze coin from either Parium or Lampsacus has Caesar's head on the obverse and on the reverse a priest ploughing with oxen; another bronze coin of the triumviral period from Thessalonica, with Octavian's head on the obverse and Caesar's on the reverse, qualifies Caesar with the term *theos*.[42] In the west the emergence of the cult is shown by two contrasting pieces of evidence from colonies. The law given to the colony of Urso, founded according to Caesar's instructions in the aftermath of his death, provides for the cult of Caesar's divine ancestor Venus (it was named *colonia Genetiva*), but has no mention of any cult of Caesar himself. On the other hand, the Caesarian colony at Lugdunum, founded by L. Munatius Plancus, issued coins with the heads of Caesar and Octavian and the legend, '*Divi Iuli, Imp.Caesar. Divi.f., Copia*'; the legend '*Divus Iulius*' also accompanies Caesar's head on the obverse of a coin from Arelate (Arles).[43] There is of course nothing surprising in the extension of a cult founded at Rome to colonies, which were communities of Roman citizens in the provinces. Nevertheless, this did mean that there was a geographical expansion of the cult in the west, parallel to that in the east.

During the triumviral period Octavian contented himself with being son of the divinised Caesar, but he paraded this status to the extent of making it part of his titulature from *c.* 38 BC onwards.[44] In 41 BC Marcus Antonius was acclaimed, according to Plutarch, as Dionysos Charidotês and Meilichios (Joygiver and Gracious) in Asia, especially at Ephesus. He was later called New Dionysus at Athens, where he and his wife Octavia were 'divine benefactors' (*theoi euergetai*).[45] Before his war with Octavian he assembled all the Dionysiac artists on Samos for a festival and subsequently gave them Priene as a home. In Egypt, as Cleopatra's consort, he would have been Osiris, the equivalent to Dionysus; a stone set up by a *parasitos* of his commemorated him as 'great, unconquered god'. The story of the Dionysiac rout that was heard leaving him at night during his last days at Alexandria is another testimony to the contemporary importance of this identification.[46]

His victor, Octavian, could have simply taken over this kind of cult with his other spoils from the east. In Egypt he stepped into the place of the divinised rulers and was called *theos* there from 30 BC onwards in a seemingly automatic and casual way. He was later identified with Zeus Eleutherios (the Liberator).[47] Elsewhere he moved more deliberately and in conjunction with his family. In 29 BC the Romans in Bithynia and Asia were each permitted to have two provincial cults – of Roma and Divus Iulius at Nicaea and Ephesus respectively and of Roma and Augustus at Nicomedia and Pergamum. Two years later Augustus himself received a cult at Ephesus.[48] We hear of a number of other shrines or temples to either Augustus or to Roma and Augustus.[49] At Halicarnassus he was celebrated at the shrine of Roma and Augustus as 'the outstanding gift to men made by the everlasting nature of everything, father of the goddess Roma his fatherland, and the ancestral Zeus and saviour of the human race'.[50] Hence his divinity was made to transcend that of Roma and he took the place of the city and its people as the benefactor of the generality of men. Similar sentiments are shown in the decree of the provincial council of Asia of 9 BC, drawn up according to the proposal of the proconsul Paullus Fabius Maximus, which established a new calendar year beginning on Augustus' birthday, 23 September: the birthday could be rightly regarded as the beginning of everything, since it was the end of every individual's regret that he had been born; Augustus' birthday began the good news (*euangelia*).[51] When the people of Paphlagonia and the Roman businessmen resident there took an oath of loyalty to Augustus in 3 BC, Augustus was one of the divinities by which they took the oath. Equally fervent celebrations were made of his wife and descendants, though without the same extravagance of language.[52]

The western provinces on the whole followed the pattern of Rome, where Augustus did not appear as a god in his lifetime but his *genius* and *numen*, the divine spirit in him inherited from his ancestors, were the subject of cult. For instance, the old colony of Narbo (Narbonne) fulfilled the vow of an altar to his *numen* in AD 12–13.[53] It is interesting that the cult was proposed on account of a specific service that he had done the city by bringing together the courts of the senate and plebs there.[54] In Africa there are *flamines* and other evidence for the cult of Augustus in his lifetime, while in Spain the altar to Augustus at Tarraco was famous thanks to the emperor's joke about the appearance of a palm shoot there.[55] One of the grandest shrines was the altar to Rome and Augustus at Lugdunum, founded next to the confluence of the Rhine and Saône by Augustus' stepson Drusus. This was intended for the provincial council of the sixty-four communities belonging to the three Gallic provinces conquered by Julius Caesar and it became the focus of a cult-centre, including a theatre which also functioned as a political meeting-place.[56] A similar altar was placed at Ara Ubiorum for the Germans then regarded as permanent subjects of Rome.[57]

When Augustus finally died, the senate's decree that he should receive a temple at Rome as a god seems to have been passed with the minimum of trouble.[58] The following year the Spaniards were allowed to construct a temple to Augustus at Tarraco and this was then a model for the rest of the empire.[59] Augustus' wife Livia had already received divine honours in his lifetime, as had his grandsons C. and L. Caesar and Agrippa Postumus, as well as their father M. Agrippa.[60] Under Tiberius such honours to living members of the imperial family continued, while cults of Augustus and Livia were combined in that of the Augusti; at the same time there developed a general cult of the imperial household as the *domus divina*.[61] Tiberius himself might declare his reluctance to receive divine honours, but in practice even he received shrines and cult in his lifetime – at Smyrna and in Lycia, Cyprus, Judaea and Africa.[62]

The imperial cult was not forced on a reluctant empire. As we have seen, requests were made to the emperor to initiate a cult: indeed, on some occasions we may suspect that cults were begun without permission. The extravagant language of decrees, strained though it may appear, does not seem to have been dictated from above. On the other hand, it is appropriate to speak of orchestration. Cults were allocated to cities in Asia and Bithynia by Augustus in 29 BC and the general form, which they were to take at each place, was prescribed. The proconsul of Asia got the credit for inventing the later calendar-reform, but we may wonder if the original idea was his. In the west the establishment of the cult of the *numen Augusti* suggests careful control by the emperor of the inclinations of his subjects. Furthermore, it is clear that political capital is derived from the imperial cult. It is drawn into the oaths of loyalty required from subjects.[63] In the shrines of legionary headquarters images of the emperors shared the space of the gods. Disloyalty to the ruling house was translated into impiety to the gods and, as became sadly evident under Tiberius, solecisms in treating words and objects related to the emperors were interpreted as disloyalty.[64]

Meanwhile, the performers in theatres and festivals retained their high profile in Roman eyes. Under Augustus we have evidence of the writing of encomia, presumably for public consumption by contrast with the more private satisfaction provided by the laudatory epigrams of Crinagoras of Mytilene.[65] Those who hymned Augustus at Pergamum in the temple of the province of Asia were paid out of a fund to which all the cities of Asia contributed according to an arrangement prescribed by Augustus himself; their privileges were confirmed by Claudius. Ephesus established *hymnodoi* of its own for Augustus, Livia and the imperial house at some expense to the city itself, and this institution was reformed by the proconsul Paullus Fabius Persicus in Claudius' reign, the duties being transferred to young men (*ephêboi*) of suitable age, status and education.[66] It appears from communications by Claudius to the Dionysiac Artists that they had been united in one worldwide organisation under Augustus: ultimately they were to have a new base in Rome itself. They were also linked with the Association of Victors in Sacred Contests, first attested under the triumvirate.[67] The later importance of this association under the Principate may well have fluctuated, if we can trust the scatter of evidence. After a period of comparative obscurity they returned to prominence under Trajan, Hadrian and Antoninus Pius, especially since the emperors came to receive cult in the form of New Dionysus. A cult of Dionysus Choreios was also established by a revived Athenian association at Eleusis with the support of Hadrian, and Antinous seems to have been incorporated into the cult-figure after his death.[68]

The wealth of documentation about the imperial cult diminishes considerably after the reigns of Augustus and Tiberius. However, this should not be necessarily taken as a sign of its diminished importance in provincial life. The age of deep gratitude, belief in a new era and ingenious invention of honours was past. What remains is consolidation in the form of routine, whose significance best appears when it is challenged by dissenters such as Christians.

13

CONCLUSION

In the middle of the second century AD Aelius Aristeides, a provincial from Asia, perceived Rome as a world state: that is, he did not simply, like Polybius, record the fact that Rome had subjected most of the known inhabited world, but he conceived it as a community and a fortress on a macrocosmic scale. Rome's defences were in his view a double perimeter, which, like city-walls kept at bay those incompatible with the community. What lay inside he regarded as a single civic society.[1] It can be argued of course that he was overimpressed by the elite circles in which he himself moved, where intellectuals could confront emperors and provincial governors, where many provincials had been granted Roman citizenship and some of them membership of the senatorial or equestrian orders.[2] However, it is still worth investigating more generally the validity of his view.

The foregoing chapters have tended, while pursuing coherence, to highlight diversity. Roman citizenship in the second century AD was still not a unifying factor but a distinction and privilege. Although Roman law was entrenched inside colonies and *municipia*, elsewhere it coexisted with various forms of local law. Roman magistrates in all provinces but Egypt seem to have adapted the procedures of the Roman civil law, while individual provincials may have found Roman legal formalities in sales, leases and other contracts attractive, simply because it was easier to get them enforced by a Roman magistrate. However, substantive law varied from province to province and even from city to city.

Apart from the standardised constitutions in colonies and *municipia*, the political structures in cities and villages had a family resemblance, one to another, up and down the empire. There were permanent councils or local senates, whose members (*decuriones* or *bouleutai*) held office for life, and annual magistrates in theory elected by the citizen body. However, the discretion permitted to the popular assembly in passing decrees varied: in the Latin west the assembly seems to have been a cipher, except for its function of electing magistrates; in some Greek cities, especially Athens and Rhodes, it had a more important place, even if this fell short of its position in classical Athens. In Athens, indeed, traditional institutions were carefully preserved and not merely as window-dressing: the need for the Areopagus, the Council of Five Hundred and, on occasion, the assembly to co-operate must have affected the balance of the constitution.[3]

In most communities we may suspect that a wealthy and powerful local inner circle tended to determine local politics, even if from time to time they came under pressure from below. We can glimpse this from the conflicts at Athens which Marcus Aurelius had to settle and from the orations of Dio of Prusa.[4] However, we do not have the inside story about how any particular local political issue was settled. When a constitution was established on a Roman pattern, such as those attested by the inscriptions on bronze from Spain, the laws themselves rendered it difficult to make any innovation whatsoever in local politics without a broad consensus among the *decuriones*. The negative would have tended to outweigh the positive, and the static nature of communities throughout the empire would have preserved their essential similarity one to another.

If we regard the Roman empire as a conglomerate rather than a unified society, then the basic similarity in local organisation did at least entail that the elements were compatible with one another. However, this was not all. The introduction of members of local elites into the governing circles of the empire, where common political status and shared intellectual culture tended to bind them into a single social class, created a unity at the highest level, though this must be qualified by the consideration that provinces contributed senators and *equites* in very differing proportions. From this elite there descended chains of patronage which might reach comparatively insignificant political units in the empire. Yet here too these linkages were unevenly distributed. There is thus an accidental element in the social forces which held the empire together. Against this background the importance of the imperial cult stands out in high relief: it was *inter alia* an institution for inculcating unity with a universal application, even if its modes of operation varied. It helped to provide social and institutional coherence through the provincial councils. However, its weakness lay in its traditional close association with Rome's military domination and, if this was uncertain, the rationale of the cult was fatally undermined.[5]

The analysis so far, it may be argued, is superficial. We have been considering forms of coherence, when we should have been seeking reasons for coherence. If it was in the interest of the communities of the empire to hold together, this outweighs any inadequacy in formal institutions. In this book the subject of economic coherence has not been discussed. One reason is that there exists an excellent recent work on the social and economic aspects of the Roman empire;[6] another is that the hopeless inadequacy of the evidence foils even the subtlest techniques of investigation. It has been argued by Hopkins that, although this was not its overt purpose, the empire during the late Republic and early Principate promoted an increase in production and trade in the Mediterranean. This was because the inhabitants were forced to produce for the market in order to obtain the money with which they paid their taxes to Rome. Hopkins connected this with a documented rise in the issue of coinage.[7] For my present purpose what matters is not whether there was an increase in production, which I am prepared to concede, but whether there was an increase in inter-provincial trade and of what kind this was.[8] For it is this which would have made the regions of the empire more integrated and interdependent.

Amidst the paucity of evidence there is relatively plenty that Italy and Rome in particular were major importers of food and raw materials. The transport of grain was the major form of commerce throughout the ancient world. The dependence of Italy on imported grain, under the Principate largely from the provinces of Egypt and Africa, is well known.[9] We must also take into account the vast imports of oil (especially Spanish), attested by the Monte Testaccio at Rome, the import of certain base metals like copper and tin, the luxury building-stone brought to Rome from the ends of the Mediterranean and the spices and perfumes of the east, this last small in bulk but highly expensive.[10] The import of precious metals should not perhaps be taken as evidence of the economic dependence of Italy, since this occurred through an exercise of sovereign power, being an imperial monopoly. In the reverse direction there may have been a significant export trade from Italy in some products, for example, wine.

However, as Hopkins pointed out, the major item in the corresponding movement of economic value from Rome and Italy to the provinces is likely to have been sheer cash, available to the emperor through taxation and the rents of his private estates and to other persons through their estates, through any public salaries they were paid and to some extent through commercial enterprise. Much of the cash acquired by individuals commercially may also have been a spin-off from taxation money, for instance profits from public contracts or business deals with those who received public salaries. Hence it is not unfair to suggest that the previous extraction of money from the provinces in taxes and rents made a major contribution towards Italy's imports.

Thus there is an economic nexus, but one in which in the last analysis the profits are on one side. Its endurance depended on the coercion of the imperial power and it can hardly be used, therefore, as an indicator of any economic integration and coherence apart from that resulting from conquest and military force.[11] One may also question the importance of this nexus in the economy of the empire as a whole and its relation to total production. The export of goods was not the only way that provincials could regain the money yielded in taxation and rents to those in Italy. Some of that would have been regained through wealthy Italians investing in the provinces, especially in land. This is a phenomenon which is well-attested from the second century BC onwards.[12] Under the Principate even land in Egypt was in part opened to private ownership by men from the Roman elite.

Of course there was inter-provincial trade. Not all grain and metals went to Rome or Italy and we can trace the movement of cheap pottery over long distances between provinces.[13] The Roman peace, even if it could not eliminate piracy and brigandage entirely, would have assisted both long- and short-haul transport and there is evidence of an increase in trade between certain sections of the empire (for example, between Britain and Gaul), which might otherwise not have existed. Yet it is hard to assess how much was due to the existence of the Roman empire. Interestingly enough, it has been recently argued that some of the most interesting developments in trade came about not inside the empire, but at its frontiers, where the products of the empire as a whole could be exchanged for those of 'barbarian' peoples and the frontier organisation provided a spring-board for the procurement of resources from outside the empire.[14] In short, it would be rash to see a single economy in the empire and thus to use the economic interests of the provinces as a justification of the perpetuation of the empire, or to make the provincials' perception of a common economic interest a cause of its coherence.

A similar answer might be given to the objection that I have neglected the unifying effects of culture. No one would doubt the importance in its own right of the development of a binary literary culture in the Greek and Latin languages, available as a whole to the elite through their linguistic knowledge and to a lesser extent to many more. The same may be said of the artistic languages of painting, sculpture, mosaic and architecture which the provinces shared, though often with strong local variations (visible, for example, in Celtic and Palmyrene sculpture and African mosaic). Yet we must remember that the growth of Hellenism as a common Mediterranean culture began when the area was still divided politically – even in the west it reached Gaul via Massilia (Marseilles) before the Roman conquest of *c.* 120 BC, and it reached Numidia before the final destruction of Carthage. Rome herself became gradually Hellenised over the centuries of the Republic, absorbing the new culture at increasing speed as her power and wealth grew. Thus, although a common culture was encouraged by the development of the Roman empire, it was not in origin dependent on this. Moreover, culture would have been assimilated by the recipients according to their needs: it was not crammed down their throats by a superior force. Nor did it contain any unambiguous political or moral imperatives relating to the empire itself. Greek and Latin literary culture would keep its place as long as it was attractive: it could not replace political links which were weak or broken.

One reaction to these arguments for a persistent diversity, which tend to subvert the view of the empire as a social unit, might be to accept their truth, as far as they relate to the first two centuries of the Principate, but to point out that subsequently institutional coherence at least was in some ways increased. Almost all free members of the empire received citizenship, which led to the disappearance of some of the legal anomalies between peoples of the empire. We find also in the early third century an intensification of the imperial bureaucracy.[15] Then, after the third-century crisis the dominate of Diocletian and his successors introduced a more pervasive bureaucracy, while Constantine sought to embrace the empire in a new universal religion. The difficulty here is that it is a well-established and plausible view that this enforced coherence did not work, combining oppression with inefficiency through its corruption. Indeed, it has been argued that the fall of the empire was the result of an attempt to reverse the trend of its decline.[16] It was only the armies that could hold the empire together, and in fact the corruption of the military worked in the opposite sense towards disintegration.

Alternatively, it may be suggested that Aelius Aristeides' view was a myth, or rather an aspiration. Augustus and certain of his successors had tried to create an integrated whole (*'cuncta inter se conexa'*, as Tacitus put it),[17] but this integration was essentially a matter of armies and taxation, never the creation of a society. The grants of citizenship and high rank in Roman society would be seen in this light more as a reward for favoured people than the creation of some kind of world elite. Even Caracalla's largesse of Roman citizenship to the mass of provincials did the majority of them little good, since the legal class distinction between *honestiores* and *humiliores* once more separated them into an inferior class.[18] What remained was the historical fact of conquest and the force of Roman *imperium* (this is illustrated in Appian's *Roman History*, written in the mid-second century AD, which documented the subjection of each region of the empire, but did not pursue their history further). Roman domination under the Principate was usually elegantly clothed in ceremonies of the imperial cult, the *adventus* of proconsuls and the succession of the assizes.[19] However, its military origin and basis were palpable.

John Adams in an essay written about the time of America's Declaration of Independence pointed out that, whereas Wales and Scotland were constitutionally linked to England, the American colonies were treated merely as subjects of the English monarch: this was naked sovereignty, for which no legal justification could be given.[20] This was in effect also true of the relationship of the provincials to Rome and the emperor in particular. When all Italy became Roman, the communities there not only received a local constitution, but were given a defined relationship to Rome through incorporation in a voting tribe and through legislation about matters such as the census and the kind of lawsuits that might be judged locally. It was not so in the provinces, even where a community was given a Roman constitution. In what survives of the law from Urso or the Flavian municipal law, we find no definition of their relationship to the representative of Roman authority in the province, the governor, and, in view of the fact that the governor is never explicitly mentioned in the Flavian law and only once, in passing, in the law from Urso, it seems unlikely that this definition was ever made in detail (see Chapter 8).

I would draw the same conclusion from the exchange of letters between Pliny and Trajan concerning the claim of the colony of

Apamea that it had a *privilegium* and a most ancient tradition (*mos*) of administering its public affairs independently.[21] It seem improbable that there was a clause in the charter of the colony concerning the occasions on which the proconsul might exercise his *imperium* there since, if there had been, the Apameans would have cited it. If neither colonies nor *municipia* like Irni had a formalised relationship with the governor, still less did the non-Roman *civitates*. In short, in the provinces a community was either subjected to the *imperium* of the governor without qualification or claimed exemption from it, whether it was a colony or a free city. The latter had at least the advantage of having its freedom spelt out in the law or *senatus consultum* which established its status. However, as we have seen, even this free status had to give way before *imperium*, if the general authority of Rome was to be maintained.[22] In the majority of communities, who accepted their subjection, it was not surprising that this acceptance led to requests for intervention by a Roman magistrate in local affairs. Some of this was self-interested exploitation of Roman power against rivals in the community; on other occasions it may have simply arisen from a wish for certainty: an explicit command was better than a nebulous autonomy.

The lack of formal relationships between provincials and Roman authority (except the negatively defined status of the free city) had to be compensated by the practice of petition or appeal to the emperor. These practices have now been meticulously investigated from the emperor's point of view and it has been shown that in effect the emperor defined his relationship to the provincials through them.[23] But petitions and appeals have a more obvious and primary function as the way communities tested the extent and nature of the governor's and emperor's power over them. If the emperor was seeking to define himself in his responses, the provincials were seeking to define their position in their pleas. Replies were publicised in the provinces and kept in dossiers, many of them ultimately to fill the pages of the Roman law books.[24] Yet, however precious these are to us now, what they describe in context are variations on the theme of absolute monarchy. The Romans were happy with the sovereignty inherent in their notion of *imperium* and did not wish to formulate the connection between rulers and ruled, between centre and periphery in any other terms.

If we judge the Roman empire in Roman terms, as an organisation for providing security, it maintained an excellent record in the first two centuries AD, and, as a monarchy, it developed a tradition of government in the provinces which enabled it in many ways to survive and surmount the variations in ability of successive emperors. It was not its function to be a *res publica*, to perform the socio-political functions of a civic community, a *polis* or *civitas*.[25]

Is this too reductionist a view of the society of the early empire? The various links between ruler and ruled and between communities, however deficient when considered in isolation, are far from insignificant when taken cumulatively. Peter Brown has argued that the cohesion of the empire depended on a web of social relations:[26] such a web could have been strong, even if the threads composing it were extremely fine. The administration may be characterised materially as a network of personal relationships and formally as casuistry which developed into a law of precedent. This at least made a contrast with the naked force of Roman conquest and also with the naked force which too frequently typified the actions of potentates towards the humble in their own local societies. However, this last point tends to subvert the image of a civil society: civilised behaviour was not usually extended to dealings with those in the lowest orders.[27] Moreover, even the relationship between central and local elites was not so firmly grounded that it could stand the strain of divergent interest; when the government needed men, money and grain and the provinces had willy-nilly to provide them.

Perhaps in the end the most important lesson we should learn from the Roman empire is not to claim too much for it. Roman power did bring coherence, but not the coherence of a city, a nation-state or even a league of states with a regular constitution. The fact that we tend to idealise it as a universal society owes something to contemporary statements, such as those found in Aelius Aristeides, but far more to a tradition which grew up in the late empire, of which we are the heirs – one which sprang first from the Christian view of Rome as a world-empire, whose destiny it was to prepare the way for the kingdom of God.[28] According to this perception, when, under Constantine, the Christian world and the Roman world became coterminous, *ipso facto* Christendom became a universal society. This ideal was resurrected by the church both at the time of Charlemagne and during its subsequent efforts to control the Holy Roman Empire. Needless to say, the ideal was not shared by the Frankish and German emperors who understood their empires in a sense more akin to that of *imperium* in pagan Rome: for them empire was related to military victory and signified a sovereignty which overtopped those of city-republics and of other princes. Yet, whether empire was then seen from the Christian point of view as a universal society or from the political point of view as a sovereignty created by conquest, this relationship was not elaborated politically. The notion of a universal society remained an aspiration and a claim rather than a reality, much as it had been in the second century AD.

NOTES

INTRODUCTION

1 Pol.1.1.5, 3.10, 4.1–5, 63.9, 64.2; 6.2; 8.2.3–4.
2 Cic.*Mur*.75 (cf. Plut.*Ti.Gr*.9.5; App.*BCiv*.1.11 for similar thoughts said to have been in a speech of Tiberius Gracchus'); Lyc.*Alex*.1226–82, on which see now West (1984), arguing the passage's interpolation into the third-century play by south Italian Dionysiac artists later in the Republic.
3 Augustus, *RG praef*.; Verg.*Aen*.1.278ff.; 6.851ff.; cf. Nicolet (1988). Arist.*Pol*.1.1254 a14ff.
4 *RRC*, 397, 403.

1 THE GROWTH OF EMPIRE

1 There are many accounts of the growth of Roman power abroad in the early and middle Republic. Among the most useful are G. de Sanctis, *Storia dei Romani*², vols II–III (Florence, 1960–7); J. Heurgon, *The Rise of Rome* (London, 1973); and Toynbee (1965), vol. I. For later developments see, e.g., C. Nicolet (ed.), *Rome et la conquête du monde Méditerranien 2/ Génèse d'un empire* (Nouvelle Clio 8 (2), Paris, 1978); Gruen (1984); Badian (1958) and (1968); Sherwin-White (1984).
2 Pol.1.3.6; 15.9.2–4, 10.2.
3 Plut.*Arat*.12.6; *IG*, IX.2.858 with Livy, 42.17.2; cf. L. Moretti, *Iscrizioni Storiche Ellenistiche* (Florence, 1976), II. 95 (Chyretiai); *ILLRP*, 245 (Lindos); and B. Helly, in *Les bourgeoisies municipales italiennes* (Naples, 1983), 355–80; Livy, *Per*.14.
4 See Chapter 3, pp. 36–40.
5 Cf. Derow (1979).
6 *IOSPE*, I² 402 (= *RGE*, 30).
7 I*Macc*.8.1–3, 11–16.
8 *Syll*.³ 656 (= *RGE*, 26).
9 *SEG*.30.1079; Livy, 42.17.2. Note also, e.g., Cn. Pandosinus in the *SC de Thisbensibus* (*RDGE*, 2 = *RGE*, 21), lines 53–4, and cf. note 3 above.
10 Pol.30.20.2–9; 30.31.10; Strabo, 10.5.4 (486); 14.5.2 (668); F. Coarelli, 'L' "Agora des Italiens" a Delo: Il Mercato dei Schiavi', in F. Coarelli, O. Musti and H. Solin (eds), *Delo e l'Italia* (*Opusc.Inst.Rom.Fin*.II) (1982), 119–45.

11 Pol.36.9.

12 Pol.36.10.5; 38.9ff; Livy, *Per*.50–1; Paus.7.12–14; cf. Accame (1946); Ferrary (1988), 186–209.

13 *Lex agr.*, lines 49ff. (with Lintott, *JRLR*, commentary *ad locc.*); *Vir. Ill.*73.1; cf. Brunt (1971), 577–80. On the organisation of the province see pp. 30–1, 41. For contemporary developments in Gaul and Spain see, e.g., Richardson (1986); and Clemente (1974).

14 *Lex prov.praet.* Delphi A6, B4; Cnidos III.22–5, 35–7. cf. Hassall, Crawford and Reynolds (1974), 219; Lintott (1976a) 81–2.

15 Cyrene: Livy, *Per*.70; cf. App.*BCiv*.1.111.517–18; Sall.*Hist*.2.43M. cf. Reynolds (1962). Egypt: Cic.*Leg.Agr*.1.1; 2.41–2; Badian (1967); contrast Braund (1983).

16 Caes.*BG*.esp.5.22.4–5.

17 Jord.*Get*.11.67–8; *Syll.*³ 762.

18 Dio, 48.24–6; 39–41; App.*BCiv*.5.65.276; *RRC*, 524 = EJ 8; cf. Reynolds (1982), 11–12; EJ, 20 (*RDGE*, 59), 303 (*RDGE*, 60 = *RGE*, 91).

19 *RG*, 26.1.

20 On Celts and Germans Strabo, 4.4.2 (196); 7.1.2, 2.1–2 (290, 293–4) inc. Poseid. *FGH*, 87 F31. A recent general account of these operations in Gruen (1990).

21 R. Syme, *Danubian Papers* (Bucharest, 1971), 17, 137; Wilkes (1969), 48–9.

22 Verg.*Aen*.1.278–9; Zanker (1988), esp. chs 4–5.

23 *ILS*, 212 = Smallwood, *GCN*, 369, lines 37ff.; Ael.Arist.14 (*To Rome*), 200–348; cf. Oliver (1952).

2 ELEMENTS OF EMPIRE

1 Dion.Hal.4.49; 6.95.2–3; Festus 166L; Cic.*Balb*.53. cf. Sherwin-White (1973a), 3–37, 190–9.

2 Sherwin-White (1973a), 96–118; Salmon (1969), 55–69; Toynbee (1965), vol. I, 141–71.

3 The relevant texts were collected by Taübler (1913), 45ff., but his material must now be supplemented. Note especially the inscriptions from Methymna (*Syll.*³ 693 = *IGRR*, I.2), Astypalaea (*IGRR*, I.1028b), Callatis (*ILLRP*, 516) and that recently discovered from Maroneia (*SEG*, 35.823). For a recent discussion see Ferrary (1991).

4 Livy, 22.57.10; 27.20.3; *lex agr.*, lines 21 and 50. cf. Livy, 34.56.3–6.

5 Pol.21.32; Livy, 38.11; Proculus, *Dig*.49.15.7.1. cf. Sherwin-White (1973a), 120–3; Badian (1958), 25–6; Gruen (1984), 25ff.

6 R. Lopez Melero, J.L. Sanchez Abal and S. Garcia-Jimenez, *Gerion*, 2 (1984), 265–323 = Richardson (1986), 199–201. On *deditio* see Dahlheim (1968), 5–82, for the most comprehensive account before the publication of this inscription.

7 Cf. the appeal to *fides* when protection was sought within communities, A.W. Lintott, *Violence in Republican Rome* (Oxford, 1968), 11–16.

8 Pol.20.9.10–11; Livy, 36.27.8. For *pistis/fides* in the Greek world see

Pol.5.50.8; Livy, 22.17.1–5; 23.16.7–11; 28.7.12; 32.16.14; 43.22.2; Gruen (1984).

9 Cic.*Off*.I.35.

10 Gai.*Inst*.1.25–6; 3.74; *P.Giss*., I, no. 40, col. I (= *FIRA*, I, no. 88, line 9; *lex rep*., line 1.

11 Roman practice commended by Philip V of Macedon to the Thessalians (*Syll.*[3] 543.26ff). See, e.g., Sherwin-White (1973a); Galsterer (1976), 41ff.; Humbert (1978). Samos – R. Meiggs and D.M. Lewis, *Greek Historical Inscriptions*, 94.

12 'Common Peace Treaties' – Ryder (1965). League of Corinth – M.N. Tod, *Greek Historical Inscriptions*, II.177.

13 *SEG*, 22.339b–c; Tod, *GHI*, II.144, line 24; 147, lines 16 and 26; 277, line 11 (cf. ps.Dem.17.10 and 15).

14 See, e.g., *OGIS*, 44–5; *SEG*, I.366, 16f.; II.536; *P. Cairo Zeno*, III.341a; T. Wiegand (A. Rehm), *Milet*, I.3, no. 139; *IG*, XII.5.1065; Jones (1940), 104ff.

15 Diod.Sic.16.82.3.

16 Diod.Sic.22.10; Plut.*Pyrrh*.22–3; Dion.Hal.20.8.

17 Caes.*BG*.6.12–13; cf. 1.4.2; 1.31.3ff; 7.40.7; Poseid., *FGH*, 87, F17, 18; Diod.Sic.5.29.2.

18 References now conveniently collected by Nicols (1980).

19 Welles, *RC*, nos 10–13, 18–20; *SEG*, II.663; Y.H. Landau, *IEJ*, 16 (1966), 54–70; *OGIS*, 55 (cf. M. Wörrle, 'Epigraphische Forschungen zur Geschichte Lykiens II', *Chiron*, 8 (1978), 201–46); Rostovtzeff (1957a), 336ff.

20 On socio-economic inequality see A. Fuks, 'Patterns and Types of Social-Economic Revolution in Greece from the Fourth to the Second Century BC', *Anc.Soc.*, 5 (1974), 51–81; de Ste Croix (1981), app. IV. The extent to which the great powers consistently favoured one class in the cities against the other has been much debated. Recently scholars have tended to agree that this was not true of the period before 146 BC, though they have not agreed about alternative interpretations. See Briscoe (1967); Deininger (1971); E.S. Gruen, 'Class Conflict and the Third Macedonian War', *AJAH*, 1 (1976), 29–60; *idem* 'Philip V and the Greek *Demos*', in *Ancient Macedonian Studies in Honor of Charles F. Edson* (Thessaloniki, 1981), 169–82.

21 Welles, *RC*, no. 51; *Syll.*[3] 410.16; *OGIS*, 229.13ff; 338.12; cf. index by Rostovtzeff (1957a), s.v. *cleroi* and cleruchs; *CAH*[2], VII.1, 124–5, 157–8, 189ff., 197ff.

22 C. Mossé, *Athens in Decline 404–86 BC* (London, 1973), 114ff., 126ff., 143ff. Rhodes was institutionally a democracy (Cic.*Rep*.1.47; 3.13), but Strabo viewed it as a state in which the poor were looked after by their betters (14.2.5, 652–3C). On the survival of institutional democracy see now Ferrary, 'Les romains de la république et les démocrates grecques', *Opus*, 6–8 (1987–9), 203–16. For the attachment of Cos to democracy see S. Sherwin-White, *Ancient Cos* (*Hypomnemata*, 51, Göttingen, 1978), 20ff.

23 See, e.g., Cic.*Fam*.10.33, 34 and 35; 15.1 and 2. Welles, *RC*, nos 56–61, 71–2; in private correspondence *P.Zeno*, II.59060; 59251 (= *Sel.Pap.*, I, nos 88, 92); cf. *Sel.Pap.*, I, nos 96–7, 99.

3 THE ORGANISATION OF EMPIRE

1 Pol.3.4.2–3; 16.27.2–3 and 34.4; 22.1.3 and 4.9; 23.2.6 and 8.2; 36.9.6;
Derow (1979). The language of power, nevertheless, had a geographical
component, even if the perceptions and approach to space were
somewhat different to ours, see Nicolet (1988); N. Purcell, 'The Creation
of Provincial Landscape: the Roman Impact on Cisalpine Gaul', in Blagg
and Millett (1990), 7–29. This chapter develops ideas originally put
forward in Lintott (1981b). For a recent thoroughgoing investigation of
the notion of *imperium* both in foreign and domestic politics see
Richardson (1991).

2 *RG*, 30.1–2.

3 See e.g., Pol.32.10.10–12; Diod.Sic.31.28, 32, 34; App.*Syr*.47.244 for the
overthrow of Ariarathes V of Cappadocia by Orophernes; Pol.36.14;
App.*Mith*.4.9–7.23 on the fall of Prusias II; Sherwin-White (1984), 40ff.

4 Cf., e.g., *lex rep.*, lines 69, 72, 79–80; *lex agr.*, line 46; similarly Livy,
24.9.5; 43.11.8 for the jurisdiction of the urban praetor. This is the
standard interpretation of the term *provincia*. I am not convinced by the
alternative view (that in origin the term means a space associated with
planned conquest) put forward by Bertrand (1989). Etymological arguments seem far more secure and the use of the term for an urban post
seems to be at least as old as the third century BC.

5 Livy, 32.28.11; Artemidorus of Ephesus, *ap*.Stephanus, s.v. *Iberia*.

6 *RDGE*, 44 (= *RGE*, 37); *Syll.*³ 683.64–5; *Claros I*, Polemaios decree col. II,
lines 50–1, 53–4; Menippos decree col. I, 39; col. II, 4.

7 *Lex prov.praet.* Cnidos III.4ff. – first sense; II.20; III.22ff.; IV.7ff., 26ff.,
Delphi B.21, 29, C.8 – second sense; Cnidos III.26; IV.8–11 – third sense.

8 Campaigning: Sall.*Hist*.1.133–4; 2.36–7, 80; 4.18–9M; cf. *IGB*, I².314a =
RGE, 73 (Mesembria); Cic.*Pis*.38, 84ff.

9 Cic.*Pis*.50; contrast *Rab.Post*.20.

10 R. Syme, 'Observations on the Province of Cilicia', *Roman Papers*
(1979), vol. I, 120–48 at 121–4 (= *Anatolian Studies presented to W.M.
Buckler*, 299–332); Levick (1967), 21. cf. W.M. Ramsay, *Historical
Commentary on Galatians* (London, 1899), 103–7.

11 App.*Mith*.105.495; Strabo, 12.1.4 (535C); Cic.*Fam*.13.73.

12 *Fam*.15.2.6; 3.6.6.

13 *Fam*.15.2.4; 13.73. Deiotarus – e.g., *Att*.5.17.3; 18.2 and 4; 20.9; 6.1.14;
Fam.15.1.6, 2.2, 4.5, 7 and 15.

14 Jos.*AJ* 17.320–1; *BJ*, 2.97; Pliny, 5.81–2; cf. Rey-Cocquais (1978), at 48–
53; *idem*, *AAS* (1973), pp. 39ff., no. 2, lines 27–30.

15 Jos.*AJ* 14.74–9; *BJ*, 1.156–7; 399–400.

16 Hence it is supposed that he was technically liable to a charge of *maiestas*
on his return to Rome (cf. E.S. Gruen, *The Last Generation of the
Roman Republic* (Berkeley/Los Angeles, Calif. 1974, 495). The only
evidence to support this in the ancient sources concerns his attack on
Germanic peoples (Suet.*Caes*.24.3; App.*Celt*.18.3; Plut.*Cato mi*.51.1–5;
Caes.22.4; *Crass*.37.2), where Cato's protests and the suggestion that
Caesar was exceeding his remit sprang out of allegations (not
unfounded) that he had broken a truce.

17 Caes.*BG* 1.10.1 and 5; 44.7; 45.2.
18 Poseidonius, *FGH*, 87, F18; cf. Caes.*BG* 7.4.1 on Celtillus, Vercingetorix's father.
19 Caes.*BG* 1.35.4.
20 Luttwak (1976), ch. 1.
21 I take the legislator to have been the son of M. Cato Nepos (cos. 118), who, according to Gellius (13.20), was curule aedile and praetor before dying in Gallia Narbonensis.
22 Livy, 43.1.4–10.
23 Sandford (1939); Sherwin-White (1984), 271ff.
24 Cic.*Pis*.48–50; cf. *Fam*.1.1 and 2; *QF* 2.2.3.
25 Cic.*QF* 3.4.1; *Rab.Post*.20.
26 Pliny, *Ep*.10.79.1 and 4, 80; Strabo, 12.3.1 (541); Dio, 37.20.
27 Cic.*2Verr*.2.32ff., 90, 125 (cf. Val.Max.6.9.8); *Fam*.13.48; *RDGE*, 65, D83 (= *RGE*, 101, VII, 83).
28 Pol.18.42.5, 44.1; Livy, 33.30ff.; 38.37ff.; cf. *RDGE*, 9 (= *Syll.*^{3} 674 = *RGE*, 38), lines 51–3; *RDGE*, 10B (= *Syll.*^{3} 688), line 6; Pol.21.24.9; Livy, 37.55.7.
29 Livy, 45.17–18, 29–30. *Formula* – 45.26.15, 31.1, 32.7.
30 Pliny, *HN* 3.37. Note also Reynolds (1982), no. 15, lines 13–14 for Hadrian exempting Aphrodisias from the *tupos* of the province (cf. no. 14, line 3). The term is also used for other political lists (Livy, 38.9.10; 39.26.2).
31 App.*Iber*.43–4; Livy, 40.35.4, cf. 43.2.12 for a regular 5 per cent levy in 171, which apparently did not exist in Cato's time; see Richardson (1976), 149; Strabo, 3.4.13 (162–3C).
32 Cic.*Att*.6.1.15; Val.Max.8.15.6.
33 Phrygian dioceses – Cic.*Fam*.13.67.1; Sicilian cities – *Verr*.3.13ff.; 5.56.
34 The precise point at which the African section begins is open to argument (see the commentary in *JRLR*), but it must have begun by line 48.
35 Pliny, *HN* 5.25; Eumachos of Naples, *FGH*, 178, F2; App.*Lib*.54.235; 135.639–41; *lex agr.*, line 77.
36 Piganiol (1954); A. Caillemer and R. Chevallier, 'Les centuriations de l'Africa Vetus', *Annales*, 9 (1954), 433–60; Chevallier (1958).
37 Strabo, 14.1.38 (646); *RDGE*, 12 (= *RGE*, 45), line 9; App.*BCiv*.5.4; H.B. Mattingly (1972).
38 *ORF*, no. 48, fr. 44 = Gell.11.10.1; Cic.*Verr*.3.12.
39 Livy, 45.17.8 and 26.12ff.
40 Vell.Pat.2.97.4; 117.3–4; Dio 56.18.1–2. Note also the altar at Cologne (*Ara Ubiorum*), Chapter 12, n. 57.
41 Livy, 30.15.11; 31.11.11–12; Tac.*Ann*.4.26.
42 Treaties with defeated kings: Pol.18.42; 21.17.3ff., 24.2ff., 42.6ff.; Livy, 33.25; 38.38. Masinissa – Livy, 30.15.11; 31.11.11–12.
43 See for contrasting strong and weak interpretations of treaties and the meaning of *societas*, Sherwin-White (1984), 58ff.; Gruen (1984), ch. 1, esp. 52ff.; for a new analysis of treaties, Ferrary (1991).
44 Livy, 43.6.10; 44.16.7; *RDGE*, 22 (= Bruns, no. 41), lines 7 (Latin), 25 (Greek).

45 Mellor (1975); Braund (1984), 25–6; Errington (1987).

46 *ILLRP*, 174–181a, b. cf. Degrassi (1962), vol. I, 415ff.; Lintott (1978), 137–44; Jos.*AJ*, 14.389; *BJ*, 1.285.

47 Livy, 37.54.17; Proculus, *Dig.*49.15.7.1. General reservations – Brunt (1988), 382ff.; Braund (1984), 5ff., 182ff.; contrast J.W. Rich, 'Patronage and Interstate Relations in the Roman Republic', in Wallace-Hadrill (1989), 117–35 for a critique and reformulation of the view that the Roman empire was a form of *clientela*.

48 Reynolds (1982), no. 3, lines 49ff.

49 *Syll.*³ 656 (= *RGE*, 26), lines 20ff.; Reynolds (1982), no. 5, lines 17ff.; *REG* (1898), 258ff. line 30; Pol.30.4.3–5. cf. M. Gelzer, *The Roman Nobility*, trans. R. Seager (Oxford, 1975), 86ff.; D. Braund, 'Function and Dysfunction in Roman Imperialism', in Wallace-Hadrill (1989), 137–52. A particular form of patronage introduced by Rome was that of the advocate appointed to assist plaintiffs with an extortion case, see *lex rep.*, lines 9–12; *JRLR*, commentary ad loc.

50 Sall.*Jug.*7.4–9.2.

51 *Lex.rep.*, line 1; Caes.*BG* 2.14.1–2; Sall.*Jug.*24.10; cf. for the Greek perception of being in *fides* the decree from Oropos (*Syll.*³ 674, lines 11f. and 22).

52 Pol.31.10.7 and 11.4ff.

53 Pol.2.11.17; Livy, 30.15.11.

54 Pol.21.18.

55 Pol.29.27; 30.1–2; 30.18–19 (cf. Livy, 45.44.19–21; cf. ibid., 1–18 for the Roman version more complementary to Prusias).

56 Sall.*Jug.*14.1; Aug.*RG* 27.2; Suet.*Aug.*48; Dio, 38.38.4.

57 Jos.*AJ* 14.74; *BJ*, 1.154; 1.399–400. However, Braund (1984), 63–4, is generally doubtful about whether Herod or any other client king paid tribute to Rome.

58 *Bell.Alex.*65.4.

59 Cic.*Att.*6.1.3.

60 Pliny, *HN* 5.2.3; cf. Mackie (1983a).

61 Quoniam (1950).

62 *B.Afr.*56.3; cf. 32.3; 35.4; Gascou (1969), at 555ff. for a Marius Gaetulicus at Theveste. cf. Brunt (1971), 577.

63 Dio, 54.3.1.

64 Strabo, 17.3.25 (840); cf. Suet.*Aug.*48.

65 Tac.*Ann.*11.31; 14.40; *Hist.*3.45; Stat.*Silvae* 5.2.42ff.

66 *RIB*, 91; cf. J. Bogaers, *Britannia*, 10 (1979), 243–54; Tac.*Agric.*14.2.

67 Cic.*Verr.*3.13; 5.83. I find it difficult to follow Ferrary's argument (1988, 6ff.) that being *immunes et liberae* was somehow an inferior status to freedom (i.e., mere freedom from taxes and corvées), when outside Italy *immunitas* is usually the greatest privilege that accompanied *libertas*, while inside Italy it was not conceded to Rome's theoretically autonomous allies.

68 Pol.18.46.5; cf. 44; also *RDGE* 34 (= *RGE*, 8), 19–21 for the formula agreed between Rome and Antiochus III to define the status of Teos.

69 Pol.4.84; 15.24 – Philip V. Welles, *RC*, 15, 21ff.; Z. Tashliklioglu and P. Frisch, 'New Inscriptions from the Troad (1)', *ZPE*, 17 (1975), 101–6,

lines 13ff. (with Ferrary and P. Gauthier, 'Le Traité entre le Roi Antiochos et Lysimacheia', *Journ.Sav.* Oct.–Dec. (1981), 327–45) – Antiochus II. P. Herrman, *Anatolia*, 5 (1965), 34ff., lines 18–19 – Antiochus III. cf. *Syll.*³ 390 for Ptolemy II and the Island League; Tod, *GHI*, 185 = Harding, 106, lines 3–4; *GHI*, 186 = H., 103, line 3 – Alexander the Great.

70 Pol.18.43; Livy, 33.27–9; 34.51.4–6; *RDGE*, 9 (= *RGE*, 38), 51ff.

71 Pol.24.9. For a recent attempt to interpret the Roman concept of freedom in this period see Yoshimura (1984).

72 Livy, *Per.*82.

73 Ferrary (1985).

74 On the changing concept of freedom see Bernhardt (1971).

75 Cic.*Verr.*3.13, 172; 4.72; 5.56, 83.

76 *Verr.*5.49f.; *AE* (1973), no. 265.

77 *Syll.*³ 748 = *RGE*, 74, 17ff.; *IG*, IV.1.66, 25ff. and 44ff.; cf. IV.1.63 = *RGE*, 51.

78 See *IGRR*, I.1692 (Elaea); IV.1028b (Astypalaea); *IG*, IV.1.63 (Epidaurus); *SEG*, 35.823 (Maroneia).

79 Pol.30.4–5; cf. V. Kontorini, 'Rome et Rhodes au tournant du IIIe s.av. J-C. d'après une inscription de Rhodes', *JRS*, 73 (1983), 24–32, for some obscure diplomatic activity involving the two states.

80 *Claros I*, Polemaios decree II.50ff., Menippos decree I.23–II.7; Cic.*Att.*1.19.9, 20.4; *Prov.Cos.*7; *Pis.*37, 90.

81 *Flacc.*70–83; *QF.*1.2.10; *Att.*6.1.5ff.; *Fam.*13.54, 55, 56, 61; cf. ibid., 26 and 28. See Peppé (1985).

82 Cic.*Verr.*3.12; *lex agr.*, lines 77–80.

83 See, e.g., *Verr.*3.53, 56, 93, 200; *Flacc.*34, 42, 51–2; Contrebia – G. Fatas, *Contrebia Belaisca II: Tabula Contrebiensis* (Zaragoza, 1980); Richardson (1983); Birks, Rodger and Richardson (1984).

84 Festus, 86L; Livy, *Per.*41; App.*Iber.*43.179; Degrassi (1962), vol. III, 129ff.

85 Caes.*BG* 1.3.4; 4.12.4; 7.31.5.

86 *BG* 1.16.5; 7.32.3–4. cf. EJ, 340 = Braund, *AN*, 656.

87 *BG* 1.30.4; 4.65; 5.24; 5.56.1–3; 6.3.4; 6.44. cf. ibid., 7.1.4; 63.5; 75.1 for those summoned by his Gallic opponents during Vercingetorix's revolt.

88 *2Verr.*2.154.

89 Paus.7.16.10; cf. *SEG*, 15.254, if this is rightly dated to *c.* 120 BC.

90 *OGIS*, II, 438 = *RGE*, 58; Reynolds (1983), no. 5, lines 21–4; *RDGE*, 52 = *RGE*, 77, line 43; *RDGE*, 57 = RGE, 85, lines 3–4.

91 Lines 77, 79–80.

92 Picard (1966); cf. *idem* (1969–70); and J. Février, *Cahiers de Byrsa*, 7 (1957), 119–24.

93 Gai.*Inst.*1.25–6; 3.74; *FIRA*, I, no. 88, line 9; cf. A.H.M. Jones (1960), 127–40, criticising Mommsen's view that all provincial communities were *dediticii*.

94 Vell.Pat.2.120.2; Mommsen, 'Der Begriff des Limes', *Ges.Schr.*, V.456–64; Fabricius (1927), at 573–5; B. Isaac, 'The Meaning of *Limes* and *Limitanei* in Ancient Sources', *JRS*, 78 (1988), 125–47.

95 Tac.*Ann*.1.50; 2.7; *Agric*.41.2; *Germ*.29.4; *Acta Fratrum Arvalium*, 2 August AD 213, p. 197 Henzen, line 21.
96 *RG*, 30.1–2.
97 Mann (1979); and *idem*, 'The Frontiers of the Principate', *ANRW*, II.1 (1974), 508–33; Brunt (1990), 433–80.
98 See, e.g., Salway (1981), 95ff.; Todd (1981), 113ff.
99 Poidebard (1934); Mouterde and Poidebard (1945); Kennedy and Riley (1990). For a general study of Rome's political and military strategy in this area see Isaac (1990).
100 Baradez (1949); R.G. Goodchild and J.B. Ward-Perkins, 'The *Limes Tripolitanus* in the Light of Recent Discoveries', *JRS*, 39 (1949), 81–95; and R.G. Goodchild, 'The *Limes Tripolitanus* II', *JRS*, 40 (1950), 30–8. For a study of economic relations across frontiers see Cunliffe (1988).

4 GOVERNMENT AND THE GOVERNOR

1 See, e.g., Pol.1.11.2–3, 63.1; 15.1.3; 18.42.4; Livy, 31.7–8; 33.25.7.
2 Rich (1976).
3 Livy, 42.7–9, 21–2.
4 Livy, 43.1.4–10. I do not discuss here the attempts by *popularis* politicians to assert the people's sovereignty over matters in the empire. On this see *CAH*, IX, 2nd edn (forthcoming), ch. 3.
5 Pol.18.44; Livy, 45.17–18, cf. 45.26 on Illyricum.
6 Livy, 43.2.12; Poseidonius, *FGH*, 87, F59 (= 265 Edelstein-Kidd); Cic.*2Verr*.4.9; *lex agr*., lines 54–5. cf. Crawford (1977), p. 51.
7 *Lex prov.praet.*Cnidos III.3–15; *lex Ant.Term*. II.13ff.
8 Cic.*2Verr*.2.32ff.
9 Cic.*Att*.6.1.15.
10 *2Verr*.3.93–101.
11 *2Verr*.3.138–9. On the monarchic element in the Roman constitution, not surprisingly stressed by Polybius, since it was most visible in magistrates abroad, see Richardson (1991) and A.W. Lintott, 'Democracy in the Middle Republic', *ZSS*, 104 (1987), 34–52 at 43 and 49.
12 *RDGE*, 10 and 14.
13 *RDGE*, 9 = *RGE*, 38.
14 *RDGE*, 15, lines 15ff.
15 Reynolds (1982) no. 15; *RDGE*, 23 = *FIRA*, I, no. 36 = *RGE*, 70. cf. Cic.*Att*.1.19.9; 20.4 for Sicyon's appeal in 61 BC.
16 Asc.89C – Catiline; Cic.*QF* 2.12.2–3 – Gabinius.
17 Livy, *Per*.20; 32.27.6, 28.11.
18 Cic.*Att*.1.13.5, 15.1.
19 Cic.*Att*.1.16.8, cf. 18.2, and *MRR* on 78 BC.
20 Cic.*Fam*.3.6.3.
21 Dio, 40.30.1, 56.1, cf. 46.2 for a previous *s.c.* to this effect.
22 Sall.*Jug*.73.7 – Marius; *MRR*, on 67 and 66 BC; Livy, 26.18–19 – Scipio; cf. e.g., 29.13.1; 30.2.1 on his immediate successors in Spain.
23 For example, Livy, 30.1.1–2; 42.4.1f.; 43.12.1; Sall.*Cat*.26.4.
24 Sall.*Jug*.27.3; Cic.*Dom*.24; *Prov.Cos*.3; *Fam*.1.7.10.

25 Cic.*Fam*.1.9.25; *Att*.4.17.2, 18.4; Dio, 39.14.3; 41.43.2. cf. Giovannini (1983), 44–56.
26 Pol.6.12.8, 13.2. *Ornare provinciam* – Cic.*Att*.3.24.1; 4.17.1; *QF*.2.3.1; *Fam*.1.7.10; 8.4.4; *Prov.Cos*.28; *Balb*.61.
27 Cic.*Att*.2.6.2, 16.4.
28 Crawford (1985), 116ff., 152ff.
29 Ibid., 84ff.
30 Livy, 40.35.4.
31 Plut.*Pomp*.25.6.
32 Cic.*Att*.5.13.2, 15.2.
33 Cic.*Att*.11.1.2; *Fam*.5.20.9, cf. *Rab.Post*.40 for *pecunia permutata* by Rabirius Postumus.
34 F. Braudel, *The Mediterranean in the Age of Philip II*, trans. S. Reynolds (London, 1972), 508ff.
35 *Lex prov.praet*. Cnidos II.13–32 (cf. IV.5–31 for instructions to governors of Macedonia about using them); cf., e.g., Livy, 42.31; 43.12. On the probable allocation of legions under the Republic from 218 to 49 BC see Brunt (1971), 416–72. It is hard to judge the quantity of auxiliary (allied) troops used either before or after the Social War, when the Italians became eligible for the legions. For the end of the Republic see Saddington (1982), ch. 2.
36 See Livy, 40.35.6ff. for men being withdrawn in 180 BC after six years' service.
37 App.*Mith*.64.265; Dio, 36.14.3, 16.3, 46.1; Caes.*BG*.1.7.2, 10.3. cf. Plut.*Caes*.12.1 for the two legions Caesar took over in Hispania Ulterior in 61 BC; and see in general Smith (1958), chs 2–3.
38 Cic.*Att*.5.15.1, 18.2; 6.1.14; *Fam*.15.4.3. Cf. Caes.*BG*.7.7.5, 65.5 for recruitment in southern Transalpine Gaul, apart from the levy in Cisalpine in 7.1.1.
39 Cic.*2Verr*.2.34; 3.28, 136; Catull.10.
40 Cic.*Div.Caec*.39, 55–8; *2Verr*.2.44; 3.168; 5.114. For a slightly garbled report of the beginning of the allocation of quaestors to provinces by *sortitio* see *Dig*.I.13.1.2 (Ulpian). Presumably there was a time when consuls and praetors chose their preferred member of the quaestors elected for that year.
41 *2Verr*.2.44.
42 Mommsen, *Staatsr*.I³, 570, n. 3. For example, Cicero was quaestor in Sicily at the minimum age in 75 BC. On the situation earlier, see Astin (1958), esp. 36ff. Augustus – Dio, 52.20; cf. Mommsen, *Staatsr*.I³, 576, n. 3.
43 Cic.*Att*.5.6.1, 11.3; 6.3.1, 4.1, 5.3, 6.3.
44 *QF*. 2.14.3; *Fam*.7.8.1; *Rab.Post*.19.
45 Caes.*BG*.1.24.4; Catull.29.3. Cf. N. Magius, Pompey's equivalent (Cic.*Att*.9.13a).
46 Caes.*BG*.1.39.2–4; Cic.*Fam*.7.5.2, 13.2.
47 Cic.*2Verr*.1.73.
48 *Flacc*.49; *Att*.5.21.6.
49 Early known examples in Britain in late first century AD – *ILS*, 1011, 1015 = MW, 311, 309.

50 Catull.28; cf. Caes.*BG*.1.39.2: 'those who had followed Caesar from the city *amicitiae causa*'.
51 Plut.*Ti.Gr*.4.5. cf. Sall.*Jug*.64.4; Cic.*Cael*.73; *Planc*.27; Tac.*Agric*.5.1.
52 Cic.*2Verr*.1.67; 2.27; 3.187; *QF* 1.1.13. On these posts see Jones (1960), ch. 10.
53 Cic.*Div.Caec*.29; Pliny, *Ep*.4.12.
54 Cic.*QF* 1.1.13. For the *decuriae* cf. *lex Cornelia XX quaest*. (*CIL*, I.^{2} 587 = *FIRA*, I, no. 10), I.5–II.6, here concerned with the *apparitores* of the treasury quaestors at Rome.
55 Cic.*2Verr*.1.71; 2.69ff.; 3.154; *QF* 1.2.1ff; *Att*.2.18.4, 19.1.
56 Cic.*Att*.4.16.12; *Fam*.3.7.4–5. Demetrius – Plut.*Cato mi*.13.1–9; *Pomp*.40.1–9. Trogus – Justin, 43.5.11–12; cf. *1Macc*.6.15; Jos.*AJ* 17.82; *IGRR*, IV.17.12; and Malitz (1987), at 52–4.
57 Cic.*2Verr*.3.69; cf. 28, 138–9 and 2.33, 75. See also *QF* 1.1.11–12.
58 EJ, 300 = *RDGE*, 57 = *RGE*, 85.
59 Oliver (1946); trans. Levick, *GRE*, no. 9.
60 Cic.*Att*.5.14.2.
61 Caes.*BG* 1.54.3; 5.1.5; 7.1.1; *RDGE*, 24A.
62 Cic.*2Verr*.5.29.
63 *2Verr*.5.39ff.; *AE* (1973), no. 265. Verres was also invited to intervene in southern Italy (*2Verr*.5.39ff.).
64 *Flacc*.27–33.
65 *Att*.5.20.2–3. cf. Tac.*Ann*.11.20 for Corbulo digging a canal to keep his men occupied.
66 *Lex prov.praet*.Cnidos IV.5–31.
67 App.*Iber*.99.430.
68 Livy, 34.51.4–6; *RDGE*, 9 = *RGE*, 38, 51ff.; *RDGE*, 33 = *RGE*, 4.
69 Livy, 45.29.4, 32.2.
70 *RDGE*, 43 = *RGE*, 50, 6ff. cf. Ferrary (1988), 189, n. 228.
71 Cic. *2Verr*.2.123; cf. *ILLRP*, 320; *IG*, XIV.952.
72 *2Verr*.2.122.
73 *2Verr*.2.131ff.
74 *Att*.5.20.9, 21.9; 6.2.4–6; cf. 5.17.6 for Appius Claudius at Tarsus. cf. Marshall (1966); and, on the development of the diocese system in Asia, Burton (1975).
75 *Lex prov.praet*.Cnidos IV.32ff.
76 Cic.*2Verr*.2.32ff., 90, 125 (cf. Val.Max.6.9.8).
77 *Claros I*, Polemaios decree, p. 13, II.51ff., Menippos decree, p. 63, I.29ff; Cic.*Att*.6.1.15; Val.Max.8.15.6.
78 See A. Watson, *Law Making in the later Roman Republic* (Oxford, 1974), ch. 3, 31–62.
79 App.*Iber*.43.179; 44.183.
80 Richardson (1983); Birks, Rodger and Richardson (1984).
81 *2Verr*.2.31–4 is essentially concerned with private cases. It appears from *Verr*.2.68ff. that it was legitimate for a governor to try a capital case regarding a citizen of a *civitas libera* (Halicyae, cf. 2.166). For his powers over offenders *contra rem publicam* see 2.94, 3.68.
82 The criticisms of the view of Kunkel (1962, 79ff.), mounted by Garnsey (1966), 167–89 at 177ff., seem to me valid.

83 Cic.*Att*.6.1.15; *tab.Contreb.*, cf. note 80 above. For Roman governors normally using the forms of Roman civil jurisdiction, including the two-part process see Mitteis (1891), 132; Wlassak (1919). Their view is borne out in a number of passages considered below. See also Chapter 9 with note 29.

84 Cic.*QF* 1.2.7–8; *Att*.6.1.15, 2.4; Cato, *ORF*, no. 8, frr. 51, 132, 173, 203; C. Gracchus, *ORF*, no. 48, frr. 23 (= Plut.*C.Gr*.2), 10, 26, 27.

85 EJ, 311, I and 312 = Braund, *AN*, 543 and 545.

86 *Lex rep.*, line 86; *frag.Tar*.5; *FIRA*, I, no. 35 = *RDGE*, 22 = *RGE*, 66, Lat.3ff., Gk. 19ff.; no. 55, 53ff.

87 Cic.*2Verr*.5, esp. 18ff., 72ff., 158ff.; Pliny, *Ep*.2.11.2.

88 Cic.*2Verr*.2.32.

89 Ibid., 31–2; cf. 66.

90 *2Verr*.2.37–42, 44.

91 Ibid., 2.68ff.

92 Ibid., 3.28ff, 117.

93 Ibid., 3.90, 152; 5.108.

94 Ibid., 3.28–30, 55ff., 69, 138–9; cf. 2.71–5.

95 *Att*.6.1.15.

96 *Att*.6.1.15; Val.Max.8.15.6. The main treatment in English of Cicero's edict remains Marshall (1964). For a recent comprehensive study with full bibliography see Peppé (1991).

97 Or indeed that he provided the Greek judges with a *formula* to provide a framework for their judgements (see pp. 58, 64).

98 *Att*.5.21.11; 6.1.5–6.

99 *Att*.6.1.15.

100 See, e.g., F. de Zulueta, *The Institutes of Gaius* (Oxford, 1953), vol. II, 94ff., 133ff.; J.A. Crook, *Law and Life of Rome* (London, 1967), 119, 173ff.

101 *Att*.5.21.9; 6.2.4. For Cicero's negotiations and arbitrations see 5.21.1–2; 6.1.16; 6.2.5.

102 *OGIS*, 437, III.58ff.; *Claros I*, p. 13, Polemaios decree, col. II, 51ff., p. 63, Menippos decree, col. I, 29ff.; *RDGE*, 70 = EJ, 317 = *RGE*, 108.

103 *Claros I*, p. 64, Menippos decree, col. I, 42ff.; Cic.*2Verr*.1.85.

104 Cic.*2Verr*.1.73–6; *QF* 1.2.4–7.

105 Cic.*QF* 1.2.10–11.

106 *QF* 1.2.10: 'Is it customary that a praetor makes a judgement that a debt is owed?' Cicero's point is that, as a magistrate, Quintus' job is to perform jurisdiction, not actually to judge cases. It is thus implied that governors in this period were expected to behave like civil magistrates at Rome, rather than to investigate cases by *cognitio* procedure.

107 Cic.*Flacc*.71; see also 74f. for Flaccus and Apollonis, 76ff. for interventions there by other praetors.

108 Ibid., 40, 43, 48–9; cf. 11.

109 See ibid., 74 for the use of Latin legal terms in recounting an action under Greek law.

110 EJ, 311 = Braund, *AN*, 545 = *RGE*, 102, I.4ff. and IV.

111 Cf. *SEG*, IX.5.

112 Plut.*Cim*.1.6. Interestingly, the case was the murder of a Roman citizen

and his local supporters at Chaeronea after brutal behaviour by the Roman.

113 Even at Rome judicial verdicts were not regularly appellable under the Republic (and appeal was specifically excluded in the laws establishing *quaestiones*). On *provocatio* as a form of appeal see Lintott (1972).
114 Cic.*2Verr*.1.84–5; *Claros I*, p. 64, Menippos decree, col. I, 42ff.
115 *RDGE*, 43 = *RGE*, 50, 23ff.; EJ, 311 = *RGE*, 102, II.
116 Cotton (1979); Cic.*Fam*.13.26 and 28.
117 *Fam*.13.56.
118 *Att*.1.19.9, 20.4; *Prov.Cos*.7; *Pis*.37, 90.
119 *2Verr*.3.132ff.
120 This is generally held to be implicit in Asc.3C, but see Ewins (1955) for some doubts.
121 Cic.*Att*.5.11.2 with Suet.*Jul*.28; Asc.3C for Pompeius Strabo's concession of Latin rights to Transpadanes; Caesar's grant of citizenship – Dio, 41.36.3.
122 *Frag.Atest*. (*FIRA*, I, no. 20); *lex Rubr.Gall*. (*FIRA*, I, no. 19).
123 Laffi (1986).
124 Crawford (1989a).
125 Lintott (1972).
126 Cic.*2Verr*.2.95 and 100.
127 Ibid., 2.109.
128 See note 86 above.
129 *RDGE*, 23 = *RGE*, 70; Cic.*Flacc*.79.
130 *Att*.2.16.4.

5 TAXATION AND CORVEES

1 Pol.6.21.5; Livy, 27.9.7 and 13; App.*BCiv*.1.7.30; *lex rep*., lines 77 and 84; *frag.Tar*.4; Nicolet (1978).
2 Livy, 45.18.7 and 29.4; 45.26.14.
3 Pol.18.46.5 and 15; Livy, 33.32.5; *lex agr*., lines 79–80; App.*Lib*.135.640.
4 Livy, 23.48.7.
5 LIvy, 22.37.6; 23.38.13.
6 Cic.*2Ve: r*.3.13; 4.72; 5.83. See p. 20 for the likely status of cities in the Punic domain in Sicily in the third century bc. Note also Tyndaris' claim to belong to a group of seventeen communities (*2Verr*.5.124), perhaps an early division of Roman Sicily outside Hieron's territory.
6 Centuripium – *Bull.Ep*. (1965), no. 499.
8 Cic.*Div.Caec*.39, 55–8; *2Verr*.2.22.
9 Livy, 31.29.6–7; 26.40.15–16.
10 Livy, 26.21.11–12; cf. Cic.*Phil*.2.101; *2Verr*.3.97 and 108–11; *Leg.Agr*.2.57.
11 Cic.*2Verr*.3.13; 5.49–50; App.*Sic*.5. On the system see pp. 75–6.
12 Livy, 41.17.2; cf. Cic.*Scaur*.21 for the *frumentarium crimen* brought much later against Scaurus; *Scaur*.45 for the free cities; *Bell.Afr*.98 for a later tithe increased to an eighth.
13 Livy, 23.48.4–5.

14 Pol.9.25.9; Livy, 28.25.9–10 and 34.11 (tribute for pay); 29.3.5.

15 Richardson (1976); for a different view W.V. Harris, *CAH*, VIII² (1989), 129f.

16 Livy, 34.9.12ff.; *ORF*, no. 8, fr. 154.

17 Livy, 40.35.4; App.*Iber*.43.179, cf. 44.182; Strabo, 3.4.13 (162–3).

18 Livy, 43.2.12 – the identification is suggested by Richardson (1976), 149.

19 Strabo, 3.2.10 (147–8) = Pol.34.9.8; Diod.5.36.2–38.

20 Livy, 34.21.7; Richardson (1976).

21 Crawford (1985) 91–7, 340–2.

22 Livy, 45.18.7; 29.4; Cic.*Leg.Agr*.1.5; 2.50.

23 Livy, 45.18.3–4; 29.11; 158 BC – Cassiodorus *Chron. sub anno.*

24 App.*Lib*.135.639–41; *lex agr*., line 77, cf. 75–82 and the commentary in *JRLR* on the African section *passim.*

25 *2Verr*.3.12.

26 *CIL*, I² 2500 = Nicolet (1980), lines 21–2; *RDGE*, 22 = *RGE*, 66. Latin 11, Greek 23.

27 Cic.*Phil*.2.101; *Verr*.3.13, 97, 108–10, 147–51; *Leg.Agr*.2.57.

28 Cic.*2Verr*.3.13, 18–19. For a helpful series of discussions of grain-production and taxation in Sicily see Pritchard (1970), (1971) and (1972).

29 Welles, *RC*, 41, lines 5 and 8; 48.D3; 51.17f.; *OGIS*, 229.101; 55.18 (the tithe here is a legitimate exaction by contrast with previous abuses).

30 App.*BCiv*.1.7.27.

31 Cic.*2Verr*.3.36, 38, 55, 113.

32 *Lex agr*., lines 53, 56, 90. Mitteis, Wilcken, *GCP*, I.1.175ff.; I.2, nos 241ff.

33 Cic.*2Verr*.3.70ff. (in kind – 72, 75, 113; monetary equivalent – 90; resident *decumani* – 77, 90, 91).

34 *2Verr*.3.35ff.; charge – 3.116–18 contrast *Rab.Post*.30 referring to Egypt.

35 *2Verr*.3.36–7, 181. Pritchard (1970), 359 for the argument that the obligation lay on the *decumani.*

36 Varro, *RR*, 2.*Praef*.3, cf. Col. 1.*Praef*.20; Cic.*2Verr*.3.172; *Dom*.25; *Planc*.64; *Fam*.13.75, 79.

37 On this problem see Rickman (1980), 38ff., esp. 41; C. Nicolet, 'Le *Monumentum Ephesenum* et les dîmes d'Asie', *BCH*, 115 (1991), 465–80, esp. 473ff.

38 Cic.*2Verr*.3.13; *Att*.5.13.1; App.*BCiv*.5.4.18–19.

39 App.*Mith*.83.376; Plut.*Luc*.20.3–4; *lex portorii Asiae*, line 72.

40 Herrman and Polatkan (1969), lines 21–6; Dio, 42.6.3; App.*BCiv*.5.4.19.

41 Cic.*Att*.5.14.1; 6.1.16; *lex portorii Asiae*, lines 22ff.; EJ, 191 = Braund, *AN*, 738. *Tabellarii: Att*.5.15.3, cf. 16.1 Brunt (1990), 377 believes that the *publicani* were responsible to some extent for collecting the direct taxes from all the provinces, but in his view all contracts except those for Sicily were let at Rome. The evidence for the last proposition (Cic.*Leg.Agr*.2.56) is manifestly rhetorical exaggeration (it ignores Sicily) and so is by itself unsafe. Badian (1972), 79 believes that in provinces other than Asia and Sicily the agreements between *publicani* and cities over direct taxation were made in the province under the governor's supervision. For general references to contractors for direct

taxation from the triumviral period see EJ, 302 (= *FIRA*, I, no. 56), 15ff.; EJ, 301 = *RDGE*, 58, II.33–5.

42 *Cic.Att*.5.16.2; *Fam*.3.8.3–5; 15.4.2. See especially Cicero's comment in *Fam*.3.8.5 as printed in Watt's OCT: *'ne in venditionem tributorum et illam acerbissimam exactionem, quam tu non ignoras, capitum atque ostiorum inducerent[ur] sumptus minime necessarii'*; and cf. *Flacc*.20 on the bankruptcy of cities. For similar problems in a Greek city in the Hellenistic period see *Syll*.³ 495.50ff. – the decree of Olbia for Protogenes.

43 *RDGE*, 59.6ff.

44 *Caes.BCiv*.3.32; cf. *Cic.Att*.13.6.1 for a tax on columns in Italy.

45 *Syll*.³ 1000; *BCH* (1922), p. 301.

46 *IG*, V.1.1432; cf. A. Wilhelm, *JOAI*, 17 (1914), 48ff.; Giovannini (1978), 115ff.

47 *Cic.Flacc*.80; *Fam*.8.9.4.

48 *Flacc*.91; cf. *Fam*.13.56.2 for Cicero's request that the cities of Heraclea and Bargylia should be required to give security for their debts to Cluvius with their revenues (*fructus*), which might imply that Cluvius would be given the right to collect the taxes himself, but more probably that he had first claim on any proceeds from their sale.

49 *Cic.QF* 1.1.33; cf. *OGIS*, 46 (Halicarnassus).

50 *Inschriften v.Priene*. 111.14ff. and 112ff.; *QF* 1.1.33.

51 *App.Lib*.135.641; *Jos.AJ* 12.142; 13.59.

52 *App.Syr*.50, cf. *BCiv*.5.4.18 (where Antonius argues, in the speech retailed by Appian, that it would have been easier to collect a tax based on a personal valuation, *timēma*, than the tithes). There are a number of references to poll-taxes paid by Greek and Macedonian cities in the Principate but some are clearly local taxes and none look like the main source of Roman revenue in the area – *IG*, XII.5.724, 946; *IGRR*, IV. 181; *Arch.Delt*., 2 (1916), 148; *JOAI*, 41 (1954), 110–18.

53 *Jos.AJ*. 14.74.

54 Dio, 42.6.3; *App.BCiv*.5.4.19; Badian (1972), 99f.

55 *Cic.Prov.Cos*.9–10; *Pis*.41; *QF* 2.11.2. Contrast Dio, 39.56.5–6; *Jos.AJ* 14.87–91, 104.

56 *Jos.AJ*. 14.206; cf. 201.

57 Festus, s.v. *scripturarius*, 446L; *lex agr*., lines 14–15, 24–6, 85–6, 88–9; Mitteis, Wilcken, *GCP*, I.2, nos 242–3, cf. 245–7 from the Roman period.

58 *Lex agr*., lines 66, 82–9.

59 *Cic.Phil*.2.101; *2Verr*.3.97, 108–10.

60 *2Verr*.3.57, 114.

61 Cf. V.M. Scramuzza, 'Roman Sicily', *ESAR*, III.225–377 at 329.

62 *Lex agr*., lines 49 and 66 with the commentary in *JRLR*.

63 The view of Mommsen in his commentary on *lex agr*. (reprinted in his *Ges. Schr*., I, 127ff.). For *ager quaestorius* see Sic.Flacc.154Lach = 116Thul.

64 De Martino (1956). cf. M. Gelzer, *Kl.Schr*.II.82 and M. Weber, *Römische Agrargeschichte*, 150ff. See also M. Kaser, 'Die Typen des römischen Bodenrechts', *ZSS*, 62 (1942), 1–81 at 7ff.

65 Lines 73–4 – the normal procedure, when purchases from the public treasury occurred.
66 Lines 99ff. cf. *RDGE*, 22 = *RGE*, 66, Latin 11, Greek 22.
67 Cic.*Leg.Agr*.2.38ff., esp. 48–51; cf.1.3–6.
68 *Leg.Agr*.2.56–7; cf. 1.10.
69 *Leg.Agr*.2.50.
70 Rostovtzeff (1910), 285ff.
71 Frank (1927), esp. 148–9.
72 Cf. M. Rostovtzeff, 'Notes on the Economic Policy of the Pergamene Kings', in W.H. Buckler and W.M. Calder (eds), *Anatolian Studies presented to Sir W.M. Ramsay* (London, 1923), 359–90 for the fiscal and economic structure of Pergamum.
73 Cic.*Leg.Agr*.2.57.
74 Jos.*AJ* 13.49.
75 Diod.34/5.2.2ff. (Poseidonius, *FGH*, 87 F108); 36.3.2ff.
76 Cic.*2Verr*.3.167–72.
77 Lucil.26.671–2 Marx = 650–1 Warmington; cf. 27.722–3M = 753–4W for his comment on the evasion of *portoria* by exporters.
78 For censorial regulations controlling grazing see *lex agr.*, line 86, where it is attractive to restore a reference to where it could take place; see commentary in *JRLR ad loc.*
79 *Lex agr.*, line 26 excludes the imposition of tax on cattle moving on the drove-roads of Italy, but it may have only applied up to a certain head of cattle. Moreover, the chapter of the law may be taken to imply that there had been taxes on such movements previously.
80 Cic.*Att*.5.15.3; 11.10.1.
81 Cagnat (1882), 1ff.
82 Bruns, 14 = *RGE*, 62, col. II, 31ff.
83 Livy, 32.7.3 (*venalicium* = the genitive plural, *venaliciorum*; cf. the commentary of J. Briscoe, *Commentary on Livy XXXI–XXXIII* (Oxford, 1973); *Dig*.50.16.203; cf. *lex portorii Asiae*, lines 60, 81ff.; *CIL*, VIII.4508.11, 22.
84 Dio, 37.51.3–4; Cic.*Att*.2.16.2, cf. *QF* 1.1.33 for alleged *iniuriae* by *portitores*; Suet.*Caes*.43.1.
85 Livy, 38.44.4.
86 *RDGE*, 2 = *RGE*, 21. 17–20; *RDGE*, 18 = *RGE*, 63. 95–9, 103–5. cf. *RDGE*, 23 = *RGE*, 70. 22ff.
87 cf. note 82 above.
88 *Lex portorii Asiae*, lines 88ff.
89 Suet.*Tib*.49.2. Contrast EJ, 333 = Braund, *AN*, 649.14–15; Smallwood, *NTH*, 453 = *Syll*.[3] 837.9–10; *NTH*, 454(b) = *OGIS*, 502.
90 *OGIS*, 629 (cf. Matthews (1984); Smallwood, *NTH*, 458; Levick, *GRE*, no. 82); *CIL*, VIII.4508; R. Cagnat, *JRS*, 4 (1914), 142–6 = *AE* (1914), no. 234; *Dig*.39.4.16.7.
91 Caes.*BG* 1.18.3–4; 3.1.1–2; 3.8.1; Strabo, 4.6.7 (205).
92 Cic.*2Verr*.2.169–72, 182, 185; 3.167 (cf. *ILS*, 1549 for a parallel to Chilo's title); *Fam*.13.65, cf. 13.9.2; *Att*.11.10.1.
93 Cic.*Prov.Cos*.10; *Imp.Cn.Pomp*.16; *Font*.19–20 (cf. 32 for the friendship between Fonteius and the *publicani*); De Laet (1949), 106.

94 Cic.*Imp.Cn.Pomp*.15; cf. *Pis*.87; *Sest*.94; *Prov.Cos*.5; Aquileia and Tergeste – *ILLRP*, 199, 243; cf. *ILS*, 1862 and *CIL*, III.447 for similar slaves at Miletus and Iasos; right to search – Cic.*Leg.Agr*.2.61; *Vat*.12.

95 Cic.*2Verr*.2.185; *Font*.19–20; *Att*.2.16.4. The view of P. Middleton, 'The Roman Army and Long-Distance Trade', in Garnsey and Whittaker (1983), 75–81, that some of the tolls in Gaul were on wine for the army has become somewhat unlikely in view of the exemption for goods carried for public purposes in the Republican section of the tax law from Ephesus (*lex portorii Asiae*, lines 58ff.).

96 Cf. note 90 above.

97 Tac.*Ann*.13.51; 15.18; *lex portorii Asiae*, esp. line 11 for the rate of tax, lines 68ff. for reference to the last Attalid, 72ff. and 84ff. for the contracts let in 75 and 72 BC, 32ff. and 68ff. on customs posts, 58ff., 72ff. and 88ff. on exemptions, 99ff., 105ff. and 123ff. on the procedure for letting contracts.

98 Cic.*2Verr*.3.167; *ILS*, 1549; cf. Cic.*Prov.Cos*.12; Pliny, *Ep*.5.34. On *publicani* in general see Kniep (1896); Badian (1972); Cimma (1981); Nicolet (1979); Brunt (1990), ch. 13.

99 Pol.6.17.2–4; cf. *Tab.Heracl*.73–6. *Pace* Nicolet (1971), the traditional view that Polybius' last phrase in the passage refers to the registration of property as security for tax-collection still seems best, nor should one view those involved as *secondary* guarantors: it may be simply that their liability was limited; it may be that without specifically registering properties with the treasury their *dignitas* was inadequate to provide a guarantee.

100 Cic.*Leg.Agr*.1.7; 2.56. For consular auctions cf. note 97 above for the auctions of 75 and 72 BC (with Cic.*Verr*.3.18); and see *lex agr*. lines 89; *Tab.Heracl*.73–4; Ovid, *Ex Ponto* 4.5.19–20, 9.45–6.

101 Festus, 137L; Cic.*2Verr*.1.141; Suet.*Caes*.20.3. cf. Nicolet (1979), 82ff.

102 Pol.6.17.4; cf. *lex portorii Asiae*, lines 123ff.; *lex Flav.mun*.cap.63–5; *praedia subsignare* – *lex agr*., lines 73–4, 83–4, cf. 46 and 100 for *mancupes*, *praedia* and *praedes* in different contexts. See also Cic.*Dom*.48; *Schol.Bob*.Cic.*Flacc*.80, 106St. Egypt – Nicolet (1971) discusses a Ptolemaic papyrus (Wilcken, *Griechische Ostraka*, I.553–4).

103 *Lex agr*., lines 74; *Schol.Bob*.Cic.*Flacc*.80, 106St; *lex Flav.mun*.cap.65.

104 *ILLRP*, 518, I.5–8, II.13–19.

105 *Lex portorii Asiae.*, lines 123ff.

106 Cic.*2Verr*.1.143; *Quinct*.76; Livy, 43.16.2; cf. Cic.*Dom*.48; *lex Flav.mun*.cap.65.

107 Cic.*Rab.Post*.4; *Vat*.29; PsAsc. on *2Verr*.1.142–3, 253St; Val.Max.6.9.7. cf. Cimma (1981), 91.

108 *Lex agr*., lines 85–9; *lex portorii Asiae, passim*; Cic.*Prov.Cos*.12; *2Verr*.5.53; *ND* 3.49; Varro, *RR*, 2.1.16; Pliny, *HN* 33.78; Gai.*Inst*.4.28; *Dig*.50.16.203. Contractor's percentages – Cic.*2Verr*.3.116; *Rab.Post*.30.

109 Cic.*Att*.6.2.5; *lex Urs*.cap.82; Hyginus 79Thul = 116–17 Lach; *Dig*.49.14.3.6.

110 Macr.*Sat*.1.12.7, 14.1; *Dig*.39.4.15.

111 *Lex agr*., lines 15–18, 70. There would not have been time between the earliest possible date for the enactment of the *lex agraria* (early January

111) and 15 March 111 for the various operations required by the law to
be completed before the next Ides of March.

112 Cic.*Planc*.33.
113 See notes 97 and 100 above.
114 Cic.*Att*.4.11.1; cf. 9.1; 6.2.5.
115 *Lex portorii Asiae*, lines 99ff., cf. 144ff. Intercalation – cf. note 110.
116 Cic.*Att*.1.17.9, 18.7; 2.1.8, 16.2; Suet.*Caes*.20.3; App.*BCiv*.2.13.
117 Cic.*Planc*.32; *Schol.Bob*.157St on *Planc*.31; cf. Nicolet (1980), 111ff. on
     lex de Delo, lines 21–2.
118 Cic.*Flacc*.32.
119 In *QF*. 1.1.33, written in the winter of 60–59, Cicero discusses the correct
     way to handle *publicani*, especially when they have an unfavourable tax
     contract. He writes in general terms and may not be referring particu-
     larly to the current situation: indeed he may be hinting obliquely at
     Quintus' past behaviour towards the company which was in difficulties in
     61.
120 App.*BCiv*.2.13; *lex portorii Asiae*, lines 68–9.
121 Nicolet (1979). So also more briefly Badian (1972), 69f.
122 Gaius in *Dig*.3.4.1; cf. e.g., Pliny, *Ep*.10.33.3, 34, 92–3, 96.7; *Dig*.47.22.
123 *Lex Flav. mun*.cap.65; *lex portorii Asiae*, lines 99–100, 105–12, 123–8. (I
     assume that, contrary to the view of the original editors, the *authentes* in
     lines 109 and 123 is a legal representative, *cognitor*, not the contractor
     himself. The latter is regularly described by a phrase referring to his
     lease of the customs-dues.)
124 Livy, 42.1.7–12.
125 *ORF*, no. 48, fr. 48 = Gell.10.3.2.
126 Hor.*Sat*.1.5.45ff. For Greek *parochē* – Pol.32.13.2; *OGIS*, 262
     (Baitocaice), 22ff.
127 *ILLRP*, 454; *lex agr*., lines 11–12 with commentary in *JRLR*.
128 EJ, 302 = *FIRA*, I. no. 56, 15ff., cf. EJ, 301 = *RDGE*, 58, II.33–5.
129 *Lex prov.praet*.Cnidos III.3ff.; *lex Ant.Term*. (Bruns, 14), II.15ff.; *IG*,
     IV.1.66, cf. 63.
130 *ORF*, no. 8, frr. 132, 203; Cic.*Att*.5.16.3, 21.6–7; 6.2.4.
131 Catullus, 10.9ff.; 28.
132 Livy, 34.9.12–13; 43.2.12.
133 Cic.*2Verr*.3.188. cf. the brief reference in *Scaur*.21 and contrast the
     scrupulousness of L. Calpurnius Piso Frugi (cos. 133) in Sicily
     (*2Verr*.4.56).
134 Tac.*Agric*.19.4–5.
135 Cic.*Pis*.90; *Flacc*.56; *2Verr*.2.141ff.
136 On auxiliary soldiers in the late Republic see Saddington (1982), ch. 2.
     From the second century note *SEG*, XV.254, XXXVI.555 (the sort of
     men who made these dedications were eager to fight); M. Holleaux,
     REA, 21 (1919), 1–19 – relating both to military service and exemption
     from it.
137 Cic.*2Verr*.5.49–50; *AE* (1973), no. 265.
138 Cic.*Flacc*.27ff., 33; Caes.*BCiv*.3.32.
139 Livy, 42.1.10; Cic.*Pis*.90; cf. *QF* 1.1.9 for expenses caused by governors'
     travels.

IMPERIUM ROMANUM

140 Hdt.3.126; 8.98; cf. Xen.*Cyr*.8.6.17.
141 Jos.*AJ* 13.52; *P.Teb*.703.70ff., 215ff.; Rostovtzeff (1906).
142 Mitchell (1976).
143 A list of other documents is provided by Mitchell (1976), n. 142. Germanicus – EJ, 320(a) = Braund, *AN*, 558A; Phrygia – Frend (1956).
144 Illustrated by the fragment of C. Gracchus' speech on the *lex Aufeia* (*ORF*, no. 48, fr. 44); cf. Diod.Sic.34/5.25.
145 Jos. *AJ* 13.49; Plut. *Luc*.20.3; App. *Mith*. 83.376.
146 For plausible long-term levels of taxation see Hopkins (1980b), esp. 116ff.
147 See above note 91.

6 RESTRICTIONS ON MAGISTRATES AND THE PUNISHMENT OF DELINQUENTS

1 Recent discussions of the theorists of *imperium* which emerged in the nineteenth century by A. Giovannini and E. Badian in Eder (1990), section V.
2 Lintott (1972), 249ff.
3 Sall.*Jug*.69.4; cf. App.*Num*.fr. 3; Brunt (1988), 128f.
4 Livy, 43.2.12; *ORF*, no. 8, fr. 51; Poseidonius, *FGH*, 87 F59; *lex agr.*, line 55, with commentary in *JRLR*; cf. *Dig*.18.1.62; 48.11.8; Crawford (1977), 51. See for fuller discussions of the prehistory of the *quaestio de repetundis* Lintott (1981a) at 164ff., and *JRLR*, pp. 12–16; Eder (1969); Venturini (1969).
5 Livy, 43.4.1–6 and 7.5–10; *Per*.43; Zon.9.22.6.
6 Livy, 29.8–9 and 16–22; 34.44.6–8; cf. Lintott (1972), 256ff. Livy, 38.54–5; 42.7–8, 21–2; App.*Iber*.59.249ff.; Cic.*Brutus* 89f.; *de Or*.1.227.
7 Livy, 43.2.3ff.
8 *Lex rep.*, lines 9–12.
9 Lintott (1976b).
10 Cic.*Brutus* 81, 106; *Off*.2.95; *Div.Caec*.69; *2Verr*.3.95; 4.56; *Font*.38; *Mur*.58; Val.Max.8.1.11. *Actio sacramento/lex Iunia* – *lex rep.*, lines 74, 81; penalty of simple restitution – *lex rep.*, line 59. On the problem, Lintott (1981a), 172ff. and *JRLR*, pp. 14–16; Richardson (1987).
11 On the discovery of the fragments see Lintott, 'The So-Called *Tabula Bembina* and the Humanists', *Athenaeum*, 61 (1983), 201–14, revised in *JRLR*, ch. 5.
12 See, especially, H.B. Mattingly, 'The Two Republican Laws of the *Tabula Bembina*', *JRS*, 59 (1969), 129–43; *idem*, 'The Extortion Law of the *Tabula Bembina*', *JRS*, 60 (1970), 158–68; A.N. Sherwin-White. 'The Date of the *Lex Repetundarum* and its Consequences', *JRS*, 62 (1972), 83–99. The controversy can be followed further in *JRLR*, pp. 166–9.
13 Cic.*Div.Caec*.18; *lex rep.*, line 1 with commentary in *JRLR*.
14 *Lex rep.*, lines 2–3, 58–9.
15 For the loss of senatorial status as a penalty under other laws see *lex rep.*, line 11 and 13 and on *infamia* the commentary in *JRLR* on *lex rep.*, line 23.

212

16 *Lex rep.*, lines 3–6, 9–12, 19, 59–60, 76–7.

17 *Lex rep.*, lines 76ff.

18 *Lex rep.*, lines 30–5 with commentary.

19 Condemnation and second part of the action – *lex rep.*, lines 54–60. On the form of the trial see *JRLR*, pp. 17–25, 29–31.

20 *Lex rep.*, lines 12–27.

21 Kunkel (1962) and *RE quaestio*, XXIV (1963), 720ff.; Brunt (1988), ch. 4.

22 See, especially, E.S. Gruen, *Roman Politics and the Criminal Courts, 149–78 BC* (Cambridge, Mass., 1968); Brunt (1988), chs 3 and 4.

23 *Divinatio* – Cic.*Div.Caec.*10, 24, 47–50, 63–5, 71–3; *QF* 3.1.5, 2.1, 3.2; *Fam.*8.8.3. On the two *leges Serviliae* see Lintott (1981a), 186–97; Balsdon (1938), at 102ff.; M. Griffin, 'The *leges iudiciariae* of the pre-Sullan Era', *CQ*, n.s., 23 (1973), 108–26 at 114f.

24 Cic.*Balb.*54; cf. Lintott (1981a), 186–8.

25 Cic.*Verr.*1.34; *2Verr.*1.26; *Scaur.*29–30; *Rab.Post.*8–9, 37; *Fam.*8.8.3.

26 *Lex prov.praet.*Cnidos III.4ff.; *lex Ant.Term.*II.13ff.

27 Cic.*2Verr.*2.137ff.; 3.169 and see notes 2 and 4 above.

28 Cic.*Pis.*90.

29 Cic.*Rab.Post.*16; *Clu.*104, 153. cf. *Dig.*48.11.3 on the *lex Iulia*.

30 Dio, fr. 97, 1; cf. Cic.*Brut.*115; Athen.4.168d–e; Poseidonius, *FGH*, 87 F27; Lintott (1981a), 194–5.

31 Cic.*Verr.*1.6; *Scaur.*23ff.; *Flacc.*13ff., Asc.19, 21C (Asc.21C and *Scaur.*23 refer to the 90s BC).

32 Lintott (1981a), 197.

33 Cic.*Clu.*115–16; Lintott (1981a), 198–201.

34 EJ, 311 = *RDGE*, 31, V.97ff. (trans. *RGE*, 102; Braund, *AN*, 543); cf. Tac.*Ann.*3.67–8; *Hist.*4.45; *Dig.*48.11.7.3.

35 Cic.*Pis.*87, 90; cf. *Clu.*144, 148, 151; U. Ewins (Hall), '*Ne quis iudicio circumveniatur*', *JRS*, 50 (1960), 94–107.

36 Cic.*Fam.*8.8.3.

37 Cic.*Pis.*50, 90; *Flacc.*27ff.; *Prov.Cos.*7; cf. *lex prov.praet.*Cnidos III.4ff.; *lex Ant.Term.*II.13ff.

38 Cic.*Pis.*90; *Att.*5.10.2, 16.3, 21.5; Pliny, *Ep.*4.9.7. cf. *Dig.*1.1.18 (the plebiscite apparently forbad gifts to Roman officials except of immediate items of consumption) and Chapter 5 with note 124.

39 Cic.*Att.*6.7.2; *Fam.*5.20.2; *Pis.*61.

40 G. Archi, M. David, *et al.*, *Pauli Sententiarum Fragmentum Leidense* (Leiden, 1956), Recto 2; cf. Lintott (1981a), 204.

41 *Dig.*48.11.3, 6.1. and 7. cf. Cic.*2Verr.*4.15; *Flacc.*61ff.; Dio, 56.25.6 (an edict of AD 11 totally banning such decrees until eighty days after a governor left the province).

42 For *saevitia* see Tac.*Ann.*3.67–8; 13.30, 52; *Hist.*4.45; Pliny, *Ep.*2.11.2. Only in two of these cases was a capital penalty enforced (cf. note 34 above).

43 *Dig.*48.11.7; Pliny, *Ep.*2.11.2.

44 Cic.*Verr.*1.56 (*Div.Caec.*19's figure of 100 million sesterces perhaps roughly allows for double repayment); Plut.*Cic.*8.

7 THE IMPACT OF THE MONARCHY ON THE EMPIRE •

1 Cassiodorus, *sub anno Cn.Pap.Carbo II, L.Corn.Cinna IV*; Plut.*Sulla* 25; Cic.*Flacc*.32; *QF* 1.1.33; App.*BCiv*.1.102.474; *Mith*.61.259.

2 App.*Mith*.114.558ff.

3 App.*BCiv*.2.9.31–2; Dio, 37.49.2; Plut.*Luc*.20.6; Cic.*Att*.2.16.2.

4 Cic.*Att*.5.2.3; 11.2; *Fam*.8.1.2; Suet.*Jul*.28.3; Plut.*Caes*.29.4.

5 Caes.*BG, passim*; on *decem legati* see Cic.*Prov.Cos*.28; *Balb*.61; *Fam*.1.7.10.

6 Cic.*Pis*.48–50; *Rab.Post*.19ff., 30ff.; *QF*.2.12.2–3; 3.1.15 and 24; 3.2.1–2; 3.4.1; Dio, 39.55–63. Cf. Sandford (1939).

7 Oropos – *RDGE*, 23, lines 38–9, 42–3, 55; Cos – *RDGE*, 49B. Sullan *senatus consulta* – *RDGE*, 17, 18, 20 = *RGE*, 62–4; cf. *RDGE*, 49A about Cos.

8 Jos.*AJ* 14.143–4, 192ff.; cf. 196ff., 202ff.

9 *RDGE*, 28; cf. Jos.*AJ* 14.219 for a *SC* of 11 April 44 BC, referring to another *SC* of 9 February, which could not be recorded in the treasury at Rome before Caesar's murder. Forgery – Cic.*Fam*.9.15.4.

10 Cic.*Att*.14.12.1; cf. *Phil*.1.7ff.; 5.12; 12.12; *Fam*.12.29.2; App.*BCiv*.2.135. 563; Dio, 44.34.2; L.Varius Rufus, fr.1 (*FPL*, p. 130) = Macr.*Sat*.6.1.39.

11 Herrman (1989); Tac.*Ann*.3.60ff., esp. 63.3.

12 Xanthus – Plut.*Brut*.2.8; 30–1; App.*BCiv*.4.76–80; Dio, 47.34. Lepidus – Cic.*Fam*.10.34, 34A, 35; App.*BCiv*.3.83–4; Dio, 46.51.

13 Dio, 43.54.3; Jos.*AJ* 14.306–13; 314–18; 319–20; *RDGE*, 57 (= EJ, 300, *RGE*, 85). cf. Bleicken (1990), esp. 36ff.; Millar (1973).

14 Reynolds (1982), nos 7, 8, lines 48ff., 10, 12.

15 EJ, 301–4; cf. *RDGE*, 58 and 60 (Braund, *AN*, 535–6), with EJ, 20 = *RDGE*, 59.

16 Tac.*Ann*.1.2.

17 Millar (1966), (1977) and (1984).

18 Strabo, 10.5.2 (485); Agathias, 2.17, quoting the epigram on the statue-base dedicated to Chaeremon (see also *RGE*, 96).

19 *RDGE*, 61 = *RGE*, 95.

20 *Pace* A.H.M. Jones (1960), 6 with n. 7, who, developing an idea of H.F. Pelham (*Essays* (Oxford, 1911), 66–8), relies mainly on a highly tendentious passage of Cicero (*Phil*.4.9), '*omnes in consulis iure et imperio debent esse provinciae*' – used by Cicero to prove that Antonius could not be a proper consul because D. Brutus refused to cede him his province. Another passage used in this argument, '*quibus* [sc. the consuls] *more maiorum concessum est vel omnes adire provincias*' (Cic.*Att*.8.15.3), does not reflect known Republican practice and is anyhow irrelevant to the present problem of instructions sent from Rome.

21 For the *iussum* being some further instruction see Atkinson (1960), at 256–9 (who also thought that the first document was a *SC* – implausibly in view of the complete absence of any of the appropriate formulae). Sherk (*RDGE*, 61, p. 316) believed that the first document was an edict and thus the *iussum* mentioned later. However, he also suggested that Augustus and Agrippa were commissioned by the senate to investigate

the matter, something possible in principle but for which there is no evidence in the text. Coinage – Grant (1946), 81 B and 82ff. Note also the subordination implicit in Norbanus Flaccus' letter to the Jews (EJ, 306 = Philo, *Leg. ad Gaium*, 315; Braund, *AN*, 538).

22 Dio, 53.12.3–7.

23 Strabo, 17.3.24–5 (839–40); Dio, 54.4.1; 34.4; Syme (1979), vol. I, 144ff. on Galatia and Cilicia; *idem* (1939), 390f. on Macedonia.

24 Dio, 54.3.1–3.

25 Dio, 53.32.5; 54.28.1; EJ², 366 = *P. Colon.*, I.10.

26 12 BC – Jos.*AJ* 16.160–5 (cf. Bowersock (1964); with *AE* (1906), 1 on Censorinus as a legate in Bithynia–Pontus). See also *AJ* 16.172–3 for Iullus Antonius writing a letter to Ephesus saying that the Jews had quoted Augustus' permission to them to observe their ancestral customs. Cyrene – *SEG*, IX.8 = EJ, 311, nos I, II and V = Braund, *AN*, 543, *RGE*, 102.

27 Millar (1977), 217ff. The evidence for *subscriptiones* is sparse. They may not have begun as early as Augustus' reign, but quite probably did. See Mourges (1987); and on their later history, and essentially *ad hoc* nature, see Turpin (1991), discussing *inter alia* the replies publicly displayed by Septimius Severus (*PColumbia* 123).

28 Dio, 53.14.4; Mitchell (1976) (= *AE* (1976), 653); Gonzalez (1984), fr.I, lines 15–16 (cf. Tac.*Ann*.2.43.1). See in general Burton (1976).

29 *RDGE*, 67 (EJ, 312) = *RGE*, 103.

30 *Dig*.48.6.7; Paul.*Sent*.5.26.1–2.

31 Dio, 51.19.6. See Lintott (1972) at 263ff.

32 Suet.*Aug*.33.3 refers to appeals from foreigners. On the subsequent history of appeal see Millar (1977), 507–16; Burton (1976); Garnsey (1966).

33 *Acts*, 25.11–12. General references to the practice may be found in Suet.*Aug*.33.3; *Cal*.16.2; *Claud*.14; Dio, 59.18.2.

34 *PP*, 30 (1975), 102–4 and *IGRR*, IV, 1044; cf. Burton (1976). For the general principle of approaching the governor first, see *Dig*.1.18.8 (cf. *ILS*, 6092 = AJ, 61, lines 9–14 –Vespasian's reply to the Saborenses). For the flexibility of conditions for appeal, see *IG*, V.1.21.

35 *AE* (1962), 288, lines 5–6; Oliver (1970), document 1 with pp. 37ff.; C.P. Jones (1971). Among juristic texts see especially *Dig*.49.1–13 (*Dig*.49.1.29 = *POxy*, XVII.2104 and XLIII.3106 is a letter of Alexander Severus stressing the right of appeal) and 28.3.69 for an appeal for mercy by a condemned man.

36 *Lex imp.Vesp*. (EJ, 364 = Braund, *AN*, 293), esp. lines 29ff. (this clause retrospectively ratifies earlier acts of Vespasian, but the implication of the whole text is that the *lex* itself is giving authority to future acts); *lex Irnit*.XIX, lines 18ff., XX, lines 33ff., B, lines 10ff.; Gai.*Inst*.1.4–5; *Dig*.1.4.1.

37 Strabo, 17.3.25 (840).

38 EJ, 307 = *RDGE*, 26, col. II, 36ff. = *RGE*, 97; EJ, 311, no. V; Tac.*Ann*. 4.43.1; cf. *RDGE*, 23.

39 Tac.*Ann*.1.11; Suet.*Aug*.101. For the date see EJ, 52 (from *Fasti Oppiani*, *Amiternini* and *Antiates*). An attempt to recalculate this (K. Wellesley, 'The *Dies Imperii* of Tiberius', *JRS*, 57 (1967), 23–30) in order to allow

more time for Drusus' journey to Illyricum is unnecessary, since Drusus could have taken ship from Ancona to Aquileia.

40 For *rationes imperii* see Suet.*Cal.*16.1; for the advice Tac.*Ann.*1.11; *Agric.*13.

41 On censuses Brunt (1990), 329–39; Neesen (1980), 36ff.

42 In favour of a calculated general strategy Luttwak (1976); in favour of a calculated strategy on the northern frontier Syme, *CAH*, X¹, 351ff.; Wilkes (1969), 48–9; in favour of old-style expansion Mann (1979); Wells (1972), ch.1; Brunt (1990), 433–84; Isaac (1990), ch. 9; in favour of opportunism Gruen (1990); and *CAH*, X², ch. 4.

43 Strabo, 4.5.3 (200–1).

44 Tac.*Ann.*2.26.3.

45 *Cursus publicus* – Suet.*Aug.*49 (cf. *ILS*, 5903ff. for later inscriptions using the term). On the lack of intelligence about frontier areas and what lay beyond and the difficulty of implementing a coherent policy, Millar (1982).

46 Tac.*Ann.*3.47.1; cf. 40–6.

47 EJ, 311, no. V; *ILS*, 212 = Smallwood, *GCN*, 369 = Braund, *AN*, 570; Tac.*Ann.*11.23–5; 13.50–1.

48 Tac.*Ann.*1.72.3; 3.68; 4.21.3. Amid the considerable *maiestas* bibliography note especially Levick (1976), 180–200 (although the view of the *lex Iulia maiestatis* there must be treated with caution); Allison and Cloud (1962); Chilton (1955). The fullest treatment, that of R.S. Rogers, *Criminal Trials and Criminal Legislation under Tiberius* (Middletown, 1935), is undermined by its determination to attribute to Augustan legislation the developments of later case law.

49 Tac.*Ann.*3.38.1, 66.1; 4.13.2, 19.4.

50 Pliny, *Ep.*2.11–12; 4.9; 5.20; 6.5; 6.13; 7.6. See in general Brunt (1990), 53–95 = 'Charges of Provincial Maladministration under the Early Principate', *Historia*, 10 (1961), 189–227.

51 Dio, 53.13.2ff.

52. Dio, 53.13.2; cf. Tac.*Ann.*12.60.3; Ulpian, *Dig.*1.17.

53 For the term 'public provinces', Tac.*Ann.*13.4.2; cf. Millar (1989).

54 Dio, 53.13.2–4, 14.5.

55 Ibid., 53.14.2; cf. 40.56.1–2.

56 *Legati pro praetore* – ibid., 53.13.5–7 (examples in EJ, 199, 201, 207, 208, 209, 211, 268); quaestors and *legati* – 53.14.6–7.

57 Ibid., 53.15.2–3.

58 Ibid., 53.15.4–6, 16.1.

59 The one possible example known to me is an anonymous citizen of Tabai who sat on the judicial *consilium* of P. Cornelius Dolabella (cos. 44), when the latter was proconsul of Asia and is also said to have been honoured as *dikaiodotēs* (Robert (1937), 324–8). However this man is unlikely to have been a *legatus iuridicus*, appointed to be on the governor's staff. For later evidence for *iuridici* see *ILS*, III.1, pp. 365–6.

60 Tac.*Ann.*4.15.2.

61 EJ, 191 = Braund, *AN*, 738.

62 Pliny, *HN* 3.91; Gabba (1986), at 77f.

63 *Lex portorii Asiae*, lines 72–3; cf. Hyginus 205L = 168–9Thul (the

fractions there may be regarded as rent; so, e.g., E. lo Cascio, 'La Struttura Fiscale dell' Impero Romano', in Crawford (1986), 29–59 at 46–7; but see in general Neesen (1980), 45ff.).

64 *Lex portorii Asiae*, lines 8ff., esp. 58–87.
65 Ibid., lines 88ff., 98ff., 103ff., 109ff.
66 This was clear from Tac.*Ann*.13.50–1, before the *lex portorii* was discovered. Note the dedication to M. Plautius M.f. Silvanus (proconsul of Asia *c.* AD 6) by *publicani 'e[x pecunia] phorica'* (*AE* (1968), 483). Recent scholars who have stressed the continuing importance of *publicani* include Cimma (1981); and Brunt (1990), ch. 13.
67 Cic.*Att*.6.2.5.
68 Tac.*Ann*.2.47.4 (the name rests on an emendation and is not certain). See in general on the post of *curator* Burton (1979).
69 For *conventus* see Habicht (1975); Burton (1975). For the advantages see, e.g., Dio Chrys.35.15; 38.26; 40.33.
70 Dio, 54.32.1; Suet.*Claud*.2.1; EJ, 119, 120; *CIL*, XIII.1036, 1042–5; *CRAI*, (1958), 106.
71 Dio, 56.25.3 for festival; EJ, 105, lines 14, 22ff; *Coll*.11.7.1–2; *CIL*, VIII.17639 = AJ, 152; *AE* (1946), 180; *AE* (1954), 241; Tac.*Ann*.1.78; 14.31. cf. Millar (1977), 385ff.; Deininger, (1965), esp. 21ff., 33ff.
72 Tac.*Ann*.15.20; Pliny, *Ep*.7.6.1; cf. 3.4.2; 5.20; 6.13. 2.
73 *CIL*, XIII.3162 = AJ, 140.
74 Pol.6.19.2; cf. App.*Iber*.78.334 (the proportions of cavalry and infantry service in *Tab.Heracl*.100–1 reflect a different period and different concerns: in any case they do not necessarily presume the completion of cavalry service). On this point see Brunt (1990), 193, 203; and more generally on the nature of the Republican army Keppie (1984).
75 For evidence for conscription see Brunt (1971), ch. 22; for length of service and instances of professionalism, Smith (1958).
76 Brunt (1990), ch. 9, 188–214. AD 6 – Vell.2.111.1; Pliny, *HN* 7.149; Dio, 55.31; cf. 57.5.4; Tac.*Ann*.1.31; AD 9 – Dio, 56.23.2–3; under Tiberius – Tac.*Ann*.4.4.2; Vell.2.130.2. Cf. Livy, 6.12.4; Suet.*Aug*.25.2.
77 Dio, 54.25.5–6; 55.23ff. and 31.1. Earliest evidence for the ban on marriage – Dio, 60.24.3; fullest discussion – J.B. Campbell, 'The Marriage of Soldiers under the Empire', *JRS*, 68 (1978), 153–66. For other aspects of soldiers' conditions of service see Campbell (1984), 207ff.
78 Legionary distribution – Tac.*Ann*.4.5; Dio, 55.23ff. For the pattern of recruitment see Forni (1953).
79 Tac.*Ann*.14.27; *Hist*.2.74.1; 80.3. The regional pattern of recruitment is already visible under Augustus in EJ, 261 = *ILS*, 2483. See also MacMullen (1988), 537, fig. 13.
80 Examples of *beneficiarii* in *ILS*, III.1, pp. 479–80.
81 Examples of *stationarii* – Pliny, *Ep*.10.77–8; *ILS*, 9072–3, 9087, 9089; Robert (1937), 285; Keil and von Premerstein (1910), no. 101; Mitteis, Wilcken, *GCP*, II.2, nos 111, 115, 122–5, 278; cf. *GCP*, I.1, 413f.
82 Examples of *frumentarii* – Smallwood, *NTH*, 334(a) and (b) = *ILS*, 9473, 2365; cf. *ILS*, III.1, 488–9; Keil and von Premerstein (1914), 11, no. 9; on *speculatores* see Suet.*Aug*.27, 74; Plut.*Galba* 24; Dio, 77.17; and other evidence collected by Hirschfeld (1913), 576–612.

83 Local military officials – EJ, 243–4; Smallwood, *GCN*, 258; Strabo, 4.6.4. (203); public works – EJ, 263–4; *GCN*, 448–9; Smallwood, *NTH*, 394; P.A. Brunt, *ZPE*, 13 (1974), 161; later *praepositi* – *RIB*, 583, 587; *ILS*, 2768–9, 3251; *ILT*, 880.
84 Tac.*Ann.*1.9.5.

Appendix to Chapter 7

1 Mitteis, Wilcken, *GCP*, I.1, 8ff., 146ff.; E.G. Turner, 'Ptolemaic Egypt', *CAH*, VII².1, ch. 5.
2 Dio, 51.17; Tac.*Ann.*2.59; *Hist.*1.11; Arr.*Anab.*3.5.7. See in general on Roman Egypt Mitteis, Wilcken, *GCP*, I.1, 34ff., 153ff., 185ff.; Bowman (1986); Foraboschi (1986); S.L. Wallace, *Taxation in Roman Egypt from Augustus to Diocletian* (London, 1938). On the transition from Ptolemaic to Roman Egypt see Lewis (1970).
3 Dio, 53.13.2; *Dig.*1.17.1; Tac.*Ann.*2.59; 12.60. cf. Brunt, 'The Administrators of Roman Egypt', *JRS*, 65 (1975), 124–47 = Brunt (1990), 215–54.
4 *FIRA*, III, no. 166 = *P.Ryl.*II.74 for edict of M. Petronius Mamertinus (prefect, AD 133–7), issued when he was holding *conventus* for the *nomoi* beyond Coptos. For court-proceedings, cf. *POxy*, XXXVI.2757, XLII.3015.
5 Strabo, 17.1.12 (797C); *FIRA*, III, 171(a). For the *iuridicus*, cf., e.g., *FIRA*, III, nos. 65, 166; for the *idios logos*, EJ, 245 = *ILS*, 2690, Smallwood, *GCN*, 391 = *OGIS*, 669, col. ii, 44, and especially his rule-book, 'Gnomon', ed. W. Schubart, *BGU*, V (Berlin, 1919), abbreviated in *FIRA*, I, no. 94; cf. *POxy,* XLII.3014.
6 For lower officials see, e.g. Smallwood, *NTH*, 253 = *ILS*, 2728; *Sel.Pap.* II.243, 246, 248–9, 257, 260, 303; Bowman (1986), 65ff.
7 Mitteis, Wilcken, *GCP*, I.1, 287ff; Tomsin (1961).
8 For these estates see, e.g. Tomsin (1961), 84, with n. 16; Smallwood, *GCN*, 440 = Mitteis, Wilcken, *GCP*, I.2, 176.

8 CITIES, MUNICIPALITIES AND LOCAL GOVERNMENT

1 For Alexander see Plut.*Mor.*328E (seventy cities); cf., e.g., W.W. Tarn, *Alexander the Great* (Cambridge, 1948) vol. II, 232ff. Seleucus is said to have founded fifty-nine cities within his kingdom (App.*Syr.*57).
2 See B.H. Warmington, *Carthage* (London, 1960), ch. 3.
3 See Frederiksen (1976); A. la Regina, 'I territori sabelli e sannitici', *DArch*, 4/5 (1970/1), 443–59.
4 Galsterer (1971b), (1979); Mackie (1983b); Blagg and Millet (1990), sect. III, chs 10–12 (by S. Keay, N. Mackie and J.C. Edmondson). For pre-Roman communes see Barker and Lloyd (1991), chs 4, 5, 6.
5 Clemente (1974).
6 Sherwin-White (1973a), ch. 10, 251ff., ch. 15, 360–79.
7 Paus.10.4.1 and 32.10.
8 For Roman *vici* see Vitr.5.1ff; Tac.*Germ.*16; Frederiksen (1976); *fora*

and *conciliabula* in Italy, *lex rep.*, line 31 with the commentary in *JRLR*; the same in Gaul, Actes du colloque 'Le *vicus* Gallo-romain', *Caesarodunum*, 11, *numéro spécial* (1976); Drinkwater (1983), 179–83, 203–4; in Britain, Burnham and Wacher (1991); Mauretanian *pagi* and *castella*, *ILS*, 6884ff.

9 Wightman (1985), 91ff.

10 App.*Illyr.*22; *Syll.*³ 880 = AJ, 131; cf. *Syll.*³ 888 = AJ, 139 for a village in Thrace which may have formed part of an imperial estate. cf. AJ, 21ff.

11 Jos.*AJ* 18.2.3; *OGIS*, 488, 527, 609, 769; AJ, 142–4, cf. 122; Welles, *RC*, nos 69, 70 (= *OGIS*, 262); G. Bean, *Anat.Stud.*, 10 (1960), 71, no. 124. cf. Harper (1928).

12 AJ, 74 = Bruns, no. 114; AJ, 93 = Bruns, 116 = Levick, *GRE*, no. 111; AJ, 111, esp. lines 9ff.; AJ, 142 = Keil and von Premerstein (1914), 37f.; contrast Peyras (1975) for a popular lessee of an estate belonging to the local *res publica* of Biha Bilta in a later period.

13 Frontin.45–6Thul; *Dig.*50.1.38.1; 50.6.6.10–11; *CJ* 5.62.8; Millar (1977), 179–81. This seems to have been a problem peculiar to the imperial estate, not affecting large estates owned by communities (note 12 above) or private individuals such as those mentioned by Strabo (5.3.2; 8.5.1).

14 Plut.*Mor.*814F; cf. Phil.*V.Soph.*1.25.532 for Polemon's advice to Smyrna.

15 Cic.*2Verr.*2.122–7.

16 Pliny, *Ep.*10.79.1; 80; 112; 114; 115.

17 Bruns, no. 8 = *FIRA*, I, no. 16; cf. Galsterer (1971a).

18 Bruns, no. 18 = *FIRA*, I, no. 13.

19 Cic.*ND* 3.74; *Off.*3.60; cf. Crawford (1989a).

20 Frederiksen (1965).

21 Lines 159ff.

22 *Lex mun.Tar.* (Bruns, no. 27 = *FIRA*, I, no. 18), lines 39–42; cf. *lex Urs.* (Bruns, no. 28 = *FIRA*, I, no. 21), chs 77–8; *lex Flav.mun.* (Gonzalez, 1986), ch. 82.

23 Lines 83–8; cf. 126–40.

24 The law only refers to current practice of these trades, but, if there were infamy attached to them, it would have remained with those who had practised them in the past. For such a contract cf. the [*Lex de munere publi*]*co libitina*[*rio*] from Puteoli and Cumae, *AE* (1971), no. 88 = L. Bove, 'Due Nuove Iscrizioni di Pozzuoli e Cuma', *RAAN*, 41 (1966), 207–39; cf. Bove (1967).

25 Bruns, no. 27 = *FIRA*, I, no. 18. On the development of municipal laws see Galsterer (1987), emphasising that there is no single standard model of a municipal law.

26 cf. note 22 above.

27 *Lex Urs.*ch. 75; *lex Flav.mun.*62; Smallwood, *GCN*, 365 = *ILS*, 6043.

28 Lines 7–31. cf. the surviving letters of the next column (the word *testamento* suggests freedmen manumitted by testament).

29 Ateste fragment – Bruns, no. 17 = *FIRA*, I, no. 20; cf. line 9 for '*ex h(ac) l(ege) n(ihilum) r(ogatur)*' revealing that the law was passed in a Roman assembly; line 12 for the reference to the *lex Roscia*. In *Tab.Heracl.*111 the *actio doli* appears after the *actio iniuriarum* in the list (but not here

in line 3). For opposing views on the date of the Ateste fragment see Crawford (1989a); and Laffi (1986), at 18–22.

30 Lines 10–21. For the recalling of cases to Rome see Chapter 4, pp. 66–9.
31 Bruns, no. 16 = *FIRA*, I, no. 19. See the recent detailed studies of Laffi (1986); F.J. Bruna, *Lex Rubria, Caesars Regelung für die richterlichen Kompetenzen der Munizipalmagistrate in Gallia Cisalpina* (Studia Gaiana, 5) (Leiden, 1972).
32 *Lex Rubria*, chs 20, 21 and 22.
33 Ch. 21, line 19, ch. 22, lines 27–8.
34 Ch. 21, lines 21ff.
35 References in Galsterer (1987), 183–4; Crawford (1988), at 135, notes 5–6.
36 Bruns, no. 28 = *FIRA*, I, 21. Cf. Gabba (1988).
37 Ch. 75, cf. *lex mun.Tar.*, lines 32–5; ch. 80, cf. *lex mun.Tar.*, lines 21–5; ch. 91, cf. *lex mun.Tar.* 26–31.
38 Chs 101, 125; cf. *Tab.Heracl.*, lines 135–41.
39 See Crawford (1989b). On *tumultus Italicus/Gallicus* see *lex Urs.* ch. 67.
40 Gonzalez (1986); cf. Bruns, no. 30 = *FIRA*, I, no. 23 (*lex Salpensana*), *FIRA*, no. 24 (*lex Malacitana*).
41 See Gonzalez (1986), 150–1; Bruns, no. 31; *AE* (1984), no. 507; *AE* (1989), no. 510.
42 Pliny, *HN* 3.30.
43 *Lex Irnit*.69; *Mal*.69.
44 Gonzalez (1986), 181, lines 33ff.
45 Gell.*NA* 16.13.4ff.
46 Chs 64–74 and 125–8.
47 Cf. the elaborate rules in *Tab.Heracl.*, lines 135–40.
48 *Lex Urs*.ch. 75; *lex mun.Tar.*, lines 32–8. *lex Urs*.ch. 67; *lex mun.Tar.*, lines 21–5.
49 *Lex Urs*.ch. 129, cf. 82, 96.
50 The initial lacuna would have dealt with the composition of the citizen-body and its religious affairs, the missing Tablet V with the local senate, what cannot be reconstructed of Tablet VI with elections.
51 Burton (1979).
52 *Lex Urs*.chs 127, 130–1. The *album* containing the rules for jurisdiction of the provincial governor appears in *lex Irnit*.ch. 85.
53 *Lex Irnit*.ch. 84, cf. 69 concerning suits for the recovery of public money.
54 *Lex Irnit*.ch. 74; cf. *lex Urs*.ch. 106.
55 See chs 26, G, J, 62, 67, 74, 75, 90, 96 and especially ch. 69 for procedure. cf.*lex Urs*.ch. 95.
56 *Lex Osca*, lines 8–13; *Tab.Heracl.*, line 119; *lex Urs*.ch. 102. The public contract with the undertaker of both funerals and executions at Puteoli and Cumae need only imply the capital punishment of slaves (see note 24 above). Simshaüser (1973), 175ff. adduces Cic.*Clu*.41, 125, 127, but these passages only show quasi-judicial decisions by a local senate. Capital trials could occur in communities other than colonies and *municipia* under the Principate (Plut.*Mor*.815A; Apul.*Met*.3.2ff.; Lucian, *Demonax*, 11).
57 *Lex Arae Narbonensis* (EJ, 100 = *ILS*, 112), lines 30–1.
58 *ILS*, 6090 = *FIRA*, I, no. 92 (Tymanda) shows the general principles; for

the constitutional elements in *civitates peregrinae* cf., e.g., *ILS*, 5516 = EJ, 348, 6095 = EJ, 355, 6099 = EJ, 354, 6798, 6816, 6827, 6831, 6898, 7045. The most comprehensive account of local administration remains Liebenam (1900), II, 174ff.

59 These arrangements have their origin under the Republic; cf. those of the Sicilian cities (Cic.*2Verr*.2.122–7). For the pattern see *Tab.Heracl.*, lines 83–8; *lex Irnit*.ch. 31ff.; for the function of the *quinquennalis*, e.g., *ILS*, 6121.

60 *Sufetes* in, e.g., *ILS*, 6100; *ITrip*, 321 = EJ, 346; *vergobretus* in *ILS*, 7040 = EJ, 340.

61 See Livy, 34.51.6 on Flamininus, who chose the senate and the judges from those with the highest property-qualification.

62 Illustrated in, e.g., the *SC de Thisbensibus* (*RDGE*, 2 = *RGE*, 21); cf. *SEG*, XXV.445 = *RGE*, 17.

63 Paus.7.16.10; Fabius Maximus' letter to Dyme (*RDGE*, 43, lines 9–17).

64 See, e.g., *Syll.*³ 768, 786, 797, 1262; *OGIS*, 441, 562; *SEG*, I.329, XVIII. 293; AJ, 46 = *IG*, IX.2.261 on a league assembly.

65 Poseidonius, *FGH*, 87, F36 (Athen.*Deip*.5.48–53, 211D–15B); App.*Mith*.109; Paus.1.20.5; Plut.*Sulla* 12–13.

66 Pliny, *Ep*.10.114–15.

67 EJ, 98 (*OGIS*, 458; *SEG*, IV.498), line 83; *IGRR*, IV.1.188.

68 Wörrle (1988), 96ff., lines 92 and 109ff.

69 Cf. AJ, 122 = *IGRR*, III.409 for the distinction between *ekklēsiastai* (members of the assembly) and *politai* (citizens) in a community which has newly attained city-status; Dio Chrys.34.21 for the so-called linen-workers, poor men outside the citizen-body of Tarsus.

70 *Lex Flav.mun.* (*Mal.*), chs 50–9; AJ, 122 = *IGRR*, III.409 for the distinction between *ekklēsiastai* and *politai* in a community which has newly attained city-status.

71 AJ, 65a = MW, 464, col. 2, lines 3–4.

72 *SEG*, XXIV.614.

73 Note especially Dio Chrys.31, 34, 40 and 43 (for the democracy at Rhodes *Or*.31; cf. AJ, 52 = *IG*, XII.1.2; *Syll.*³ 810); Plut.*Mor*. 798–9, 813D, 815C–D.

74 See Geagan (1967), esp. 32ff., 41ff. and 83ff.; *idem* (1971), at 101ff. (= *SEG*, XXVI.120) for an inscription which in the editor's view referred to a Sullan reform (alternative datings – J.H. Oliver, *GRBS*, 13 (1972), 101–2; E. Badian, *AJAH*, (1976), 115–17).

75 Cic.*Balb*.28–30; *Phil*.5.14; 8.27; Rawson (1987).

76 For three generations of free birth later in relation to office-holding see Marcus' letter to Athens, Oliver (1970), document 1 – re-edited in C.P. Jones (1971) – lines 59–60, 74–9, and lines 30–5, 57–81, 94–102 for Marcus' general uneasiness over the slipping standards for citizenship. See Dio, 54.7.2 on corruption in granting Athenian citizenship in Augustus' time and on the whole issue Oliver (1970), 47–9.

77 Tac.*Ann*.2.55; *IG*, II² 1013, 1103; *Syll.*³ 796B; *SEG*, XV.108 = Smallwood, *NTH*, 443; cf. *IG*, II² 1069, 1072, 1077–8, 1103; Oliver (1941), no. 26; and see Oliver (1970), 44–65.

78 cf. Geagan (1967), 86–8 for restrictions on speech in the assembly.

79 Oliver (1941), esp. 1–8 on origins, and inscriptions nos 31–2 for organisation; *idem*, 'New Fragments of Sacred *Gerousia* 24 (*IG* II² 1108)', *Hesperia*, 30 (1961), 402–3 (ibid., 231–6, no. 31 for the fragments themselves published by B.D. Meritt); and *idem* (1970), 92ff.

80 *Syll.*³ 842; Oliver (1970), 119f.; Spawforth and Walker (1985–6).

81 Dio, 69.16.2; cf. *lex Irnit*.ch. J (Tab. VC, lines 10ff). Strabo, 10.4.22 (484C), contrasting the archaic Cretan constitutions with the present supremacy of Roman ordinances in Crete, as in other provinces, suggests that intervention of precisely this sort, adapting rather than suppressing existing constitutions, had been the rule since Augustus' time.

82 Pliny, *Ep.*10.110–11; *lex Urs*.ch. 134.

83 *Lex Urs*.ch.106; *lex Irnit*. ch. 74 (cf. Asc.7C; Suet.*Iul.*42; *Aug.*32; *Dig.*22.3.2; 47.22; *ILS*, 4966, 6720, 7190, 7212); Pliny, *Ep.*10.33; 34; 92–3.

84 *AE* (1962), 288; *ILS*, 6092 = Bruns, no. 81 = *MW*, 461).

85 Pliny, *Ep.* 10.79.1; 80, 112, 114, 115.

86 Ibid., 79. 1–2, 112.1, 114.1–2; cf. *Tab.Heracl.*, lines 83–8, 108–34; *lex Urs*. ch. 124; *lex Irnit*.chs 30–1; and for the currently huge numbers of councillors Dio Chrys.40.14.

87 Pliny, *Ep.*10.112.1–3, 113, 114.1.

88 On these see Chapter 11.

89 Dio Chrys.38.1; 39.1; 41.6–7.

90 Pliny, *Ep.*10.115.

91 Ibid., 10.110.1 for the constitution at Amisus (for those elsewhere cf. Dio Chrys.43.2; 44.1; 45.1; 48.1–2). On the *lex Cornelia* see note 67 above.

92 Pliny, *Ep.*10.92–3; cf. 33–4 and the references in note 83. It should be noted that exceptions could be made for those concerned with a public utility, such as the fire-brigade that Pliny wished to create at Nicomedia, and those whose purpose was funerary (see especially *ILS*, 7212 = *FIRA*, III, no. 35, lines 10ff. for a relevant *SC*).

93 *Ep.*10.110–11; *lex Urs*.134; cf. on the illegal holding of public property or funds, *Ep.*10.17A and B, 23, 54–5; *Syll.*³ 833; *Dig.*8.11.1; 50.4.6.1.

94 *Ep.*10.108. cf. the edict of Ti. Iulius Alexander (Bruns, no. 72 = Smallwood, *GCN*, 391, lines 18ff.) for the provincial treasury. Sherwin-White (1966), ad loc. quotes Paul.*Sent.*5.12.10 (cf. 5.38.1) on the priority of the *fiscus*. But does this apply to a municipal treasury? According to Marcian (*Dig.*50.1.10), only if a specific privilege has been conceded.

95 *Lex mun.Mal.* chs 63–6. Spitzl (1984), 89 on ch. 64, thinks that the immediate execution allowed here should not be assimilated to the *privilegium exigendi* in a creditors' gathering. Yet the principle of community priority remains the same.

96 *Lex Irnit*.ch. 84. The classical jurists recognised local jurisdiction but do not seem to give it such a wide scope (e.g., Paulus, *Dig.*50.1.28).

97 Pliny, *Ep.*10.95–6.

98 *Ep.*10.72–3.

99 *Ep.*10.65–6. For Trajan's solution being closer to Greek law see the commentary of Sherwin-White (1966), ad loc., following Volterra (1939). Mitteis (1891), 107, 127–8, believed it to be according to Roman principles – according to which, as also in the law of some Greek cities,

the exposure of a free child could not extinguish its status (cf. *Gnomon of Idios Logos*, paras 41 and 107 with Taubenschlag (1944–8), vol. I, 55, but the foster-parents were repaid. On Roman *alumni/ae* see the case of Petronia Iusta (*Tab.Herculan*.16 in G. Pugliese Carratelli, *PP*, 3 (1948), 165–84) with the revised interpretation of Arangio-Ruiz (1959).

100 *Ep*.10.31–2. cf. *Dig*.48.19.8.11–12 for criminal *venatores*. See by contrast *Ep*.10.58 for Flavius Archippus being condemned to the mines by a proconsul.

101 *Ep*.10.17A.3–4; 28.2–3 and *passim*.

102 Cic.*Att*.6.2.5; Smallwood, *GCN*, 380. cf. Burton (1979).

103 *Lex Urs*.chs. 65, 69, 72, 80–2, 134; *lex Flav.mun*.60–5; 77–80.

104 Pliny, *Ep*.10.110.

105 Dio Chrys.40; 43; 44.

106 Plut.*Mor*.813 D–F; cf. Dio Chrys.34.38–9.

107 See e.g., *OGIS*, 493; *Syll*.³ 850; AJ, 71, 87; *AE* (1977), 801; ILS, 6680, lines 9ff. cf. Liebenam (1900), 471ff.

9 ROMAN AND INDIGENOUS LAW

1 *AE* (1979), no. 377; Richardson (1983); Birks, Rodger and Richardson (1984).

2 Cic.*Flacc*.74; *2Verr*.2.50; *Fam*.13.19; and see below for the evidence for the Principate.

3 See Galsterer (1987).

4 Cf. *frag.Vat.* (*FIRA*, III, 41), 112 for Roman law in a *municipium* elsewhere.

5 *FIRA*, III, nos 49, 87–9, 92, 132, 137, 150, 157–8; Turner (1956) – the tablet is from the first half or middle of the third century AD.

6 *PYadin* 28–30, published in Lewis, Yadin and Greenfield (1989), reviewed by Goodman (1991).

7 On this see Tomulescu (1987).

8 *PDura*, no. 26.

9 *Tab.Pomp*.13; J.G. Wolff (1979).

10 *PYadin* 11, 17–21; cf., e.g., *PYadin* 10, 37, on which see Lewis, Katzoff and Greenfield (1987), at 230ff.

11 *Actio tutelae* – *PYadin* 28–30. cf. H.J. Wolff (1980). *Vadimonium* – *PYadin* 26, cf. 25. *Vadimonium* between Roman citizens involved *stipulatio* and *sponsio* (see, e.g., *Tab.Herculan*.16 (Chapter 8, note 99); *Tab.Pomp*. 32–3, 36, 38, 41, 70), but *fide rogare* and *promittere* could be substituted for a foreigner; see Bove (1979), 21ff. For eastern polygamy cf. Mitteis (1891), 28, 221–2.

12 As in *FIRA*, III, no. 170.

13 Mitteis, Wilcken, *GCP*, II.1, 36–40; II.2, nos 50–6; Taubenschlag (1944–8), I, 382, 411.

14 Mitteis, Wilcken, *GCP*, II.2, nos 280–2, 312–3; *PLouvre* 13–14; *CPRain*.I, no. 18; Mitteis (1891), 56ff., 223.

15 For a fragment of a Greek translation of a demotic Egyptian law-code, *POxy*, XLVI.3285 (cf. G. Mattha, *The Demotic Lawcode of Hermopolis*

West (Cairo, 1975); for decisions by Roman officials that Egyptian cases fell under Egyptian law see *FIRA*, I, no. 60 (a) and (b); *POxy*, XLII.3015; cf. Mitteis (1891), 40ff., 54ff., 180ff., 230ff., 380ff.

16 *PBrux*.I.1–21; Taubenschlag (1944–8), I, 111–12 with further references; cf. Gai.*Inst*.3.59–62; Just.*Inst*.2.10.1; Ulp.*Reg*.5.6. On endogamic marriages see Hopkins (1980a).

17 *FIRA*, II.753ff. (e.g., paras 1, 20, 36–7, 92); Mitteis (1891), 29ff., 79ff.

18 *PDura*, 26 (contrast 27), 30. For earlier legal syncretism, a contract in the Syriac language, but Greek in form see Goldstein (1966).

19 *PYadin*, 18; *Murabba'at*, 18, 19. Contrast *CPJ*, I, 20, 24, 25; II, 149, 413–14. See Volterra (1963); Rabello (1980).

20 Smallwood, *NTH*, 443 = *SEG*, XV.108; XXI.501, lines 47ff. See in general on the Athenian constitution at the time Geagan (1967); and Oliver (1970), 44ff.

21 Smallwood, *NTH*, 444 = *SEG*, XXI.502 = *IG*, II/III^2 1103, lines 7ff. cf. ibid., 1104.

22 *IG*, IX^2 1100b, line 11.

23 Gai.*Inst*.I.193.

24 A. Hauvette-Besnault and M. Dubois. 'Inscriptions de Tralles', *BCH*, 5 (1881), at 344–5, line 15; Phil.*V.Apoll*.8.7.12; Mitteis (1891), 358. Cf. Phil.*V.Apoll*.1.13 for the age of majority varying from city to city.

25 Pliny, *Ep*.10.65–6; cf. Chapter 8, p.51 with note 99.

26 Plut.*Mor*.814F.

27 Oliver (1970), document 1; C.P. Jones (1971), line 43.

28 Gai.*Inst*.I.86.

29 For the argument that a provincial governor in private cases tended to play the part of the magistrate at Rome, performing jurisdiction rather than judging, see Chapter 4, pp. 57–8, 64–5 with notes 83, 106–7. The evidence from the Republic in summary is: *lex prov.praet.*Cnidos IV, 33–5; Cic.*2Verr*.2.32–3; *Flacc*.70; *QF*. 1.2.10; *Att*.6.1.15 (where Cicero's edict implies procedure parallel to that of jurisdiction at Rome); *SC de Asclepiade* (*RDGE*, 22 = *FIRA*, I, no. 35 = *RGE*, 66), Latin 7ff., Greek, 18ff.; *Tabula Contrebiensis* (cf. note 1 above). For the Principate we have the Fourth Cyrene Edict (EJ, 311 = *SEG*, IX.8, IV, lines 65ff.), where *cognitio* by the proconsul is only in question in capital cases and not all of those. cf. Mitteis (1891), 132; and for the use of *iudices* or *recuperatores* Dio Chrys.35.15; *CJ*, 3.8.2., 42.1; 7.53.2. See also Phil.*VS* 1.524 for a court of 100 at Sardis, reminding us of the centumviral court at Rome.

30 *Dig*.47.12.3.5 (Ulpian); contrast *CJ*, 8.53.1 on the allowance to be made for local *consuetudo* by a provincial magistrate.

10 ROMAN CITIZENSHIP

1 *Syll.*^{3} 543 = S.M. Burstein, *The Hellenistic Age from the Battle of Ipsos to the Death of Kleopatra VII* (TDGR, 3), no. 65, lines 26–39.

2 Livy, 41.8.9–11; Cic.*Att*.4.18.4 (cf. on the *lex Papia* of 65 BC, Cic.*Balb*.52; *Off*.3.47; *Arch*.10; *Schol.Bob*.175St; Dio, 37.9.5). For an example of a man

using this route to become a freedman in the emperor's service in the second century AD see *POxy*, XXVI. 3312.

3 Livy, 38.36.7–8; *lex Iulia* – App.*BCiv*.1.20.86–7; 23.99; Vell.Pat.2.20; Gell.4.4.3; Cic.*Balb*.21.

4 For *connubium* and *commercium* Livy, 8.14.10; Cic.*Caec*.102; Dion.Hal.6.95; Festus, 426, 474–5L (cf. for the meaning of *commercium* Cic.*2Verr*.3.93). See in general on the romanisation of Italy, Sherwin-White (1973a), chs 2, 3 and 4 with the appendix on pp. 190–214; Brunt (1971), chs 5 and 6; *idem*, (1988), ch. 2; Humbert (1978); Galsterer (1976).

5 Livy, 39.3.4–6 (187 BC); 41.8.6–12 and 9.9–11 (177 BC); 42.10.2–3 (172 BC); Asc.3C.

6 Livy, 26.40.3ff.; cf. *Syll*.³ 585, line 86; *lex rep*., lines 78–9 with commentary in *JRLR*; Cic.*Balb*.53–4.

7 *ILS*, 8888; Cic.*Balb*.46, cf. 50 on Pompeius Strabo's grant to P. Caesius of Ravenna. Note also Sisenna fr. 120 Peter for the *lex Calpurnia* allowing enfranchisements on account of *virtus*.

8 See in general Taylor (1960).

9 Cic.*Balb*. esp. 6, 19; *Arch*.29; *Syll*.³ 752, 755; cf. Justin, 43.5.11 on Pompeius Trogus; Caes.*BG* 4.12.4 on Piso Aquitanus; and in general Badian (1958), appendix B, pp. 302ff.

10 Strabo, 14.2.15 and 24 (656, 659–60); *Syll*.³ 761; *SEG*, II.547–8.

11 Asc.3C; Dio, 41.36.3; *FIRA*, I, no. 20, lines 12–13.

12 Cic.*Att*.14.12.1; contrast Pliny, *HN* 3.91, where only a few cities have Latin rights and these were formerly free cities.

13 Brunt (1971), ch. 14, pp. 204ff.; Wilson (1966); *SC de Asclepiade* (*RDGE*, 22 = *FIRA*, I, no. 35, Latin, 3ff., Greek, 12ff.

14 Pliny, *Ep*.10.114.1.

15 Cic.*Balb*.28–30, with Rawson (1987).

16 P. Otac[ilius] Arra[nes f.] – A. Pantoni and A. Gianetti, 'Iscrizioni latine e greche di Montecassino', *Rend.Acc.Lincei*, ser. viii, 26 (1971), 427–44, at 434, no. 8.

17 For example the family of the poet Valerius Catullus and their social milieu, see Wiseman (1987), 335–48.

18 Cic.*Phil*.5.14; 8.27.

19 EJ, 302.

20 *Lex rep*., lines 78–9; *ILS*, 8888.

21 EJ, 301 = *RDGE*, 58 = *RGE*, 86, II, lines 20ff.

22 EJ, 311 = *RGE*, 102, III.

23 Roman citizens are not exempted in *lex Flav.mun*.chs G and 83. For the law's probable dependence on an Augustan *lex Iulia municipalis* see Gonzalez (1986), 150.

24 Seston and Euzennat (1971), at 472–3; *salvo iure gentis* (lines 13, 19–20, 37) is also to be restored in line 9 of *P.Giss*. 40 (Mitteis, Wilcken, *GCP*, II, 2, no. 377). Cf. Sherwin-White (1973a), 312, 336, 380ff., and *idem*, (1973b).

25 Cf. Frederiksen (1984), chs 10 and 11.

26 Dio, 41.24.1; 48.45.3; 49.16.1; cf. Livy, *Per*.110; Gell.16.13.4.

27 Pliny, *HN* 3.7 refers specifically to ten *municipia civium Romanorum* in Baetica.
28 Smallwood, *GCN*, 407(a) and (b); Pliny, *HN* 5.11 and 20, cf. 3.146 for an *oppidum Claudium* in Noricum.
29 Gai.*Inst*.1.96; *ILS*, 6781. cf. Sherwin-White (1973a), 251ff.
30 *IGRR*, IV.1276; *OGIS*, 470; Bowersock (1965), 119.
31 Hybreas – *SEG*, II.547–8; the Gauls – *CIL*, XIII.2805; Livy, *Per*.139; cf. *CIL*, XIII.1042–5 for C. Iulius Victor from Saintes.
32 Tac.*Ann*.1.58.1; Vell.Pat.2.118.2; *ILS*, 1977.
33 Suet.*Aug*.40.3.
34 *CRAI* (1971), 472–3, line 22, cf. 21, with Sherwin-White (1973b).
35 Sen.*Apoc*.3, cf. 9; *ILS*, 211 = Smallwood, *GCN*, 369 = Braund, *AN*, 570, col. II, 1ff.
36 For example, the military units rewarded by Marius and Pompeius Strabo (note 7 above).
37 Sherwin-White (1973a), 244ff.
38 Dio, 60.17.7 for the general rule about nomenclature and Claudius' permission for exceptions to be made. cf. Alföldy (1966).
39 Examples of Ti. Claudii who were enfranchised foreigners, not ex-slaves: *PIR*, C 787 (cf. Smallwood, *GCN*, 370, 105ff.), 812, 840, 889, 912, 937, 943, 959, 969, 1021, 1050 (cf. Tac.*Hist*.1.68).
40 Suet.*Claud*.25.3.
41 Dio, 78.9.5.

11 THE WORKINGS OF PATRONAGE

1 Badian (1958); Saller (1982); Brunt (1988), chs 7–8; Wallace-Hadrill (1989).
2 Chapter 3 with notes 48–51.
3 Cic.*Div.Caec*.2–3; *Verr*.1.16; *2Verr*.4.25; *Att*.2.1.5; 14.12.1; *Fam*.13.30, 32, 34–9; Plut.*Cic*.31.5; 32.1–2. cf. Livy, 26.32; Cic.*2Verr*.2.102, 110, 113; 4.6, 25, 48; Badian (1958), ch. 7.
4 Asc.3C; Cic.*Att*.5.11.2; Suet.*Jul*.8; Dio, 41.36.3; *FIRA*, I, no. 20, lines 12–13.
5 Pompeian patronage survives in Transalpine Gaul (Caes.*BG* 5.36; *BCiv*.1.34.3; 35.4–5 – for the patronage of the Domitii Ahenobarbi there cf. Cic.*Div.Caec*.6; *2Verr*.2.118). On Spain see *BCiv*.1.29.3; 2.18.5–7; *B.Hisp*.1.1–4; contrast 42.2 for Caesar's patronage through his quaestorship and praetorship.
6 *ILLRP*, 1068.
7 cf. Nicols (1980).
8 Nineteen examples, see, e.g., *ILS*, 6098, 6099, 6099a, 6100.
9 *ILS*, 6102, 6104, 6105.
10 Nicols (1980), 547ff.
11 *AE* (1961) no. 96, (1917), no. 239; *ILS*, 6096, perhaps also 6097, 6107, 6108 (since the men concerned have no Roman tribe named and may therefore be Latins).

12 Caes.*BG* 1.4.2, 31.3ff.; 2.2.4, 13.2; 6.4.2, 12.1–2; Poseidonius, *FGH*, 87, F17 and 18.

13 See, e.g., EJ, 216, 217; also P. Wuilleumier, *Inscriptions latines des trois Gaules, Gallia* Supp. 17 (1963), no. 229 for L. Caesar as patron of Lugdunum.

14 *Syll.*[3] 656 (= *RGE*, 26), lines 20ff.

15 Reynolds (1962), nos 2 and 3, lines 49ff.

16 Eilers (1991), 167–78.

17 Examples are EJ, 201 = *SEG*, VI.646; EJ, 203 = *OGIS*, 763; Smallwood, *GCN*, 245a = *Syll.*[3] 811; *SEG*, IX.56; XIV.644–5, 647, 650; XV.662; XVI.700; XVII.573; XVIII.260; 588; XX.730; *IG*, IV.14; VII.268, 311, 331; IX.1.722–3; XII.5.285, 698,756–7; *IGRR*, I.654; IV.253.

18 Cf. *IGRR*, IV.292, lines 24 and 39.

19 For example Lugdunum and Vienne in AD 68–9 (Tac.*Hist*.1.64–6, 77; 2.66).

20 Plut.*Mor*.814C.

21 Pliny, *Ep*.4.9, esp. 6, 8, 17; cf. Ulpian in *Dig*.1.16.6.3.

22 *RDGE*, 57 (= EJ, 300, *RGE*, 85); Reynolds (1962), no. 10; cf. ibid., no. 36 and appendix V, pp. 156ff.

23 Smallwood, *GCN*, 370, lines 107ff. For a recommendation that did not work see Reynolds (1962), no. 13, line 5, where Augustus says that he would have liked to do a favour to the Samians on account of his wife but regrets that he cannot.

24 Pliny, *Ep*.3.4.4; cf. note 16 above.

25 Fronto, *Ad Ant.Pium* 8; Tac.*Dial*.5.5.

26 Bowersock (1965), 30ff.

27 Bowersock (1969), 43ff.

28 *PIR*, C 812 – Balbillus; Phil.*VSoph*.1.22.521ff. – Dionysius (who became a satrap and *eques*); Dio Chrys.7.66; 40.13; 41.6; 45.1–2; Phil. *VSoph*.1.7.488. cf. C.P. Jones (1978), esp. chs 2 and 6.

29 Phil.*VSoph*.1.21.520, 25.531 (cf. Dio Chrys.40.1.14 for earlier gifts). Polemo's influence is attested in an inscription from Smyrna (*IGRR*, IV.1431, line 33).

30 *SEG*, XVII.315 = Smallwood, *NTH*, 488; *ILS*, 6988 = AJ, 107; *ILS*, 6680.

31 Pliny, *Ep*.2.13; 9.28; 10.4.

32 Fronto, *Ad Amic*.1.3. cf. Saller (1982), 145ff., 172ff.; Champlin (1980), 13ff.; MacMullen (1988), 83–4.

33 *ILS*, 212 = Smallwood, *GCN*, 369; Tac.*Ann*.11.22–3; 12.23; Afer (from Nimes) – Tac.*Ann*.4.52; *PIR*, D 126; Asiaticus (from Vienne) – *Ann*.11.1; Jos.*AJ* 19.102, 159, 252; Graecinus – *Agric*.4.1. cf. *AE* (1946), no. 94 = EJ[2], 371.

34 Wörrle (1988), 55, 96ff., see esp. lines 102ff. of the decree. cf. G.M. Rogers, 'Demosthenes of Oenoanda and Models of Euergetism', *JRS*, 81 (1991), 91–100, for the way the creation of this festival was negotiated with the local community.

35 Bruns, no. 86 = AJ, 110 = *CIL*, VIII.10570; *Syll.*[3] 888 = AJ, 139 = *CIL*, III. 12336.

12 PUBLICITY, THEATRE AND CULT

1 *1Macc.*8.16.

2 *Mark.*12.16; *Matt.*22.20–1.

3 Pol.18.46.5, cf. 44; Ferrary (1988), 86–7.

4 *RDGE*, 34, lines 11ff.; cf. *RDGE*, 38, lines 23ff.

5 *SEG*, XVI.486 = Derow and Forrest (1982).

6 Hellanikos, *FGH*, 4 F84 = Dion.Hal.1.72; Ogilvie (1965), 32ff. cf. Galinsky (1969).

7 Livy, 10.23.1–2 (296 BC); *RRC*, no. 235 (137 BC); cf. no. 20 (269–8 BC) for the wolf and the twins without the tree.

8 Plut.*Rom.*3.1 and 8.9 (Diokles, *FGH*, 826); Ogilvie (1965), 39–40; Galinsky (1969), 141ff.; Skutsch (1985), 190 and 193ff. on lines 31 and 34ff. – showing that Ennius retained the early tradition, whereby both Aeneas and Romulus were in effect founders of Rome.

9 Lyc.*Alex.*1226–82; West (1984).

10 Plut.*Flamin.*16.7; cf. *BCH*, 19 (1895), 554 for a priest of *Roma* and *Pistis* at Teos (thought by Mellor (1975), 51 to be late second-century).

11 Stobaeus, 3.7.12; Bowra (1957).

12 *Syll.*³ 702, lines 6–7 (*c.* 157–6 BC).

13 *Syll.*³ 631; cf. Ferrary (1988), 125ff.; L. Robert (1937), 445–50. A recently discovered example is in Malay and Petzl (1984), lines 8–13.

14 Argos – *BCH*, 88 (1964), 570; Gytheion – EJ, 102, lines 11–12. See *RE*, XXIV (1963), *Quinctius*, no. 45 (H. Gundel), 1075–6.

15 Cic.*2Verr.*2.51, 114, 151; *QF* 1.1.26; Plut.*Luc.*23; *OGIS*, 437 (= *RDGE*, 47), lines 5–6, 29–31, cf. 438 and 439.

16 *IDelos* 1950; *SEG*, XVIII.570 = Bean (1948), no. 11, lines 69ff.; *IG*, II² (1938), line 2; IV.1².629, line 6; VII.48. There were *Romaia* at Ephesus by *c.* 90 BC (*OGIS*, 437, lines 89ff.); for Chios see L. Robert (1969). vol. I, 523. cf. Mellor (1975), 99ff., esp. 105, 165ff.

17 Mellor (1975), 192ff.; F. Poland, *RE Technitai*, VA.2.2473–558; Pickard-Cambridge (1968), 279ff., 306ff. (epigraphic appendix).

18 Plut.*Alex.*72; Arr.*Anab.*7.14; Athen.*Deip.* 5.196a–203b (198c for the priest of Dionysus and the *technitai*); cf. ibid., 12.538e–9a for the artists present at Alexander's mass marriage at Susa; and see Rice (1983), 52–8. See also *OGIS*, 50–1, 164; *SEG*, XIII.586 (Paphos).

19 *SEG*, II.580 (cf. L. Robert (1937), 39ff.); P. Herrman, *Anadolu*, 9 (1965), 29ff. (*Bull.Ep.* (1969), 495–6).

20 *IG*, XI.4.1136 with 1061; *OGIS*, 326.

21 *Syll.*³ 694 = *IGRR*, IV.1692; cf. Mellor (1975), 78; and L. Robert (1987), 489–96 on the provenance of the stone and the migration of the artists.

22 Plut.*Arat.*53.

23 Ferrary (1988), 189, n. 228, 206 (on *RDGE*, 44).

24 *IG*, II².1132; *Syll.*³ 690, 704–5.

25 Tac.*Ann.*4.56.

26 Livy, 43.6.5. The cult at Elaea (note 21 above) seems to have arisen out of

the cession of the Attalid kingdom to Rome and the consequent war with Aristonicus.

27 *OGIS*, 762, line 16.

28 Reynolds (1982), no. 1, lines 2, 7–11.

29 *SEG*, XVIII.570 = Bean (1948), 46–56, no. 11, lines 69ff.

30 Ch. Habicht, *MDAI(A)*, 72 (1957), no. 65, line 6. For the dating of this material see Errington (1987). Note also *Milet*, I.7, no. 203; and *IErythrai*, II (1973), no. 207, line 11 for further evidence for this cult in the second century and see Habicht (1990) for a recently discovered statue-base and further discussion.

31 *ILLRP*, 174–81b; A. Degrassi, 'Le dediche di popoli e re asiatici al Popolo Romano e Giove Capitolino', in *idem* (1962), I, 415–44; Mellor (1978); Lintott (1978).

32 Mellor (1975), 203ff. and (1978).

33 *ILLRP*, 174–7.

34 For a comprehensive study see Habicht (1970).

35 Price (1984), 28–9.

36 Sulla – *IG*, II^2.1039, line 57; *SEG*, XIII.279; Servilius Isauricus – *IEphesos*, III.702, line 8; VII.1.3066, lines 6–7; Marcius Censorinus (*SEG*, II.549); cf. Price (1984), 42 with no. 86; Bowersock (1965), 150–1.

37 Cic.*QF* 1.1.26; *Att*.5.21.7 – Price (1984), 40 seems to undervalue this.

38 For a commemorative monument to Marcus and Quintus Cicero and their families on Samos, not certainly connected with Quintus' governorship of Asia, see Dörner and Gruben (1953). For cults of Greeks associated with Rome see Price (1984), 48.

39 *Syll.*^{3} 760 = *IEphesos*, II, 251 (other Greek evidence – *IG*, XII.2.35; XII.5.165–6, 557). cf. Weinstock (1971), 96ff.

40 Pliny, *HN* 36.69; Dio, 51.15.5; Malalas, 9.278–9, 287.

41 Dio, 44.6.4; 47.18.3ff.; Cic.*Phil*.2.110; Plut.*Ant*.33.1; J. Keil, *Forschungen in Ephesos*, IV.3 (Vienna, 1951), 280f., no. 24 = EJ^2, 377.

42 Grant (1946), 246; Weinstock (1971), plates 21,10; 30,1–2; cf. ibid., 407ff. for the later evidence.

43 *Lex Urs*.chs 70–1; Grant (1946), 207; Weinstock (1971), 408 and plate 30, 9.

44 EJ, 56, cf. 9.

45 Plut.*Ant*.24.3; 26.5; 60.4–5; Sen.*Suas*.1.6–7; *IG*, II^2 1043, lines 22–3; Raubitschek (1941).

46 Plut.*Ant*.56.5–57.1; 75.4–5; *OGIS*, 195, corrected by Fraser (1957).

47 *POxy*, XII.1453; Rea (1982); EJ, 116.

48 Dio, 51.20.6–9; cf. EJ, 122; *SEG*, XXVI.1243 (for a later temple at the Artemision see *ILS*, 97).

49 See, e.g., Dio, 57.24.6; Tac.*Ann*.4.36; *OGIS*, 456, 537; EJ, 99, lines 13–14; EJ, 114; D.M. Pippidi, *Epigraphische Beiträge zur Geschichte Histrias* (Berlin, 1962), 101–5; *IGRR*, IV.975; *MDAI(A)*, 75 (1960), 70, nos 1–2; L. Robert (1969), vol. IV, 116.

50 EJ, 98a. cf. *IG*, XII.2.656 for a high-priest of the goddess Roma and Augustus Zeus Caesar Olympios.

51 EJ, 98 = *RDGE*, 65, esp. lines 5–10, 37–40; Price (1984), 54–5.

52 EJ, 315, esp. lines 9–10. cf. EJ, 99 (I), 102, lines 9ff., 115, 128–9.

53 EJ, 100 = *ILS*, 112 = Braund, *AN*, 125.
54 Lines 30–1. It is usually argued that the institution of the provincial *flamen* of Augustus in Narbonensis should be dated under the Flavians (*ILS*, 6964 = MW, 128; cf. ibid., 129 for the dating). See on this and what follows Fishwick (1978), esp. 1214f.
55 EJ, 105a, 105b; Quint.6.3.77; *Anth.Pal.*9.307; cf. EJ, 107a.
56 Livy, *Per.*139; EJ, 119, 120; Suet.*Claud.*2.1; Strabo, 4.3.2 (192C); Dio, 54.32.1; Tac.*Ann.*3.44; *CRAI* (1958), p. 106; *Inscr.III Gaules* (Wuilleumier, 1963), nos 215–23. cf. Chapter 10 with note 31.
57 Tac.*Ann.*1.39.1; 57.2.
58 Tac.*Ann.*1.10.
59 Tac.*Ann.*1.78; EJ, 102, lines 2–9, 106, 107, 107a, 111, 124, 134a.
60 EJ, 77, lines 1–2, 115a, 127; *IEphesos*, II, 253; cf. note 52 above.
61 EJ, 88, 93, 102, lines 10ff., 123, 124, 126, 129, 130a, 131, 134a, 135–7.
62 EJ, 102(b), lines 13ff.; Tac.*Ann.*4.37.5; 38.1; Suet.*Tib.*26.1; Dio, 57.4. Contrast Tac.*Ann.*4.15.4, 55.1; EJ, 88, 115(b), 134; *AE*, (1969/70), no. 651 (cf. *ILAfr*, 558); *AE* (1963), no. 104 = EJ², 369.
63 Dio, 51.20.6–9; EJ, 98, 313. For the importance of the centre in ruler-cult see Price (1984), 53ff.; Bowersock (1965), 121.
64.Tac.*Ann.*1.74; 2.50; 3.66; 4.2; Suet.*Tib.*48.2.
65 *IGRR*, IV.33; cf. *AE* (1973), no. 494 (Thespiae); *BCH*, 98 (1974), 649; *Corinth*, VIII.1, no. 19; *Anth.Pal.*6.161, 239, 345; 7.244; 9.224; 235; 419; 562; Bowersock (1965), 36; L. Robert (1938), 22–4.
66 Smallwood, *GCN*, 372 = *IGRR*, IV.1608a (cf. ibid., 1608c for a hymn to Tiberius as a god); *GCN,* 380, col. viii.1ff., 19ff., cf. *IEphesos*, VII.2.3801 – a dedication of the *hymnŏdoi* to Claudius.
67 Smallwood, *GCN*, 373a–b; cf. *POxy*, XXVII.2476, XXXI.2610; *BGU*, 1074; *Milet*, I.3, no. 156; EJ, 300; *IGRR*, I.149.
68 See, e.g., *SEG*, VI.59, VII.825; *IGRR*, I.17–21; Poland (1934), VA.2.2517ff.; Geagan (1972).

13 CONCLUSION

1 Ael.Arist.18 Keil (14 Dindorf), 60–1, 65, 102; cf. 7, 11; translated by Oliver (1952), cf. 889.
2 Oliver (1952), 892.
3 Geagan (1967).
4 Oliver (1970); C.P. Jones (1971); Dio Chrys.31; 34; 40; 43; C.P. Jones (1978), 19ff.
5 Apart from the fact that the honorand was originally a victor in civil war, the ancestry of the cult lay in the honours to victorious generals and to Rome herself for her victories in the east.
6 Garnsey and Saller (1987).
7 Hopkins (1980b), at 112ff.
8 See K. Hopkins, 'Models, Ships and Staples', in Garnsey and Whittaker (1983), 84–105; D'Arms and Kopff (1980); C. Panella, 'La distribuzione e i mercati', in Giardina and Schiavone (1981), vol. II, 55–80.
9 See, e.g., G. Rickman, *The Corn Supply of Ancient Rome* (Oxford, 1980);

and *idem*, 'The Grain Trade and the Roman Empire', in D'Arms and Kopff (1980), 261–75; Garnsey (1988).

10 See D.J. Mattingly (1988); S. Panciera, *'Olearii'*, in D'Arms and Kopff (1980), 235–80; R. Rodriguez-Almeida, 'Vicissitudini nella gestione del commercio del olio betico da Vespasiano a Severo Alessandro', in ibid., 277–90; M. Torelli, 'Industria estrattiva, lavoro artigianale, interessi economici', in ibid., 313–23; J. Ward-Perkins, 'The Marble Trade and its Organisation: Evidence from Nicomedia', in ibid., 325–38; R. Meiggs, 'Sea-Borne Timber Supplies to Rome', in ibid., 184–96. On the effect of trade with the east see Pliny, *HN* 12.84; 6.101.

11 Hopkins' examples (1980b; 113) are all in areas where one would expect some impact of military expenditure. For other general reservations about Hopkins' thesis see Duncan-Jones (1990), 30–47.

12 See *JRLR*, ch. III, and the commentary on *lex agr.*, lines 47ff.

13 For a cautious view about the movement of lamps see Harris (1980); for a more positive view Duncan-Jones (1990), 48–58; see also A. Carandini, 'Pottery and the African Economy', in P. Garnsey, K. Hopkins and C.R. Whittaker (eds), *Trade in the Ancient Economy* (London, 1983), 145–62.

14 Cunliffe (1988), esp. 1ff., 80ff., 145ff.

15 Dio, 52.19 for the ideology. cf. *RE*, XXIII.1 (1957), *procurator*, 1240–79 at 1259–63 (H.-G. Pflaum); de Martino (1958–67), vol. IV.1.350ff.

16 For this last view, P. Brown, *Society and the Holy in Late Antiquity* (London, 1982), 61. For corruption see most recently, MacMullen (1988), 137ff. For the failure of enforced coherence see, e.g., Rostovtzeff (1957b), ch. 12; A.H.M. Jones, *The Later Roman Empire* (Oxford, 1973), vol. II, 1045ff.; de Martino (1958–67), vol. V.510ff.

17 Tac.*Ann*.1.9.6.

18 Garnsey (1970); Rilinger (1988).

19 See Nörr (1969) for its being 'Herrschaft', not 'Macht'.

20 *Novanglus or a History of the Dispute with America* (1774), in *The Works of John Adams, Second President of the United States*, 10 vols (Boston, 1856), vol. 4, esp. ch. 3, 37–8 and chs 8–12. Adams complains that the British language of empire was introduced in order to insinuate that the prerogatives of the crown of England were like those of the Roman emperor.

21 *Ep*.10.47–8.

22 Chapter 3, pp. 36–40; Chapter 8, pp. 145–33.

23. Millar (1977); Nörr (1969), 115ff.

24 *PColumbia*, 123. cf. *POxy*, XVII.2104 and XLIII.3106 = *Dig*.49.1.29.

25 Nörr (1969), 44ff.

26 Brown (1982), 38; contrast E. Gibbon, *Decline and Fall of the Roman Empire*, ch. 37.

27 Garnsey (1970); MacMullen (1974); de Ste Croix (1981).

28 R. Folz, *L'Idée d'Empire en Occident du V au XII⁶ siècle* (Paris, 1953), 12f.

BIBLIOGRAPHY

Accame, S. (1946), *Il dominio romano in Grecia dalla guerra acaica ad Augusto*, Rome.

Alföldy, G. (1966), 'Notes sur le relation entre le droit de la cité et la nomenclature dans l'empire romain', *Latomus*, 25: 37–57.

Allison, J.C. and Cloud, J.D. (1962), 'The *lex Iulia Maiestatis*', *Latomus*, 21: 711–31.

Arangio-Ruiz, V. (1959), 'Testi e Documenti IV – Tavolette Ercolanensi (Il processo di Giusta)', *BIDR*, 62: 223–45.

Astin, A.E. (1958), *The Lex Annalis before Sulla* (Coll. Latomus, 32), Brussels.

Atkinson, K.M.T. (1960), '*Restitutio in Integrum – Iussu Caesaris Augusti*', *RIDA*, 7: 227–72.

Badian, E. (1958), *Foreign Clientelae*, Oxford.

—— (1967) 'The Testament of Ptolemy Alexander', *Rh. Mus.*, 110: 178–92.

—— (1968) *Roman Imperialism in the late Republic*, 2nd edn, Oxford.

—— (1972), *Publicans and Sinners*, Ithaca, NY.

Balsdon, J.P.V.D. (1938), 'The History of the Extortion Court at Rome 123–70 BC' *PBSR*, 14: 98–114.

Baradez, J.-L. (1949), *Fossatum Africae*, Paris.

Barker, G. and Lloyd, J. (eds) (1991), *Roman Landscapes* (BSR Arch. Monogr., 2), London.

Bean, G. (1948), 'Notes and Inscriptions from Lycia', *JHS*, 68: 40–58.

Bernhardt, R. (1971), *Imperium und Eleutheria. Die römische politik gegenüber den freien Städten des griechischen Ostens*, Diss., Hamburg.

Bertrand, J.-M. (1989), 'A propos du mot PROVINCIA: Etude sur les modes d' élaboration du langage politique', *Journal des Savants* (July–Dec.), 191–215.

Birks, P., Rodger, A. and Richardson, J.S. (1984), 'Further Aspects of the *Tabula Contrebiensis*', *JRS*, 74: 45–73.

Blagg, T. and Millett, M. (eds) (1990), *The Early Roman Empire in the West*, Oxford.

Bleicken, J. (1990), *Zwischen Republik und Prinzipat: zum Charakter des zweiten Triumvirats* (Ab. Ak. Wiss. Göttingen, Phil.-hist. Kl. 3 Folge, no. 185), Göttingen.

Bove, L. (1967), 'Due iscrizioni da Pozzuoli e Cuma', *Labeo*, 13: 22–48.

—— (1979), *Documenti processuali dalle Tabulae Pompeianae di Murecine*, Naples.

Bowersock, G.W. (1964), 'C. Marcius Censorinus, *Legatus Caesaris'*, *HSCP*, 68: 207–10.
—— (1965) *Augustus and the Greek World*, Oxford.
—— (1969), *Greek Sophists in the Roman Empire*, Oxford.
Bowman, A.K. (1986), *Egypt after the Pharaohs*, London.
Bowra, C.M. (1957), 'Melinno's Hymn to Rome', *JRS*, 47: 21–8.
Braund, D.C. (1983), 'Royal Wills and Rome', *PBSR*, 51: 16–57.
—— (1984), *Rome and the Friendly King: the Character of Client Kingship*, London.
Briscoe, J. (1967), 'Rome and the Class-Struggle in the Greek States 200–146 BC', *Past and Present*, 36 (April), 3–20.
Brown, P. (1982), *Society and the Holy in Late Antiquity*, London.
Brunt, P.A. (1971), *Italian Manpower*, Oxford.
—— (1988), *The Fall of the Roman Republic and Related Essays*, Oxford.
—— (1990), *Roman Imperial Themes*, Oxford.
Burnham, B.C. and Wacher, J.C. (1991), *The 'Small Towns' of Roman Britain*, London.
Burton, G.P. (1975), 'Proconsuls, Assizes and the Administration of Justice under the Empire', *JRS*, 65: 92–106.
—— (1976), 'The Issuing of *Mandata* to Proconsuls and a New Inscription from Cos', *ZPE*, 21: 63–8.
—— (1979), 'The *Curator Rei Publicae*: towards a Reappraisal', *Chiron*, 9: 465–87.
Cagnat, R. (1882) *Les Impôts Indirects chez les Romains*, Paris.
Campbell, J.B. (1984) *The Emperor and the Roman Army 31 BC–AD 235*, Oxford.
Carandini, A. (1983), 'Pottery in the African Economy', in P. Garnsey, K. Hopkins and C.R. Whittaker (eds), *Trade in the Ancient Economy*, London: 145–62.
Champlin, E.J. (1980), *Fronto and Antonine Rome*, Princeton, NJ.
Chevallier, R. (1958), 'Essai de chronologie des centuriations romaines de Tunisie', *MEFR*, 70: 61–128.
Chilton, C.W. (1955), 'The Roman Law of Treason in the Early Principate', *JRS*, 45: 73–81.
Cimma, M.R. (1981), *Ricerche sulle società di publicani*, Milan.
Clemente, G. (1974), *I Romani nella Gallia meridionale*, Bologna.
Cotton, H.M. (1979), 'Cicero *Ad Familiares* XIII 26 and 28: Evidence for *Revocatio* or *Reiectio/Romam?*', *JRS*, 69: 39–50.
Crawford, M. (1977), 'Rome and the Greek World: Economic Relationships', *EHR*, 42–52.
—— (1985), *Coinage and Money under the Roman Republic*, London.
—— (ed.) (1986), *L'Impero Romano e le Strutture Economiche e Sociali delle Province* (Biblioteca di Athenaeum, 4) Pavia.
—— (1988), 'The Laws of the Romans: Knowledge and Diffusion', in J. Gonzalez and J. Arce (eds), *Estudios sobre la Tabula Siarensis* (Anejos de Archivo español de Arqueologia, 9), Madrid: 127–40.
—— (1989a), 'Ateste and Rome', *Quad. ticin. num. e ant. class.*, 18: 191–200.
—— (1989b), 'The *Lex Iulia Agraria*', *Athenaeum*, 67: 179–90.

Cunliffe, B. (1988), *Greeks, Romans and Barbarians: Spheres of Interaction*, London.

Dahlheim. W. (1968), *Struktur und Entwicklung des römischen Völkerrechts* (Vestigia, 8), Munich.

D'Arms, J.H. and Kopff, E.C. (eds) (1980), *The Seaborne Commerce of Ancient Rome: Studies in Archaeology and History* (Memoirs of the American Academy in Rome, 36), Rome.

Degrassi, A. (1962-7), *Scritti Vari di Antichità*, 3 vols, Rome and Venice/ Trieste.

Deininger, J. (1965), *Die Provinziallandtage der römischen Kaiserzeit*, Munich.

—— (1971), *Der politische Widerstand gegen Rom in Griechenland 217-86 v.Chr*, Berlin.

De Laet, S.J. (1949), *Portorium*, Bruges.

de Martino, F. (1956), '*Ager privatus vectigalisque*', *Studi in onore di P. de Francisci*, I: 557-79.

—— (1958-67), *Storia della Costituzione Romana*, 5 vols, Naples.

Derow, P.S. (1979), 'Polybius, Rome and the East', *JRS*, 69: 1-15.

Derow, P.S. and Forrest, W.G. (1982), 'An Inscription from Chios', *ABSA*, 77: 79-92.

de Ste Croix, G.E.M. (1981), *The Class Struggle in the Ancient Greek World*, London.

Dörner, F.K. and Gruben, G. (1953), 'Die Exedra der Cicerones', *MDAI(A)*, 68: 63-76.

Drinkwater, J.F. (1983), *Roman Gaul: the Three Provinces 58 BC-AD 260*, London.

Duncan-Jones, R.P. (1990), *Structure and Scale in the Roman Economy*, Cambridge.

Eder, W. (1969), *Das vorsullanische Repetundenverfahren*, Munich.

—— (1990), *Staat und Staatlichkeit in der frühen Republik*, Stuttgart.

Eilers, C.F. (1991), 'Cn. Domitius and Samos: a New Extortion Trial (IGR 4.968)', *ZPE*, 89: 167-78.

Engelmann, H. and Knibbe, D. (1989), 'Das Zollgesetz der provincia Asia. Ein neues Inschrift aus Ephesos', *Epig. Anat.*, 14: 1-206.

Errington, R.M. (1987), 'Thea Rome und römischer Einfluss südlich der Mäanders im 2.Jh.v.Chr.', *Chiron*, 17: 97-118.

Ewins, U. (Hall) (1955), 'The Enfranchisement of Cisalpine Gaul', *PBSR*, 23: 73-98.

Fabricius, E. (1927), '*Limes*', *RE*, XIII: 572-671.

Ferrary, J.-L. (1985), 'La *lex Antonia de Termessibus*', *Athenaeum*, 73: 419-57.

—— (1988) *Philhellénisme et Impérialisme: aspects idéologiques de la conquête romaine du monde hellénistique*, Rome.

—— (1990), 'Traités et domination romaine' in L. Canfora, M. Liverani and C. Zaccagnini (eds), *I trattati nel mondo antico: forma, ideologia, funzione*, Rome: 217-35.

Fishwick, D. (1978), 'Provincial Ruler-Worship in the West', *ANRW*, II.16.2: 1201-53.

Foraboschi, D. (1986), 'L'Egitto', in M. Crawford (ed.), *L'Impero Romano e le*

Strutture Economiche e Sociali delle Province (Biblioteca di Athenaeum, 4), Pavia: 109–25.

Forni, G. (1953), *Il Reclutamento delle Legioni da Augusto a Diocleziano*, Milan.

Frank, T. (1927), '*Dominium in solo provinciali*', *JRS*, 17: 141–61.

Fraser, P.M. (1957), 'Mark Antony in Alexandria. A Note', *JRS*, 47: 71–3.

Frederiksen, M.W. (1965), 'The Roman Municipal Laws: Errors and Drafts', *JRS*, 55: 183–93.

—— (1976), 'Changes in the pattern of Settlement', in P. Zanker (ed.), *Hellenismus in Mittelitalien*, Göttingen: 341–55.

—— (1984), *Campania*, London.

Frend, W.H. (1956), 'A Third Century Inscription Relating to *Angareia* in Phrygia', *JRS*, 46: 46–56.

Gabba, E. (1986), 'La Sicilia Romana', in M. Crawford (ed.) *L'Impero Romano e le Strutture Economiche e Sociali delle Province* (Biblioteca di Athenaeum, 4), Pavia: 71–85.

—— (1988), 'Riflessioni sulla *lex Coloniae Genetivae Iuliae*', in J. Gonzalez and J. Arce (eds), *Estudios sobre la Tabula Siarensis* (Anejos de Archivo español de Arqueologia, 9), Madrid: 157–68.

Galinsky, G. (1969), *Aeneas, Sicily and Rome* (Princeton Monographs in Art and Archaeology, 40), Princeton, NJ.

Galsterer, H. (1971a), 'Die *lex Osca tabulae Bantinae*. Ein bestandaufnahme', *Chiron*, 1: 191–214.

—— (1971b), *Untersuchungen zum römischen Städtewesen auf der iberischen Halbinsel* (Madrider Forschungen, 8), Berlin.

—— (1976), *Herrschaft und Verwaltung im Republikanischen Italien* (Münch. Beitr. z. Papyrusf. u. ant. Rechtsgesch., 68), Munich.

—— (1979), 'Zur Integration vorrömischer Bevölkerungen auf der iberischen Halbinsel', in A. Tovar *et al.* (eds), *Actas del il Coloquio sobre Lenguas y Culturas preromanas de la Peninsula Iberica, Junio 1976*, Salamanca: 453–64.

—— (1987), 'La loi municipale des Romains: chimère ou réalité?', *RHDFE*, 65: 181–203.

Garnsey, P.D.A. (1966), 'The *Lex Iulia* and Appeal under the Empire', *JRS*, 56: 167–89.

—— (1970), *Social Status and Legal Privilege in the Roman Empire*, Oxford.

—— (1988), *Famine and Food-Supply in the Greco-Roman World: Responses to Risk and Crisis*, Cambridge.

Garnsey, P.D.A. and Saller, R.P. (1987), *The Roman Empire*, London.

Garnsey, P.D.A. and Whittaker, C.R. (eds), (1983), *Trade and Famine in Classical Antiquity* (PCPS Supp., 8), Cambridge.

Gascou, J. (1969), 'Inscriptions de Tébessa', *MEFR*, 81: 537–99.

Geagan, D.G. (1967), *The Athenian Constitution after Sulla* (*Hesperia* Supp., 12), Princeton, NJ.

—— (1971), 'Greek Inscriptions' *Hesperia*, 40: 96–111.

—— (1972), 'Hadrian and the Athenian Dionysiac Technitai, *TAPA*, 103: 133–56.

Giardina, A. and Schiavone, A. (eds) (1981), *Società Romana e Produzione Schiavistica*, 3 vols, Rome and Bari.

Giovannini, A. (1978), *Rome et la circulation monétaire en Grèce au IIe siècle avant Jésus Christ*, Basle.

—— (1983), *Consulare Imperium* (Schweiz. Beitr. z. Altertumswiss., 16), Basle.

Goldstein, J.A. (1966), 'The Syriac Bill of Sale from Dura-Europos', *JNES*, 25: 1–16.

Gonzalez, J. (1984), '*Tabula Siarensis*', *ZPE*, 55: 55–100.

—— (1986), 'The *lex Irnitana*: a New Copy of the Flavian Municipal Law', *JRS*, 76: 147–238.

Gonzalez, J. and Arce, J. (eds) (1988), *Estudios sobre la Tabula Siarensis* (Anejos de Archivo español de Arqueologia, 9), Madrid.

Goodman, M. (1991), 'Babatha's Story', *JRS*, 81: 169–75.

Grant, M. (1946), *From Imperium to Auctoritas*, Cambridge.

Gruen, E.S. (1984), *The Hellenistic World and the Coming of Rome*, Berkeley/Los Angeles, Calif.

—— (1990), 'The Imperial Policy of Augustus' in K.A. Raaflaub and M. Toher (eds), *Between Republic and Empire*, Berkeley/Los Angeles, Calif.: 395–416.

Habicht, Ch. (1970), *Gottmenschtum und Griechische Städte* (Zetemata, 14), Munich.

—— (1975), 'New Evidence on the Province of Asia', *JRS*, 65: 64–91.

—— (1990), 'Samos weiht eine Statue des *Populus Romanus*', *MDAI(A)*, 105: 259–68.

Harper, G.M. jnr (1928), 'Village Administration in the Roman Province of Syria', *YCS*, 1: 103–68.

Harris, W.V. (1980), 'Roman Terracotta Lamps: the Organisation of an Industry', *JRS*, 70: 126–45.

Hassall, M., Crawford, M. and Reynolds, J. (1974), 'Rome and the Eastern Provinces at the End of the Second Century BC', *JRS*, 64: 195–220.

Herrman, P. (1989), 'Rom und die Asylie griechischer Heiligtümer', *Chiron*, 19: 127–64.

Herrman, P. and Polatkan, K.Z. (1969), 'Das Testament des Epikrates', *Sitzungsber. öst. Ak. Wiss. Phil.-hist. Kl.*, 265.1, Abh.1, Vienna.

Hirschfeld, O. (1913), *Kleine Schriften*, Berlin.

Hopkins, K. (1980a), 'Brother–Sister Marriage in Roman Egypt', *Comparative Studies in Society and History*, 22.3: 303–54.

—— (1980b), 'Taxes and Trade in the Roman Empire', *JRS*, 70: 101–25.

Humbert, M. (1978), *Municipium et Civitas sine Suffragio*, Paris.

Isaac, B. (1990), *The Limits of Empire: the Roman Army in the East*, Oxford.

Jones, A.H.M. (1940), *The Greek City from Alexander to Justinian*, Oxford.

—— (1960), *Studies in Roman Government and Law*, Oxford.

—— (1973), *The Later Roman Empire*, 2 vols, Oxford.

Jones, C.P. (1971), 'A New Letter of Marcus Aurelius to the Athenians', *ZPE*, 8: 161–83.

—— (1978), *The Roman World of Dio Chrysostom*, Cambridge, Mass. and London.

Keil, J. and von Premerstein, A. (1910), *Bericht über eine Reise in Lydien und der südlicher Aeolis* (Denkschr. Ak. Wien, 53.2), Vienna.

—— (1914), *Bericht über eine dritte Reise in Lydien* (Denkschr. Ak. Wien, 57.1), Vienna.

Kennedy, D. and Riley, D. (1990), *Rome's Desert Frontier*, London.

Keppie, L. (1984), *The Making of the Roman Army: from Republic to Empire*, London.

Kniep, F. (1896), *Societas Publicanorum*, Jena.

Kunkel, W. (1962), *Untersuchungen zur Entwicklung des römischen Kriminalverfahrens in vorsullanischer Zeit* (Abh. Bay. Ak. Wiss. Phil.-hist. Kl. n.f., 56), Munich.

Laffi, U. (1986), 'La *lex Rubria de Gallia Cisalpina*', *Athenaeum*, 64: 5–44.

Levick, B.M. (1967), *Roman Colonies in Southern Asia Minor*, Oxford.

—— (1976), *Tiberius the Politician*, London.

Lewis, N. (1970), 'Graeco-Roman Egypt: Fact or Fiction?', *Proc. XII Inter. Congr. Pap. (American Studies in Papyrology*, 7): 3–14.

Lewis, N., Katzoff, R. and Greenfield, J.C. (1987), 'Papyrus Yadin 18', *IEJ*, 37: 229–50.

Lewis, N., Yadin, Y. and Greenfield, J.C. (1989), *The Documents from the Bar-Kochba Period in the Cave of Letters. Greek Papyri, Aramaic and Nabataean Signatures and Subscriptions*, Jerusalem.

Liebenam, W. (1990), *Städteverwaltung im römischen Kaiserreiche*, Leipzig.

Lintott, A.W. (1972), 'Provocatio. From the Struggle of the Orders to the Principate', *ANRW*, I.2: 226–67.

—— (1976a), 'Notes on the Roman Law Inscribed at Delphi and Cnidos', *ZPE*, 20: 65–82.

—— (1976b), 'The Procedure Under the *leges Calpurnia* and *Iunia de repetundis* and the *actio per sponsionem*', *ZPE*, 22: 207–14.

—— (1978), 'The Capitoline Dedications to Jupiter and the Roman People', *ZPE*, 30: 137–44.

—— (1981a), 'The *Leges de Repetundis* and Associate Measures Under the Republic', *ZSS*, 98: 162–212.

—— (1981b), 'What was the "*Imperium Romanum*"?', *G & R*, 28.1: 53–67.

Luttwak, E. (1976), *The Grand Strategy of the Roman Empire*, Baltimore, Maryland.

Mackie, N. (1983a), 'Augustan Colonies in Mauretania', *Historia*, 32: 332–58.

—— (1983b), *Local Administration in Roman Spain AD 14–212* (BAR International Series, 172), Oxford.

MacMullen, R. (1974), *Roman Social Relations 50 BC to AD 284*, Cambridge, Mass.

—— (1988), *Corruption and the Decline of Rome*, New Haven, Conn.

Malay, H. and Petzl, C. (1984), 'Ehrenbeschlüsse für den Sohn des Anaximbrotos des Gordos', *Epigr. Anat.*, 3: 157–65.

Malitz, J. (1987), 'Die Kanzlei Caesars', *Historia*, 36: 51–72.

Mann, J.C. (1979), Review of E. Luttwak (1976), *The Grand Strategy of the Roman Empire*, Baltimore, Maryland, *JRS*, 69: 175–83.

Marshall, A.J. (1964), 'The Structure of Cicero's Edict', *AJP*, 85: 185–9.

—— (1966), 'Governors on the Move', *Phoenix*, 20: 231–46.

Matthews, J.F. (1984), 'The Tax-Law from Palmyra', *JRS*, 74: 157–80.

Mattingly, D.J. (1988), 'Oil for Export? A Comparison of Libyan, Spanish and Tunisian Oil-Production in the Roman Empire', *Journ. Rom. Arch.*, 1: 33–56.

Mattingly, H.B. (1972), 'The Date of the *Senatus Consultum de Agro Pergameno*', *AJP*, 93: 412–23.

Mellor, R. (1975), *THEA ROME: The Worship of the Goddess Roma in the Greek World*, Göttingen.

—— (1978), 'The Dedications on the Capitoline Hill', *Chiron*, 8: 319–30.

Millar, F. (1966), 'The Emperor, The Senate and the Provinces', *JRS*, 56: 156–66.

—— (1973), 'Triumvirate and Principate', *JRS*, 63: 50–67.

—— (1977), *The Emperor in the Roman World 31 BC–AD 337*, London.

—— (1982), 'Emperors, Frontiers and Foreign Relations 31 BC–AD 378' *Britannia*, 13: 1–23.

—— (1984), 'State and Subject: the Impact of Monarchy', in F. Millar and E. Segal (eds), *Caesar Augustus – Seven Aspects*, Oxford: 37–60.

—— (1989), '"Senatorial Provinces": An Institutionalised Ghost', *Anc. World*, 20: 93–7.

Mitchell, S. (1976), 'Requisitioned Transport in the Roman Empire. A New Inscription from Pisidia', *JRS*, 66: 106–31.

Mitteis, L. (1891), *Reichsrecht und Volksrecht in den östlichen Provinzen des römischen Kaiserreich*, Leipzig.

Mourges, J.-L. (1987), 'The So-Called Letter of Domitian at the End of the *Lex Irnitana*', *JRS*, 77: 78–87.

Mouterde, R. and Poidebard, A. (1945), *Le limes de Chalkis*, Paris.

Neesen, L. (1980), *Untersuchungen zu den direkten Staatsangaben der römischen Kaiserzeit (27 v.Chr.–284 n.Chr.)*, Bonn.

Nicolet, C. (1971), 'Polybius VI.17.4 and the Composition of the *Societates Publicanorum*', *Irish Jurist*: 163–75.

—— (1978), 'Le stipendium des alliés italiens avant la guerre sociale', *PBSR*, 46: 1–11.

—— (1979), 'Deux remarques sur l'organisation des sociétés de publicains à la fin de la république romaine', in H. van Effenterre (ed.), *Points de vue sur la fiscalité antique*, Paris: 69–95.

—— (1988), *L'inventaire du monde: Géographie et politique aux origines de l'Empire Romain*, Paris.

Nicolet, C. et al. (1980), *Insula Sacra*, Paris.

Nicols, J. (1980), '*Tabulae Patronatus*: A Study of the Agreement Between Patron and Client Community 50 BC–AD 250', *ANRW*, II.13: 535–61.

Nörr, D. (1969), *Imperium und Polis in der hohen Prinzipatszeit* (Münch. Beitr. z. Papyrusf. u. ant. Rechtsgesch., 50), Munich.

Ogilvie, R.M. (1965), *A Commentary on Livy I–V*, Oxford.

Oliver, J.H. (1941), *The Sacred Gerousia* (*Hesperia*, Supp., 6), Princeton, NJ.

—— (1946), 'A Roman Governor Visits Samothrace', *AJP*, 81: 275–9.

—— (1952), *The Ruling Power: a Study of the Roman Empire in the Second Century after Christ through the Roman Oration of Aelius Aristeides* (*Trans. Amer. Philosoph. Soc.*, 43, 4: 873–1003), Philadelphia.

—— (1961), 'New Fragments of *Sacred Gerousia* 24 (*IG*, II², 1108)', *Hesperia*, 30: 402–3.

—— (1970), *Marcus Aurelius: Aspects of Civic and Cultural Policy in the East* (*Hesperia*, Supp., 13), Princeton, NJ.

Peppé, L. (1985), *Sulla giurisdizione in populos liberos del governatore*

provinciale al tempo di Cicerone (Pubbl. Fac. Giurisprud. Univ. Pisa, 104), Milan.
—— (1991), 'Note sull' editto di Cicerone in Cilicia', *Labeo*, 37: 13–93.
Peyras, J. (1975), 'Fundus Aufidianus', *Ant.Afr.*, 9: 207–22.
Picard, G. Ch. (1966), 'L'administration territoriale de Carthage', *Mélanges d'archéologie et d'histoire offerts à A. Piganiol*, Paris, vol. III: 1257–65.
—— (1969–70), 'Le pagus dans l'Afrique romaine', *Karthago*, 15: 1–12.
Pickard-Cambridge, A.W. (1968), *The Dramatic Festivals of Athens*, 2nd edn, rev. J. Gould and D.M. Lewis, Oxford.
Piganiol, A. (1954), *Atlas des Centuriations de Tunisie*, Paris.
Poidebard, A. (1934), *Le trace de Rome dans le désert de Syrie*, 2 vols, Paris.
Poland, F. (1934), *RE Technitai*, VA.2.2473–558.
Price, S.R.F. (1984), *Rituals and Power: the Roman Imperial Cult in Asia Minor*, Cambridge.
Pritchard, R.T. (1970), 'Cicero and the *Lex Hieronica*', *Historia*, 19: 352–68.
—— (1971), 'Gaius Verres and the Sicilian Farmers', *Historia*, 20: 229–38.
—— (1972), 'Some Aspects of First-Century Sicilian Agriculture', *Historia*, 21: 646–60.
Quoniam, P. (1950), 'A propos d'une inscription de Thuburnica (Tunisie)', *CRAI*: 332–6.
Rabello, A.M. (1980), 'The Legal Condition of the Jews in the Roman Empire', *ANRW*, II.13: 662–762.
Raubitschek, A.E. (1941), 'Octavia's Deification at Athens', *TAPA*, 77: 146–51.
Rawson, E. (1987), 'Cicero and the Areopagus', *Athenaeum*, 63: 44–67.
Rea, J.R. (1982), 'Lease of a Red Cow Called Thayris', *JEA*, 68: 277–9.
Rey-Cocquais, J.-P. (1978), 'Syrie romaine de Pompée à Dioclétien', *JRS*, 68: 44–73.
Reynolds, J. (1962), 'Cyrenaica, Pompey and Cn. Cornelius Lentulus Marcellinus', *JRS*, 52: 97–103.
—— (1982), *Aphrodisias and Rome* (JRS monographs, 1), London.
Rice, E.E. (1983), *The Grand Procession of Ptolemy Philadelphus*, Oxford.
Rich, J.W. (1976), *Declaring War in the Roman Republic in the Period of Transmarine Expansion* (Coll. Latomus, 176), Brussels.
Richardson, J.S. (1976), 'The Spanish Mines and the Development of Provincial Taxation in the Second Century BC', *JRS*, 66: 139–52.
—— (1983), 'The *Tabula Contrebiensis*: Roman Law in Spain in the Early First Century BC', *JRS*, 73: 33–41.
—— (1986), *Hispaniae*, Cambridge.
—— (1987), 'The Purpose of the *lex Calpurnia de repetundis*', *JRS*, 77: 1–12.
—— (1991) '*Imperium Romanum*: Empire and the Language of Power', *JRS*, 81: 1–9.
Rickman, G. (1980), *The Corn Supply of Ancient Rome*, Oxford.
Rilinger, R. (1988), *Honestiores - Humiliores. Zu einer Dichotomie im Strafrecht der römischen Kaiserzeit*, Munich.
Robert, J. and L. (1989), *Claros I: les décrets hellénistiques*, Paris.
Robert, L. (1937), *Etudes Anatoliennes*, Paris.
—— (1938), *Etudes épigraphiques et philologiques*, Paris.
—— (1969), *Opera Minora Selecta*, 4 vols, Amsterdam.
—— (1987), *Documents d'Asie Mineure*, Paris.

Rostovtzeff, M. (1906), '*Angareia*', *Klio*, 6: 249–58.

—— (1910), *Studien zur Geschichte des römischen Kolonates* (Arch. f. Papyrusf. Beih., I,), Leipzig/Berlin.

—— (1957a), *A Social and Economic History of the Hellenistic World*, 3 vols, 2nd edn, Oxford.

—— (1957b), *The Social and Economic History of the Roman Empire*, 2 vols, 2nd edn, Oxford.

Ryder, T.T.B. (1965), *Koine Eirene*, Cambridge.

Saddington, D.B. (1982), *The Development of the Roman Auxiliary Forces from Caesar to Vespasian 49 BC to AD 79*, Harare.

Saller, R.P. (1982), *Personal Patronage under the Early Empire*, Cambridge.

Salmon, E.T. (1969), *Roman Colonisation in the Republic*, London.

Salway, P. (1981), *Roman Britain*, Oxford.

Sandford, E.M. (1939), 'The Career of Aulus Gabinius', *TAPA*, 70: 64–92.

Seston, W. and Euzennat, M. (1971), 'Un dossier de la chancellerie romaine; la *Tabula Banasitana*. Etude de diplomatique', *CRAI*, (1971): 468–90.

Sherwin-White, A.N. (1966), *The Letters of Pliny*, Oxford.

—— (1973a), *The Roman Citizenship*, 2nd edn, Oxford.

—— (1973b), 'The *Tabula* of Banasa and the *Constitutio Antoniniana*', *JRS*, 63: 86–98.

—— (1984), *Roman Foreign Policy in the East*, London.

Simshaüser, W. (1973), *Iuridici und Munizipalgerichtsbarkeit in Italien* (Münch. Beitr. z. Papyrusf. u. ant. Rechtsgesch., 61), Munich.

Skutsch, O. (1985), *The Annals of Quintus Ennius*, Oxford.

Smith, R.E. (1958), *Service in the post-Marian Army*, Manchester.

Spawforth, A.J.S. and Walker, S. (1985–6), 'The World of the Panhellenion, I. Athens and Eleusis, II. Three Dorian Cities', *JRS*, 75: 78–104, and 76: 88–105.

Spitzl, Th. (1984), *Lex Municipii Malacitani* (Vestigia, 36), Munich.

Syme, R. (1939), *The Roman Revolution*, Oxford.

—— (1979–), *Roman Papers*, Oxford.

Taubenschlag, R. (1944–8), *The Law of Greco-Roman Egypt in the light of the Papyri 332 BC–640 AD*, 2 vols, New York and Warsaw.

Taübler, E. (1913), *Imperium Romanum*, I (only volume published), Leipzig.

Taylor, L.R. (1960), *The Voting-Districts of the Roman Republic*, Rome.

Todd, M. (1981), *Roman Britain*, London.

Tomsin, A. (1961), 'Les continuités historiques dans le cadre des mésures prises par les romains en Egypte concernant la propriété de la terre', in J. Wolski (ed.), *Actes du Xème Congrès Internationale de Papyrologie*: 81–95.

Tomulescu, C. St. (1987), 'Eléments vulgaires romains dans la pratique juridique de la Dacie', *Journ. Jur. Pap.*, 19: 7–20.

Toynbee, A.J. (1965), *Hannibal's Legacy*, 2 vols, London.

Turner, E.G. (1956), 'A Roman Writing-Tablet from Somerset', *JRS*, 46: 115–18.

—— (1984), 'Ptolemaic Egypt', *CAH*, VII.1. 2nd edn: ch. 5.

Turpin, W. (1991), 'Imperial Subscriptions and the Administration of Justice', *JRS*, 81: 101–18.

Venturini, C. (1969), 'La repressione degli abusi dei magistrati romani ai danni delle popolazioni soggette fino alla *lex Calpurnia* del 149 a.c.', *BIDR*, 72: 19–87.

—— (1979), *Studi sul crimen repetundarum nell' età repubblicana*, Milan.

Volterra, E. (1939), 'L'efficacia delle costituzioni imperiali emanate per le provincie e l' instituto dell' *expositio*', *Studi di storia e diritto in onore di Enrico Besta*, Milan: vol. I, 451–77.

—— (1963), 'Nuovi documenti per la conoscenza del diritto vigente nelle province romane', *Jura*, 29–70.

Wallace-Hadrill, A. (ed.) (1989), *Patronage in Ancient Society*, London.

Weinstock, S. (1971), *Divus Julius*, Oxford.

Wells, C.M. (1972), *The German Policy of Augustus*, Oxford.

West, S. (1984), 'Lycophron Italicised?', *JHS*, 104: 127–51.

Whittaker, C.R. (1989), *Les frontières de l'empire Romain* (Centre de Recherches d'Histoire Ancienne, 85), Paris.

Wightman, E.M. (1985), *Gallia Belgica*, London.

Wilkes, J. (1969), *Dalmatia*, London.

Wilson, A.J.N. (1966), *Emigration from Italy in the Republican Age*, Manchester.

Wiseman, T.P. (1987), *Roman Studies, Literary and Historical*, Liverpool.

Wlassak, M. (1919), *Zur römischen Provinzialprozess* (Sitzungsber. Ak. Wien, Phil.-hist. Kl.190.4), Vienna.

Wolff, H.J. (1980), 'Römisches Prozessrecht in der Provinz Arabia', *ANRW*, II.13: 763–806.

Wolff, J.G. (1979), 'Aus dem neuen pompejanischen Urkundenfund: Der Seefrachtvertrag des Menelaos', *Freiburger Universitätsblätter* (Oct.): 23–36.

Wörrle, M. (1988), *Stadt und Fest in kaiserlichen Kleinasien. Studien zu einer agonistischen Stiftung aus Oenoanda* (Vestigia, 39), Munich.

Yoshimura, T. (1984), 'Zur römischen *Libertas*-begriff in der Aussenpolitik im zweiten Jahrhundert vor Chr.', *AJAH*, 9: 1–22.

Zanker, P. (ed.) (1976), *Hellenismus in Mittelitalien*, Göttingen.

—— (1988), *The Power of Images in the Age of Augustus*, Ann Arbor, Mich.

INDEX

242